Rowdy Patsy Tebeau
and the Cleveland
Spiders

Rowdy Patsy Tebeau and the Cleveland Spiders

Fighting to the Bottom of Baseball, 1887–1899

DAVID L. FLEITZ

McFarland & Company, Inc., Publishers

Jefferson, North Carolina

ISBN (print) 978-0-7864-9947-2
ISBN (ebook) 978-1-4766-2766-3

LIBRARY OF CONGRESS CATALOGUING DATA ARE AVAILABLE

British Library cataloguing data are available

Front cover: The 1895 Cleveland Spiders baseball club
(photography by John H. Ryder)

Printed in the United States of America

*McFarland & Company, Inc., Publishers
Box 611, Jefferson, North Carolina 28640
www.mcfarlandpub.com*

Acknowledgments

I would like to thank a few people and organizations that helped make this book possible.

The availability of information on the Internet has boomed in recent years, especially as it relates to baseball. One can easily find individual statistics for all players dating back to the beginning of professional baseball in 1871, while a terrific web site called Baseball Reference (http://www.baseball-reference.com) provides player game logs, box scores, and, for games of recent decades, play by play descriptions. Sean Forman and his team deserve a great deal of credit for developing this constantly expanding trove of information, and this book would have been much more difficult to write without it.

Project Retrosheet is a web site, founded in 1989 for the purpose of providing computerized play-by-play data for as many pre–1984 games as possible. It has blossomed into a site filled with useful information and is highly recommended as well. The statistics in this book come from Project Retrosheet, which in return asks only that the user includes the following statement: *The information used here was obtained free of charge from and is copyrighted by Retrosheet. Interested parties may contact Retrosheet at www.retrosheet.org.*

Other helpful web sites display digitized, searchable copies of newspaper and magazine pages, saving the researcher from hours of poring through microfilm. One is called Paper of Record, a historical newspaper search engine that features images of *The Sporting News* beginning with its inaugural issue in 1886. The Brooklyn Public Library has digitized the *Brooklyn Eagle* from the years 1841 to 1902, and the LA84 Foundation, endowed with funds left over from the 1984 Olympic Games in Los Angeles, maintains a digital archive of *Sporting Life* and *Baseball Magazine* for the 1885 to 1920 period. Also, the Library of Congress has a collection called "American Memory" (at http://www.loc.gov) that shows images of baseball cards issued between 1887 and 1914, and those images are valuable as well.

Google (http://www.google.com) has entered the digitizing market with Google Books and Google News. These archives are free, and extremely useful to any sports researcher. SABR, the Society for American Baseball Research, also maintains a site called BioProject (http://bioproj.sabr.org), to which I have contributed several articles. BioProject has posted more than 3,500 biographies of major league players of the past and the present, and the information found there has been highly useful as well.

The Eugene C. Murdock and Charles W. Mears collections of baseball books and materials at the Cleveland Public Library were, as always, invaluable. The library in downtown Cleveland has opened a center for baseball research, called the Sports Research Center, which is a welcome development to anyone who loves baseball. As usual, I received fine assistance from the knowledgeable staff members at the National Baseball Hall of Fame Library in Cooperstown, New York. I also conducted research at the University of Michigan in Ann Arbor, which houses a fine collection of newspaper microfilm, and at Bowling Green State University in Ohio.

Table of Contents

Introduction

In 2016, Cleveland's American League baseball team, called the Indians since the beginning of the 1915 campaign, played its 116th consecutive season of major league baseball. The Indians have enjoyed some success, but not much of it; they have won the World Series only twice (in 1920 and 1948) and have claimed only five American League championships. During their 116 years of existence, the Indians have enjoyed brief periods of success, surrounded by long stretches of mediocrity and sub-.500 finishes. Still, the Indians are Cleveland's team, and despite an ongoing controversy about the Indians moniker and the cartoonish "Chief Wahoo" logo, the ballclub and its long history are woven into the fabric of the city.

Few people know that Cleveland hosted a National League team more than a decade before the American League planted a franchise there.

This ballclub, largely forgotten today, had an interesting and eventful history of its own. Originally called the Blues and then the Spiders, this team played in the American Association in 1887 and 1888 and then in the National League from 1889 to 1899. The Cleveland Spiders won no pennants as we define them today (a half-title in 1892 and a post-season win in 1895 notwithstanding), but the team left its mark on the National League and on baseball itself. The mark it left was not a positive one in many ways, but it was a mark nonetheless.

The Cleveland Spiders played in baseball's roughest, toughest era. The last decade of the 19th century is often called the "Gay Nineties," but the decade was full of economic recession, labor violence, and racial segregation. Baseball was not immune from the forces that swept American society in that decade; indeed, the sport reflected both the best and the worst of the era. Baseball, which was played as a contest between gentlemen before the Civil War, had embraced the win-at-any-cost ethic that permeated the business world in the age of the robber barons. Baseball in the 1890s was a blood sport, full of cheating, intimidation, and violence on and off the field, from which the concept of sportsmanship had virtually disappeared. As historian Bill James once wrote, "The tactics of the eighties were aggressive; the tactics of the nineties were violent. The game of the eighties was crude; the game of the nineties was criminal. The baseball of the eighties had ugly elements; the game of the nineties was just plain ugly."[1]

The Cleveland Spiders were the ugliest of all.

The Spiders were led by a battling, brawling infielder named Oliver "Patsy" Tebeau, who learned to play aggressive, take-no-prisoners baseball while growing up in the tough Irish immigrant enclaves of St. Louis. Tebeau filled his team with mirror images of himself—intelligent, quick-tempered ballplayers, mainly of Irish descent, who would do anything to win and never backed down from a fight. The Spiders took their cues from Tebeau and cut a swath through the National League, with brawls, fan violence, and umpire abuse regarded as necessary components of winning baseball strategy. "My instructions to my players are to win games, and I want them to be aggressive. A milk and water, goody-goody player can't wear a Cleveland uniform," remarked Tebeau to a reporter.[2]

The Spiders played this way because it proved successful. Tebeau took over a second-division Cleveland team in 1891 and led it to the top tier of the National League, with three second-place finishes (and a half-pennant in the 1892 split-season format) as a result. The battling Spiders became, under Tebeau's leadership, one of the league's most popular attractions on the road, as the fans in other cities loved to jeer the Cleve-landers, and sometimes throw rotten fruit and soda bottles at them. The Spiders drew poorly at home, however, largely because the local authorities refused to let the team play games in Cleveland on Sundays. The hyper-aggressive ballclub refused to accept this state of affairs, and the team's attempts to circumvent, or outright defy, the local ban on Sunday ball set off another wild battle with the city itself.

The Cleveland Spiders were hated around the National League, and their style of play was harshly criticized by their contemporaries. In 1896, one of Cleveland's newspapers, the *World*, called for "less aggressiveness both on and off the ball field," else "[if] only ruffians can make successful ball players then will it also be a fact that only ruffians will interest themselves in ball games."[3] George Wright, the star shortstop of the Cincinnati Red Stockings during the 1860s, decried the Spiders' behavior on the field, especially their foul language. "It is impossible," complained the distinguished old ballplayer, "for a respectable woman to go to the games in the

National League without running the risk of hearing language which is disgraceful."[4] The Spiders have also been held in low regard by historians, including Lee Allen, historian of the Baseball Hall of Fame. In his book, *The National League Story*, Allen wrote, "Patsy Tebeau was the prototype of all hooligans and his players cheerfully followed his horrid example."[5]

The story of the Spiders is not all unpleasant. Cy Young, who won more games than any pitcher who ever lived, spent the first nine seasons of his incredible career with the team. Young was no hooligan, and neither was Bobby Wallace, a pitcher who switched positions and became the American League's best fielding shortstop of the early 20th century. The Spiders were also ahead of their time from a racial perspective, as they employed an outfielder named Louis Sockalexis, the first recognized Native American in major league ball and the first minority player in the National League. Sockalexis played for the club a full 50 years before Jackie Robinson made his debut for the Brooklyn Dodgers.

The Spiders ended their run on a sour note when the 1899 edition of the club, with its star performers replaced by low-salaried minor leaguers and semi-pros, compiled the worst record in the history of major league ball, winning only 20 of its 154 games. Shortly afterward, the Spiders were no more. They left a complicated legacy, but an interesting one.

⑂ 1 ⑂

Frank Robison
and Cleveland Baseball

*"[Frank and Stanley Robison] were friends and supporters of the
national game when love and sentiment were the only inducements
and when to back a club meant to dig down in the pockets at the close
of each season to meet the deficit which was then always in evidence."*
—Alfred H. Spink, 1911[1]

Major league baseball had a rocky beginning in Cleveland, Ohio.
When the National Association, the first true professional circuit and precursor to the National League, began play in 1871, Cleveland was represented by its most prominent local team, called Forest City. This team,
which featured future Baseball Hall of Fame inductee James (Deacon)
White, gained a spot in the Association by paying a $10 entry fee. On
May 4, 1871, Forest City played the first game in National Association
(and major league) history, losing 2–0 to the Kekionoga club of Fort
Wayne, Indiana. The game, played in Fort Wayne, drew only 200 fans.

Cleveland's Forest City club lasted for two seasons and won only 16
of its 51 games. The city's next major league entry, which played in the
National League from 1879 to 1884, was dubbed the Blues after the color
of its uniform lettering and socks. This club was anchored by Jim
McCormick, a workhorse pitcher who won 45 games (and threw 657
innings) in 1880 while also serving as manager. This team was a little more
successful, finishing third in the league in 1880 and fourth in 1883.
McCormick was so important to the Blues that the club fell apart in August
of 1884, when he and two other stars quit the team, lured away by big-
money offers from a rival league, the Union Association. The Union Association failed, and so did the Cleveland Blues, who dropped out of the
National League.

After two seasons with no major league baseball, Cleveland was ready to try again. In late 1886, the American Association, then considered a major circuit, lost its Pittsburgh franchise to the rival National League. The Association had an opening, and Cleveland, one of the fastest growing cities in the nation, was anxious to fill it. Ownership groups from three cities—Kansas City, Detroit, and Cleveland—made offers, but the Association chose Cleveland. The driving force behind Cleveland's re-entry into top-level baseball was one of the city's wealthiest young men, a 35-year-old streetcar baron named Frank Robison.

Frank DeHass Robison[2] was born in Pittsburgh in 1852 and grew up in Dubuque, Iowa. Frank and his brother Martin Standford Robison Junior, who was five years younger and always went by the name Stanley, may have played some ball during their younger days. Dubuque was a hotbed of baseball in Iowa and many key figures of the professional game, such as future Chicago baseball kingpin Charlie Comiskey, passed through the city on their way to fame. One report says that when the nationally prominent team from Rockford, Illinois, led by its teenaged pitching sensation Albert G. Spalding, played the Dubuque Excelsiors in 1869, Frank Robison manned first base for Dubuque. His Excelsiors lost by a score of 79 to 1.

The Robison brothers soon abandoned athletics and set their sights on the business world. Frank, whose father ran a farm-supply business, married well; his new father-in-law Charles Hathaway was a builder of horse-drawn streetcar lines who happened to be expanding his business during the nation's phenomenal post–Civil War urban growth spurt. Frank and his father-in-law founded a Cleveland-based firm,

Frank DeHass Robison, the streetcar magnate who brought baseball back to Cleveland (*1896 Spalding Guide*).

called Hathaway and Robison, which built streetcar lines all over the northern United States and Canada. By the early 1880s both were wealthy men, as was Stanley, a lifelong bachelor who joined his older brother in the business.

Frank's love of baseball never left him, and his financial success allowed him to invest in the sport. In 1887, Robison bought a partial interest in the new Cleveland franchise. He then built a new ballpark, called American Association Park, at Payne and East 39th streets, on one of his streetcar lines. Eventually, Frank and Stanley Robison bought out all the other part-owners of the team, and in 1891, two years after the club had joined the National League, the Robisons built another venue, League Park, at Lexington and 66th streets about a mile east of downtown Cleveland. It, too, was easily reached by streetcar. This park was a wooden structure that seated about 9,000 people. It was rebuilt in concrete and steel in 1910 and hosted Cleveland's major league baseball teams until 1946.

Frank, whose wealth secured his place in Cleveland high society, built a massive estate on the Lake Erie waterfront, where he and his wife threw lavish parties. He was a gregarious, generous sort, though his temper would erupt every now and then. The Robisons spent freely and entertained in grand style. Frank even became interested in politics and ran (unsuccessfully) for Congress as a Republican. Stanley was much less outgoing, an introverted chap who quietly tended to business. Stanley remained in the background, as did another Robison brother, J. Howard, who served as the team's business manager.

Like many baseball magnates of the era, Frank was an enthusiastic gambler. Team owners often made bets with each other, wagering a suit of clothes, a new hat, or sums of money on the performance of their clubs. Such dealings would be cause for an investigation today, but at the time no one thought it unusual, as wagering on one's own team was regarded as a form of support and confidence. The Cleveland newspapers of the era are filled with reports of the owner's many wagers (though if one of his players asked for a $100 raise, Robison would fight him to the bitter end). However, Frank sometimes used his zest for gambling to benefit his men. One day, before a key series, Robison handed his manager Patsy Tebeau $100 and told him to wager it on that afternoon's game. If Cleveland won (which they did) Tebeau was instructed to split the proceeds equally among the players.

During the early 1890s Frank Robison merged his streetcar firm with a line owned and operated by Mark Hanna, the powerful Republican kingmaker who boosted an obscure Buckeye State congressman named

William McKinley all the way to the White House. A later merger went badly when Robison's broker embezzled the proceeds from the sale, leading to several years' worth of court filings and legal motions. Frank got some of his money back, but he and Hanna had a falling out over the botched deal. This experience soured Robison on the business world, and afterward he sold his streetcar interests and directed all his attention to his baseball club.

Frank Robison was an energetic owner, but often a frustrated one. Cleveland was one of America's fastest-growing cities during the 1890s, a decade that saw its population rise to seventh highest in the nation by 1900. However, while Robison's ballclub proved one of the National League's leading road attractions, home attendance was often disappointing. Cleveland, like Pittsburgh, was a working class town, and few factory laborers or construction workers were free to attend weekday games. Most of the city's blue-collar men worked six days a week in that era, and with no Sunday baseball—banned by state law in Ohio—Cleveland's core fan base remained small. These factors put the ballclub at a severe financial disadvantage and cast doubt on the long-term viability of baseball in Cleveland.

Despite all the problems, Robison was determined to make a go of it in Cleveland. His streetcar company had faced hurdles also, and he had built it into a smashing success. He saw no reason why he could not do the same with his baseball team. Robison kept the blue color scheme employed by the previous ballclub, and so the new team was once again nicknamed the Blues.

The new Cleveland club, with an operating stock of $20,000, had four principal partners. They were Frank Robison, treasurer George W. Howe, club secretary Davis Hawley, and *Cleveland Plain Dealer* sportswriter Frank H. Brunell. These four men, along with Robison's younger brother Stanley, would sink or swim with the fortunes of the team. Major league baseball had failed in Cleveland before, and many still doubted if the city would support a top-level club, especially as bad as this virtual expansion team promised to be.

⫻ 2 ⫻

Association Blues

The Cleveland club will have two uniforms this season. One will be of white and the other of blue-gray, both with dark blue stockings and dark blue belts and blue hats with white bands.
—*Cleveland Herald*, February 27, 1887

When major league baseball expanded from 16 teams to 30 between 1961 and 1998, the American and National Leagues allowed each new club to choose experienced players from the existing clubs in an expansion draft. The American Association in 1887 provided no such assistance, and the Cleveland Blues were left to their own devices in finding suitable players.

The Blues were fortunate to land a local boy, Ed McKean, to play shortstop. McKean, who was born in Grafton, 30 miles southwest of Cleveland, in 1864,[1] started his pro career in Youngstown at age 20 after excelling in amateur and semipro ball in and around Cleveland. He fought his way up the baseball ladder, spending time in Nashville, Rochester, and Providence before landing on his hometown Blues. A right-handed batter, Ed weighed about 200 pounds, though he was only about five feet and nine inches tall. He was "deep of chest and wide of shoulder," said one newspaper report, and he was "the kind that ran to stoutness."[2] He committed a lot of errors at short, but tried for every ball, almost never missed a game, and battled the opposition from the first inning to the last. This combination of skills made him popular with the Cleveland fans.

McKean was a future star, as was Charles (Chief) Zimmer, a 26-year-old catcher from Marietta, Ohio, who joined the club late in the season. Zimmer had bounced around the minors for nearly a decade, with short, unsuccessful major league stints with the Detroit Wolverines and New York Metropolitans. At one point, he quit the sport and moved to Chicago to open a laundry business, but he couldn't stay away from the game. He hired on as captain of a team in Poughkeepsie, New York, called the Indians, which gave him his nickname. Zimmer found a home in Cleveland as a backup to the veteran catcher Pop Snyder, and would inherit the starting job before the decade was over.

John (Cub) Stricker, a mustachioed second baseman known for his hot temper, was a key addition. Stricker, who stood only five feet and three inches tall and weighed about 140 pounds, had spent four seasons with the Athletics in his hometown of Philadelphia. He didn't hit much, but fielded well and built a reputation for leadership. He was an expert umpire baiter, too, a skill that was considered valuable in that era. Stricker had spent the previous season in Atlanta, waiting for another chance at the big leagues, and the Blues were happy to offer him the opportunity.

Ed McKean joined the Cleveland team in 1887 and remained with it until 1898 (National Baseball Library, Cooperstown, New York).

Stricker and veteran outfielder Pete Hotaling, who had played for the National League Blues earlier in the decade, were reasonably solid players, but the rest of the roster was full of failed prospects and mediocre veterans. Jim Toy was a first baseman who hit .222 with almost no power, while Phil Reccius held the third base job despite a .205 batting average. The pitching staff was a disaster area, with rookies Billy Crowell and Mike Morrison expected to carry the load. The new Cleveland club was an expansion team in every sense of the word, and its main goal for its inaugural season was not to win, but simply to survive.

Catcher Pop Snyder, a 32-year-old veteran whose career dated back to the National Association days, was appointed captain of the Blues and directed the team on the field, while Jimmy Williams, late of the St. Louis Browns, took over as manager. Williams was a respected baseball man, but lost his job in St. Louis because he failed to control the hard-drinking behavioral problems who populated the Browns roster at that time. Still, the Browns were the rowdiest crew of hell-raisers in baseball, so perhaps no one could have controlled them. Williams deserved another chance, and the Cleveland job would put his skill, and patience, to the test.

The newest American Association team needed a park to play in, so Robison and his fellow directors built a new facility at East 36th Street and Perkins Avenue. Called the Cleveland Base Ball Park, its outfield dimensions were huge compared to modern parks, as the fence stood 390 feet down the line from the plate in left field and nearly 600 feet in right. The fence had a lot of space for advertising signs, and manager Jimmy Williams hired one of his nephews to sell the ads to local businesses.[3]

The club did not take a Southern spring training trip, so the players either trained themselves at home or worked out in gyms in Cleveland. The team started practicing together in mid–April, but the drainage system at the new ballpark failed, leaving the field a muddy mess and forcing the Blues to find other practice sites. They went to Mansfield and Zanesville to play teams from the Ohio State League, and when the Cleveland Base Ball Park dried out they hosted a few exhibition games there. They walloped two local semipro nines by scores of 33–6 and 28–1, but the American Association would provide much stiffer competition.

Virtually everyone expected the talent-starved new club to finish last, and the Blues played down to expectations. The league did them no favors in putting them on the road for the first 11 games of their existence, and they completed the long road trip with only a single win. In all, the Blues dropped 13 of their first 14 games, giving up double figures in runs in nearly every contest. The Cleveland club looked totally overmatched, especially in an embarrassing 28–11 drubbing at St. Louis that lasted two hours and 40 minutes, an unusually long contest in that era. The Blues' first win, a 6–4 victory at Louisville on April 26, was the lone early bright spot in what looked to be a long season.

The Cleveland home opener on Wednesday, May 4, drew about 4,000 fans, who saw the Blues lose to the Cincinnati Reds by a 10–6 count. It was close for a while, but with the Reds leading by one run in the eighth, Ed McKean booted two ground balls, the Blues made several throwing errors, and the Reds scored five times to put the game away.

The Cleveland fans were happy to see major league ball return to the city, but the Blues, as expected, sank quickly to last place and stayed there. They gave up nearly 400 more runs than they allowed, and though they posted a winning record against the equally talent-deprived New York Metropolitans, Cleveland lost 18 of its 19 games against St. Louis and 17 of 20 to Baltimore. Their fielding was poor and their pitching was worse. Fortunately, the local sportswriters refrained from criticizing the team excessively; building a real ballclub would take time, and the papers were willing to show patience.

Perhaps the most frustrating player on the team was pitcher Billy Crowell. This right-hander had compiled a stellar minor league career and was courted by at least three other teams before signing with Cleveland. Nonetheless, Crowell gave up runs in bunches in almost every game he pitched. Frank Brunell, in his *Plain Dealer* column, insisted that Crowell had good speed, a sharp-breaking curve, and was a skilled fielder. Perhaps Crowell could not adapt to the new rule, put into place for the 1887 season, which gave a batter four strikes, not three. Still, the team had no one much better, so Crowell took his regular turn on the mound.[4]

Manager Williams searched far and wide for players, and with the team short on pitching, he signed two of baseball's most famous and controversial characters. One of them was Hugh (One-Arm) Daily, who was exactly what his nickname said he was—a one-armed pitcher. Daily, an impressively mustachioed, Irish-born right-hander, lost his left hand in a gun mishap at the age of 12. He threw speedy fastballs and wide-breaking curves, but his poor fielding and hitting kept him out of the major leagues until he was 34 years old. Daily pitched nearly 500 innings for Chicago of the Union Association in 1884 and struck out 19 men in a game, and in 1883 he threw a no-hitter for Cleveland of the National League. Daily was tough on catchers (receivers were often injured by his tricky pitches) and turned 40 years old in 1887, but he had once been a star. The Blues hoped that Daily might still have some magic in his arm.

Daily's handicap caused some limitations. He was an awful hitter with the tiny bat he used, as might be expected. He also could not be relieved. In 1887, a manager could only remove a pitcher from the box by shifting him to another spot on the field and having a position player take his place (unless the opposing manager gave permission, which rarely happened). The Irishman was such a poor fielder that almost every game he pitched was a complete one, no matter how many runs he gave up. In addition, he possessed another severe handicap, one that may have harmed his career even more than the lack of a left arm.

Daily was a thoroughly miserable human being.

Daily had alienated managers, teammates, and fans at every stop with his volcanic displays of temper, highlighted by loud and animated cursing that could be heard all over the ballpark. One day, he became so upset with his catcher that he called the receiver out to the mound—and walloped him in the head with his stump. No team had ever signed him for a second season, and by the mid–1880s his teammates hated him so much that they purposely made errors behind him to prevent him from winning. When the Washington club held a press conference in 1886 to announce that they had released the one-armed pitcher, the assembled reporters stood and cheered. Daily was damaged goods, but talent was scarce, so the Blues gave him one more chance to rehabilitate himself.

Charlie Sweeney was another well-known but troubled pitcher who received a last chance with the expansion Cleveland club. Sweeney, like Daily a right-hander, was only 24 years old, but his career was on the ropes due to arm miseries and behavioral issues. In 1884 Sweeney shot to stardom with the Providence Grays of the National League, but abandoned the team in mid-season to pursue a lucrative offer in the rival Union Association. (His departure left Charley Radbourn as the Grays' only pitcher, and Radbourn wound up winning a record 59 games that season.) Sweeney won 41 games in all in 1884, but his prodigious drinking caused problems for everyone around him. He was a mean drunk, prone to fighting his own teammates, and despite his undeniable talent, *Sporting Life* dismissed him as a "whiskey-guzzling, cowardly nincompoop."[5] The St. Louis club released him in 1886 after he beat up a teammate in a clubhouse fight. To make matters worse, his heavy pitching workload destroyed his arm, and after his great 1884 season Sweeney pitched in constant pain. He wasn't a bad hitter, so the Blues signed him to play first base, perhaps in the hope that his arm would recover.

Neither man worked out. Sweeney, who played first base for the Blues on Opening Day, hit poorly, lost all three games he pitched, and fought his teammates as he had in St. Louis. Sweeney drank himself off the team by July. Daily, signed on June 13, lost his first start, won three of his next four, and then suffered an eight-game losing streak. Besides, said historian James A. Egan, Daily "was as good at drinking with his right hand as he was at throwing with it."[6] Pleading arm soreness, Daily begged off of his last few scheduled starts, and Williams released him on September 3. Neither Daily nor Sweeney ever played major league ball again.

The Association's newest team received little consideration from the umpires, as shown in its only forfeited loss of the season on July 22 in Philadelphia. In the sixth inning, the Quakers had Louie Bierbauer on first and Harry Stovey at third when Bierbauer jogged down to second to draw a throw. Catcher Pop Snyder pegged the ball to second baseman Cub Stricker, who threw home when Stovey charged down the line. Stovey looked like a dead duck, but Ted Larkin, the Philadelphia batter, interfered with Snyder and allowed Stovey to scamper back to third.

Umpire Mitchell, whose first name has been lost to history, first declared Stovey out, but changed his mind and ruled Stovey safe and Larkin out. The Blues wanted Stovey called out (though the umpire's second decision was the correct one) and when they argued, Mitchell simply forfeited the game to the Quakers and marched off the field.

Even the Philadelphia correspondent to *Sporting Life* railed against the forfeit. He complained of Mitchell's "imbecility" and asked, "Where in the world did President Wikoff fish up that latest specimen of umpirical incompetency, Mitchell, and who stood sponsor for him? The man was utterly at sea upon the rules, and his judgment of balls and strikes was faulty in the extreme. He deliberately deprived Cleveland of a game Friday by unjustly forfeiting it to the Athletics, when that club had no desire to win it that way."[7]

Attendance slowed during the summer as the novelty of the new team wore off, and rumors reached the papers that the Cleveland club was close to collapsing under a load of debt. Frank Brunell, despite his raging conflict of interest in his dual role as a team director and *Cleveland Plain Dealer* columnist, denied the rumors that the Pittsburgh club was vying to buy out the Blues. "Despite the fact that the Cleveland team has a strong tail hold in the American Association," insisted Brunell, "the season and the team is young, and I still expect to see the latter beat the flag. It is a far better team than when it began the season and will be strengthened at every point until it gets there."[8] Brunell admitted that the team was losing money, so Frank Robison and his co-owners looked for ways to sell more tickets. One option was something that would cause great controversy in Cleveland during the next decade. That something was Sunday ball.

The American Association allowed its member teams to play games on Sundays (though the National League did not), but many cities, including Cleveland, faced local and state laws that banned the practice. Still, teams such as St. Louis enjoyed much bigger crowds on the Christian Sabbath than on any other day of the week. The potential profit to be made from Sunday baseball was too much to resist, so Robison and his partners scheduled a game to be played on Sunday, August 21.

The Cleveland city council had recently passed a bill that slightly relaxed the strict Sunday "blue laws," so Robison plowed ahead with plans to test the new regulations. He chose to stage the contest at the Cleveland Driving Park, in the eastern part of the city far from downtown. With a temporary wooden ballpark hastily assembled, the Blues prepared to do battle with the New York Mets. Rain no doubt kept some fans away, but about 2,500 showed up to see the first major league Sunday game in Cleveland's history.

There was good and bad news. The good news was that a local paper, the *Plain Dealer*, reported that "the crowd was a very respectable one and there was no unnecessary noise during the game."[9] The bad news was that the Mets defeated the home team by a score of 7 to 5. What's more, a citizen from the neighborhood lodged a complaint with the police, who arrested second baseman Cub Stricker at game's end. The team paid his fine, and the Blues scheduled no more Sunday games in 1887.

The season ended mercifully in October, with the Blues in last place, 54 games behind pennant-winning St. Louis, with a record of 39 wins and 92 losses. There was nowhere to go but up.

To upgrade the first base position for the 1888 campaign, Williams hired Jay Faatz, a tall (six feet four inches) and stringy (195 pounds) minor league veteran whose only previous top-level experience came with Pittsburgh's Association club in 1884. Faatz, at age 27, was an odd-looking player, described by *The Sporting News* as "as slender as a knitting needle and long as a fence rail."[10]

As historian David Nemec has pointed out, Jay Faatz appears to have been a thoroughly mediocre ballplayer, based on his statistics alone. He was a first baseman with a low batting average and very little power, and was not much better than the league average with the glove. However, Faatz was a born leader, though his quick temper and obscenity-filled outbursts made him unpopular with fans and umpires. Though Faatz had been out the majors for three years, manager Jimmy Williams made him the field captain of the Blues at the beginning of the 1888 season. Faatz was a good baserunner and an expert at getting hit by a pitch. He could spin away from a close pitch and still manage to stick his arm in front of it. Everyone knew that he gained a lot of bases that way, but Faatz was so good at it that the league considered doing away with the rule that allowed a hit batter to take first base.

The new first baseman set the tone for the upcoming season when the Blues played a series of pre-season practice games against the minor league squad from Wheeling, West Virginia, in mid–April. All the while, Faatz and his fellow Blues razzed the Wheeling players mercilessly, keeping up a steady beat of heckling and especially vile insults. The Wheeling fans

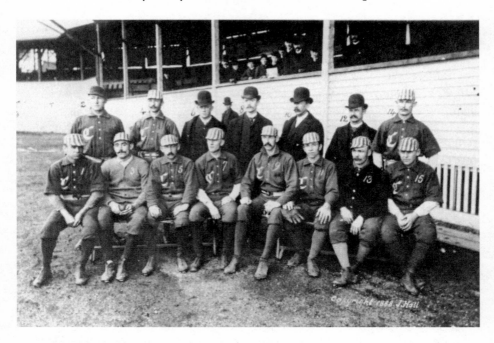

The 1888 Cleveland Blues (National Baseball Library, Cooperstown, New York).

were outraged at the Clevelanders' behavior; as the local paper reported afterward, "There were quite a number of ladies present and they were highly incensed at the ungentlemanly behavior of the visitors."[11] Perhaps Faatz should have toned it down a bit, for immediately after the game a local cop arrested him and charged him with disorderly conduct. The Cleveland captain had to post bond of $15 before leaving town. Still, the new captain had made it known that this edition of the Cleveland Blues would play in a highly confrontational fashion. They would make up for their lack of talent by dialing up the aggressiveness.

Williams also brought in a new starting pitcher. He kept Billy Crowell, who lost 31 games for the Blues in 1887, but shifted Crowell to the second slot in the rotation. The main starter for 1888 would be Edward Bakely, called Jersey because he came from New Jersey. Bakely had been a 30-game loser in the Union Association four years before and had pitched in the minors since then. Bakely was a heavy drinker, like so many players of the era, but he was a workhorse who could eat up a lot of innings. He would give the Blues a lot of quantity, if not much quality.

Thus fortified, the Blues started their second season. Forced by the league schedule-makers to play their first 12 games on the road, the Blues lost their first seven contests, with a 28–7 demolition at Philadelphia proving to be their worst performance of the year. They finally hit the winner's circle with a 10–9 win against the Athletics, then lost two more before winning six of their next seven, the best winning streak the team had yet compiled. The home opener in Cleveland on May 2 ended in a 10–1 win over the Athletics, raising hopes that the Blues might actually contend, if not for the pennant, at least for a spot in the first division.

However, the lack of talent brought the Blues down to earth. Captain Jay Faatz was not an easy man to get along with, and when Jimmy Williams criticized him in June for leaving a pitcher in too long, the two held a major screaming match that caused the manager to reinstate Pop Snyder as captain. Team morale began to dissipate as the Blues sank in the standings, and Williams lost control of his behaviorally-challenged squad just as he had in St. Louis.

One incident was particularly damaging to the club's slim chances of success. Bill Stemmyer was a right-handed pitcher who had won 22 games for Boston in 1886, but arm soreness derailed his promising career. Given a chance with Cleveland, Stemmyer took the mound and gave up 28 runs to the Athletics on April 23. A month later, he and Jersey Bakely were shooting dice with a group of patrons in a Cleveland bar when a fight broke out. Stemmyer punched a man and injured his hand, putting him on the sidelines indefinitely. Bakely escaped injury, but was so hung over the next day that he gave up 17 runs in a loss to the Browns. Williams suspended Stemmyer, who made only one more unsuccessful start and disappeared from the major leagues.

Stemmyer failed, so the Blues continued to audition new pitchers. In June, the team signed John (Cinders) O'Brien, a right-hander who had won 17 games in 19 starts for Lima (Ohio) of the Tri-State League. O'Brien pitched well enough to take the second rotation slot behind Jersey Bakely and enabled the club to release Billy Crowell, who won only five of his 18 starts.

The Cleveland owners determined that the ballclub would need an average attendance of 1,100 to break even, but as the losses mounted the fans stopped coming. The Blues were marginally improved, floating along in sixth place for much of the season, but manager Williams lost control of the team. The change in captains made little difference. Fans and players alike had become apathetic. The end for Williams came after a grueling 22-game road trip, stretching from mid–June to mid–July, which saw the Blues win only four games and drop into last place. Williams had thought about quitting for several weeks, but on July 16, after the manager received a telegram from his hometown of Columbus, Ohio, informing him that his father had died, Williams made up his mind. He resigned that day, and Frank Robison then hired Tom Loftus as the new manager.

Tom Loftus is largely forgotten today, but he was one of the most prominent and respected managers of his era. A onetime minor league outfielder who played only nine games in the majors, Loftus piloted an incredible number of major and minor league ballclubs during his career, including Cincinnati and Chicago in the National League, Milwaukee in the Union Association, and later Washington in the American League. The Cleveland post was his first sustained experience at the top level of baseball.

Amazingly, the Blues won six of their first seven games under Loftus and rose out of the cellar. The Blues soon reverted to their usual mediocrity, but in late August and early September a nine-game home winning streak boosted the Cleveland club into fifth position. The team was improving, slowly but surely, though fan support was still lacking.

In a bid to boost attendance, Blues management tested the waters of Sunday ball again. On Sunday, July 22, the Blues played a game at the Geauga Lake picnic grounds outside the city. Some 3,500 people saw the Blues defeat Baltimore that day, and one week later another crowd of 3,500 watched Cleveland lose to league-leading St. Louis. A third game at Geauga Lake, played on August 22, brought only 1,000 people, so Frank Robison moved his Sunday venue to Beyerle's Park, a site within the borders of Cleveland that hosted amateur and semipro ball on Sundays. Because those games charged admission, Robison figured that the local authorities would allow the Blues to play there on Sundays as well.

The ball field at Beyerle's was located next to the artificial lake in the middle of the park. Though seating was limited, about 3,000 people ventured to the park on Sunday, September 2 to see the Blues face off against Louisville. Many fans simply stood around the perimeter of the playing area, causing some consternation when Ed McKean belted a fly ball into the crowd in right field and circled the bases for a home run. After an argument from the Louisville nine, the umpire ruled the hit a double and sent McKean back to second. Later in the game, pitcher Jersey Bakely drove a fly over the crowd and into the lake; this hit stood as a home run, one of only two Bakely hit during his major league career. The Blues defeated the Colonels 11 to 4. Best of all, no policemen were present to interfere with the game.

The Blues played another game at Beyerle's Park the following Sunday, but this one did not count in the standings. The visiting Kansas City

Cowboys, struggling to climb out of last place, did not want another loss on their record and would only agree to play an exhibition. Cleveland won by a 7 to 5 score before 2,000 people, and that was the end of Sunday baseball in Cleveland for the next several years.

The 1888 edition of the Blues ended the season in sixth place, two notches up from their last-place finish the year before. They had some pieces in place, with McKean, Stricker and Faatz on the infield and a good catching tandem in Snyder and Zimmer. Jersey Bakely, bad behavior and all, threw 532 solid innings and compiled a 25–33 record, but the rest of the staff failed to produce. The frustrating Billy Crowell drew his release in July; picked up by Louisville, he made one start against his old Cleveland mates in early September and lost by a score of 14 to 3. That was it for Crowell, who played out the rest of his career in the minor leagues. Cinders O'Brien performed well until he was felled by heat stroke on a hot August day in Cincinnati. He missed a week, then lost 11 of his final 16 decisions and wound up with an 11–19 log. The Blues were making progress, but they needed more and better pitching.

Ed Keas was a young pitcher who showed promise, posting a 3–3 record in six late-season starts for the Spiders, but his arm could not stand the strain. He missed much of September and early October due to arm pain, and though he pitched a complete game win at Philadelphia on October 16, the next to last game of the season, his major league career was finished. Still, he provided one valuable service for Cleveland baseball on his way out the door and into obscurity. The Milwaukee club of the Western Association decided to take a chance on Keas and arranged a trade with the Blues. In return for Keas, Cleveland received a fancy-fielding center fielder named Jimmy McAleer.

⫶ 3 ⫶

The Spiders Are Born

The city is ablaze with excitement over the team and the question, "What is the score?" is being asked by everybody from the boy in dresses, nearly, to the old gens who used to play when a catch on the first bound was out. Score boards are appearing daily in all parts of the city. Fire engine houses are using their official blackboard for a score board.

— *The Sporting News*, June 1889[1]

After the end of the 1888 season, Chicago team president Albert Spalding took his White Stockings, and a selection of "All-Americas" from the other National League clubs, on an historic six-month trip around the world. The White Stockings and the All-Americas played their way to the West Coast, where they boarded a steamship and traveled to Hawaii, Australia, British India, and then to Egypt, where they played a game near the Sphinx and the pyramids. The travelers proceeded to the European continent and staged contests in Italy, France, and England. They returned to the United States in early April of 1889 to a tumultuous welcome and a series of banquets in their honor.

When the players came home, they received a big surprise.

In their absence, the National League owners had approved a payroll reduction program, which the papers called a "classification" scheme. The magnates intended to classify each player into one of five groups, labeled A to E in descending order of value and talent. Each level had its own salary cap; the maximum salary for an A player would be set at $2,500 per year, with $2,000 for a B player, $1,500 for C, $1,000 for D, and only $500 for E. This plan was nothing more than a frontal attack on player salaries, and because most of the league's biggest stars were on the other side of the world when the plan was approved, the players were powerless to object until it was too late. Not only that, but the owners, in a classic in-your-face move, rammed through a provision that required the players to pay a rental fee for the use of their uniforms.

Bad blood had existed between players and owners for years, as it had in many other industries during the age of the robber barons. The National League had introduced a limited reserve clause, binding certain players to their teams on a permanent basis, to the standard player contract in 1880. Five years later, the owners expanded the reserve clause to include every man on a major league roster, choking off the last bit of freedom the players had enjoyed up to that time. In response, John M. Ward, who not only starred at shortstop for the New York Giants but also owned a law degree, had founded the Brotherhood of Professional Base Ball Players in October of 1885. This was the first serious attempt by major league players to unionize, and though the National League had met with Ward and his Brotherhood allies in late 1887, their negotiations proved fruitless. The magnates held all the power in the player-owner relationship, and were not willing to concede a bit of it.

Some of the more cynical players believed that the world tour itself was a ruse to get Ward and other Brotherhood leaders safely out of the country to minimize interference with their salary-slashing plans. In any case, the situation added a steady flow of tension to the 1889 season, one that would explode in a full-scale player revolt by the end of the calendar year.

In the meantime, the Cleveland Blues, despite their lack of success during their first two campaigns, took a step up on the baseball ladder. The American Association was a major league, but it was definitely a lesser one, and Frank Robison no doubt intended to move into the National League as part of his long-term plan. His opportunity came after the 1888 season, when the Detroit Wolverines dropped out of the National League due to poor home support in a city that was not yet the industrial behemoth it would become during the early 20th century. Robison applied for admission to the National and was accepted as Detroit's replacement. After a five-year hiatus, Cleveland was back in the National League.

One might wonder why the National League would be so accommodating to Cleveland, as the Blues had finished eighth and sixth during their two seasons in the Association and were still weak at several positions. Besides, the circuit's previous Cleveland entry had failed only five years before, dropped from the National League due to poor attendance and player defections to the Union Association. The Association teams had charged a quarter for admission; would enough Cleveland fans be willing to pay the National League's fifty-cent rate?

Nonetheless, Cleveland had some points in its favor. The city was one of the fastest growing in the country, with its population rank rising from 21st in the nation in 1860 to tenth by 1890. A populous working-class town like Cleveland was exactly the growing market the National League wanted to claim. The city did not allow Sunday baseball, but neither did the National League as a whole, so that would be no problem, at least in the beginning. Also, team management, headed by Frank Robison, had deep pockets and a record of business success. If the team somehow failed, it would likely not be caused by incompetent ownership.

Detroit's failure was not only due to the small market in which it played. The Wolverines slugged their way to a pennant in 1887 after buying the best hitters from the Buffalo franchise, which disbanded after the 1885 campaign. The hard-hitting Detroit club was one of the league's top road attractions, and team ownership counted on balancing their books with their slice of the gate in road contests to offset the small crowds at home. The plan worked in 1887, but in 1888 the more powerful teams induced the league to change its formula for splitting gate receipts between home and road teams specifically to harm the Wolverines. The club could not survive in this new financial climate and quit the league at season's end. Perhaps this scenario showed Frank Robison that his fellow National League magnates could be as cutthroat as in any other business in the age of the robber barons.

Cleveland's previous National League team wore blue uniform letters and socks, as did the American Association entry. When the club moved into the National League in 1889, it chose a new color scheme. Team management adopted a uniform with a black top and dark gray pants with black stripes on the sides. The belts, stockings, and caps were all black too. Each player received two uniforms, and to keep a consistent look, the home and road uniforms were identical.

Frank H. Brunell, who wore several hats as a team director, baseball writer for the *Plain Dealer*, and Cleveland correspondent for *Sporting Life*, remarked that almost all the players were tall and stringy. There was not a fat one in the bunch, and some, like Jay Faatz, looked like absolute bean-poles. Brunell suggested, jokingly, that such a gangly, long-limbed collection of ballplayers in their black and gray uniforms should be called the Spiders.

And so they were. Brunell first used the name Spiders in his *Plain Dealer* column on May 12. Other papers referred to the newest National League team as the "Babes" or the "Infants," due to the presence of so many young players. In any case, few expected the Cleveland club, which had struggled for respectability in the weaker Association, to make much of a dent in the National League, at least in the foreseeable future.

To compete in the National League, Cleveland needed starting pitching, and the demise of the Detroit club allowed a very good starting pitcher to fall to the Spiders. The Wolverines sold their best players to other clubs in the circuit, and Cleveland bought the contracts of several ex-Detroiters, including those of outfielder Larry Twitchell (who led the Spiders in runs batted in that season), pitcher Henry Gruber, and left-handed catcher Sy Sutcliffe. The most important import from Detroit was an up-and-coming 22-year-old right-hander from Maryland, Ebenezer (Eb) Beatin, who added a needed dose of talent to a struggling Cleveland pitching staff.

The acquisition of Beatin was considered a coup for the Spiders, as he had been the focus of a bitter battle among three National League teams for his services only two years before. Beatin had earned notice in 1887 when he went 19–5 for Allentown of the Pennsylvania State League. After his strong showing in Allentown, the Cincinnati, Detroit, and Indianapolis clubs all laid claim to his contract, a fight that Detroit eventually won. Beatin, called the "Allentown Wonder," appeared in 12 games for Detroit in 1888 with a 5–7 record, but completed all his starts and established himself as one of the best young pitchers in the league. Cleveland manager Tom Loftus installed Beatin as his number one starter.

Beatin's best pitch was the "slow ball," which he threw with the same motion as his regular fastball and was what we would call a changeup today. Ed McKean claimed that Beatin "had the most astonishing slow ball that was ever offered up to a batter." McKean liked to tell how Harry Stovey, the Philadelphia slugger of the late 1880s, once was so badly fooled by Beatin's slow ball that he swung and missed, reset himself, and swung again, belting the ball into the outfield fence. The umpire disallowed the hit, ruling that the first swing was the only one that counted.[2]

Beatin was an important addition to the club, but two other new men would make an even larger imprint on Cleveland baseball. One was Jimmy McAleer, acquired from Milwaukee for pitcher Ed Keas in what turned out to be one of the best trades in Cleveland history.

Jimmy McAleer was born in 1864 in Youngstown, Ohio, to parents who emigrated from Ireland to Canada and then to the United States. His father found work as a boilermaker in Youngstown's steel mills, but Jimmy was determined to stay out of the factories. He graduated from high school and then set his course for a career in professional baseball.

McAleer, who stood 6 feet tall and weighed 180 pounds, was speedy and sure-handed, but was the prototypical good-field, no-hit outfielder.

One of the weakest batters in the National League, he hit below the league average in almost every season, and what little power he had left him as he grew older (in 1898, his final season with the Spiders, 84 of his 87 hits were singles). However, he compensated for his shortcomings at the plate with his brilliance in the field. Many of his contemporaries considered him the best defensive outfielder of the 1890s, and veteran sportswriter Franklin Lewis, in his definitive history of Cleveland baseball published in 1949, called McAleer "perhaps the most graceful outfielder known to the game with the exception of Tris Speaker."[3] Some say that he was the first outfielder to take his eyes off a fly ball, run to the place it would come down, and then look up and catch it. He covered vast expanses of ground in center, and the Spiders always believed that his glove work made up for his weak bat.

The other new addition left an even bigger mark on the team.

Third baseman Patsy Tebeau spoke, thought, and acted like a true son of the old sod, but was, in fact, not Irish at all. Born Oliver Wendell Tebeau in 1864, his parents were of French-Canadian and German descent. Nonetheless, the Tebeau family settled in the most Irish section of St. Louis, Goose Hill, and sent Oliver and his brothers out to find work. Oliver, at the age of nine, fell in with a group of Irish construction workers for whom he ran errands and performed odd jobs for a few stray pennies. The workers took a liking to the youngster and soon honored him with an Irish nickname. Before long "Patsy" Tebeau was bringing his lunch each day and working alongside his new brethren. He also began speaking with a brogue that he kept for the rest of his life.

By age 16, Patsy was working as an apprentice to a file maker, and his brother George, two and a half years older, was a clerk in a lumber company. However, they both were more at home on the baseball field. Goose Hill and another Irish district, the Kerry Patch, were incubators for baseball players. Baseball was the most popular sport in the city at the time, and the Irish of St. Louis produced far more than their share of star ballplayers, many of whom wound up in the National League and the American Association. It was no sport for the timid and the easily frightened, and the Tebeau brothers attacked the St. Louis baseball scene with fists at the ready. Patsy was not a big man, standing five feet and eight inches tall and weighing about 160 pounds, yet he emerged as a good hitter, a skilled infielder, and, most importantly, a born leader who never backed down from a fight.

Patsy played the infield for one of the Mound City's leading semipro clubs, the Peach Pies, with future major leaguers Jack O'Connor at catcher and Silver King on the mound. From there, he and O'Connor joined a team in Jacksonville, Illinois, where he drew the notice of Cap Anson, manager and star of the National League's Chicago White Stockings. George Tebeau wound up with the Cincinnati Reds while Patsy, at the age of 22, had a tryout with the White Stockings in September of 1887. Regular Chicago third baseman Tom Burns was injured, so Patsy filled in for 20 games, in which he batted only .162. When Burns returned in 1888, Patsy was off to Minneapolis and (later) Omaha. He performed well enough to earn a look from the Spiders, who had not yet found a third baseman of major league caliber. Tebeau claimed the position and made himself an indispensable part of the team. He played in all 136 scheduled games in 1889, batting .282 and giving the Spiders solid play at third for the first time.

Bob Gilks was another key addition. Gilks arrived in Cleveland in August of 1887 as a pitcher, but shifted to the outfield due to arm problems. Though he was a good fielder, he was never much of a hitter. He simply could not lay off sweeping curveballs on the outside of the plate. To compensate for his weakness, he hunched over in the batter's box and stood so close to the plate that his head was in the strike zone. At least this unusual stance increased his on-base percentage, for Gilks was hit by pitches on a regular basis.

Gilks, like many of the Spiders, was a scrappy fellow, and in April of 1889 his quick temper caused the National League to adopt a new rule. Gilks lived in Cincinnati, and was at home when the Spiders came to town to play the Reds in a preseason game. Gilks, following the custom of the time, was permitted to bring his uniform to the Reds' clubhouse and dress there. However, during the game Cincinnati pitcher Tony Mullane barely missed Gilks' head with two fastballs, causing Gilks to loudly threaten Mullane on the field. The argument continued in the Reds' dressing room, with Gilks grabbing a bat and going after Mullane. It turned into a brawl, and the league decided that dressing in the opposing clubhouse was not such a good idea. The league banned the practice, and the ban continues to this day.

The Spiders started their 1889 season on the road, as usual, but this time they refused to be buried early. They lost their opener in Indianapolis but won their second game by a score of 10 to 4. Splitting their four contests with the Hoosiers, they won at Pittsburgh on April 29 and found themselves, with a 3–2 record, in a tie for first place. The Spiders then fell into a mild slump, losing three of their next four to close the road trip with a 4–5 mark.

Ballplayers were, then as now, a superstitious lot, and before the season was ten games old, many of the Spiders decided that they hated their black and gray uniforms. After a spate of minor injuries and a stretch of poor clutch hitting on the season's opening road trip, the players were quick to blame their unusual uniforms, calling them a "Jonah," the then-current phrase for a jinx. Team management agreed with them and contracted with the Philadelphia firm of Reach and Company for a new style. These new uniforms featured navy blue pants and shirt for home games and black pants and shirts for the road. The stockings were also black, but the dark colors were set off by a white belt, white cuffs, and "CLEVELAND" in white letters on the chest. The new caps featured white and black vertical stripes. These uniforms were ready for the home opener.

On Friday, May 3, some 3,000 fans showed up on a bitterly cold day to see Cleveland's first National League game in five years. After the usual season-opening parade with a brass band, the Spiders lost 4–0 to Chicago, managing only six hits off Bill Hutchison. However, Cleveland defeated the White Stockings on Saturday and Monday to even their record at 6–6. A few days later at Indianapolis, Eb Beatin won his own game with a three-run homer in the eighth inning. The Spiders were holding their own against National League competition, at least so far.

The New York Giants were not convinced. They apparently did not take the Spiders seriously, for when Tom Loftus' team came to New York during the second week of May, the defending champion Giants put infielder Gil Hatfield on the mound. Hatfield was famous for his strong throwing arm[4] and the Giants did not want to waste one of their regular starters against the league's newest team. Cleveland foiled their strategy by beating Hatfield by a 10 to 8 score, and followed it up with a 5–0 shutout by Cinders O'Brien the next day. After the Giants reasserted themselves by walloping Cleveland 16 to 2, catcher Buck Ewing pitched against the Spiders a day later and won.

By early June, the Spiders were the talk of the National League. Though the established teams expected Cleveland's good fortune to run out, the Spiders compiled a 16–2 streak and vaulted into second place. They did it with hustle and aggressiveness as much as with talent, gaining a reputation as a fighting ballclub that put up a battle, win or lose. In Philadelphia, Patsy Tebeau became enraged with Phillies third baseman Billy Hallman tripped baserunner Cub Stricker, though Tebeau was never shy about doing the same thing himself. Patsy punched Phillies catcher Jack Clements, touching off a fight and resulting in a $10 fine for Tebeau and a $50 fine for captain Jay Faatz.

Tebeau was a fighter, but also drew notice for trickery. He won a game with the hidden ball trick one day; while catcher Chief Zimmer fumbled with his equipment at home plate in the ninth inning of a one-run game, Washington's Walt Wilmot grew bored and wandered off third base. Tebeau, who had hidden the ball under his armpit, tagged Wilmot out to end the game, a 5–4 Cleveland win. Patsy did it again against Indianapolis on May 11, catching Louis (Jumbo) Schoeneck off the bag in the ninth inning. Indianapolis manager Frank Bancroft was so angry that he fined Schoeneck ten dollars and booted him off the team soon afterward.[5] Tebeau's hidden ball trick ended Schoeneck's major league career.

The Spiders also won with alertness, beating Washington by one run in July when Hank O'Day of the Senators delivered what should have been a game-tying single. O'Day loafed his way down the baseline, but

STRICKER, 2d B., Clevelands
COPYRIGHT BY GOODWIN & CO., 1889.
OLD JUDGE
CIGARETTE FACTORY.
GOODWIN & CO., New York.

Cub Stricker, second baseman and staunch union man (Library of Congress).

when Jay Faatz made a diving stop and threw to pitcher Eb Beatin covering first, O'Day was out and the game was over. They also enjoyed their share of sheer luck, as when Faatz hit a three-run homer in Pittsburgh that never reached the outfield. With two men on, the Cleveland captain drove a liner off third baseman Deacon White's foot. The ball ricocheted under the grandstand, and while White frantically tried to retrieve the ball, three runs scored. It was one of only three home runs Faatz hit during his entire major league career.

The Spiders gained a share of the league lead with three wins in a row against Boston in early July. Still, Tom Loftus was not fooled. He knew that the Spiders were still short on talent, and that aggressiveness and luck would only take them so far. The Cleveland manager told a reporter that he would be happy to finish above sixth place. His remarks proved prophetic when the Spiders fell to earth, losing 15 of 19 games and dropping to fourth position.

Their biggest offensive explosion of the season came in the middle of a 1–10 skid. On August 15, the Boston Beaneaters came to Cleveland and suffered a 19–8 loss, one in which the Spiders, who batted first that day, became the first major league team to score in all nine innings. Larry Twitchell hit for the cycle—the first Cleveland player ever to do so—with six hits, three of which were triples, while Patsy Tebeau belted five hits. It wasn't easy, as Jersey Bakely was "wild as a deer," according to the papers, walking four men and hitting one in the second inning. Twitchell came in to pitch and got the last two outs of the inning, and then Henry Gruber kept the Beaneaters at bay the rest of the day. The hitting outburst did not last, as Boston's John Clarkson shut out the Spiders the next day by a 13–0 score. In late August the Spiders dipped below the .500 mark and stayed below it for the rest of the campaign.

The Spiders were not yet a contender, but the National League's newest team was always ready to fight. In August, the Spiders hosted the New York Giants at the Payne Avenue ballpark. Cleveland's Jimmy McAleer belted a liner to the outfield and slid into second, avoiding the tag. Umpire Jack Powers called McAleer safe, but when Giant catcher Buck Ewing, one of the game's biggest stars, claimed that McAleer had missed first base, Powers reversed course and ruled McAleer out. The Spiders exploded in rage, and so did their fans, dozens of whom surged out of the stands and onto the field. Most of the Spiders and many of the outraged patrons pushed, jostled, and manhandled Powers until the arbiter lost his nerve and made a dash for the clubhouse. There he remained until a squadron of police officers rescued him and escorted him back onto the field. The local cops protected the umpire from the Spiders and their agitated fans for the rest of the game.

Rule-bending, like umpire abuse, was standard operating procedure for National League teams in 1889. Patsy Tebeau, the Cleveland third baseman, was an expert at shoving a runner off base (when the umpire's back was turned) and tagging him out. The sole umpire could not possibly see everything, so Patsy gained an out more often than not. In early August Tebeau pulled this stunt on Washington's Walt Wilmot (the victim of the hidden ball trick earlier in the season), and despite the Senators' loud protests, umpire Wesley Curry declared Wilmot out. The influential *New York Clipper*, in recounting the play, praised Tebeau as "smart."

The Spiders were merely copying the behavior of other National League players, even the prominent ones. Buck Ewing of the Giants, one of baseball's biggest stars, liked to drop his heavy catchers' mask in the baseline if a runner looked like he was headed for home. This trick was dangerous to the runner and incensed New York's opponents; two batters, Philadelphia's Sam Thompson and Washington's Paul Hines, smashed Ewing's mask with their bats in retaliation. Chicago player-manager Cap Anson was an inveterate umpire abuser, and in a game at Cleveland on June 15, umpire Wallace Fessenden ordered Anson out of the game, but the Chicago field boss refused to leave. Anson's belligerent attitude worked, for he bullied the umpire into letting him stay in the game. Anson went 4 for 4 to lead the White Stockings to a win over the Spiders.

The Spider infielders loved the hidden ball trick, but it didn't always work. The Spiders tried to pull it on Washington's Bill (Dummy) Hoy, a deaf mute, one day. Hoy was on second when the Spiders casually tossed the ball around among McKean, Stricker, and even center fielder McAleer. Finally, when they thought Hoy

Oliver (Patsy) Tebeau played third base for the 1889 Spiders and became manager of the team in 1891 (Library of Congress).

was napping, Stricker crept up behind the base and waited for him to wander off it. Instead, Hoy slapped the ball out of Stricker's hand and took off for third, making it safely. The Spiders protested, but the umpire let the play stand. Tebeau, the third baseman, then hid the ball under his arm and waited for his chance, but Hoy merely sat on the base until Tebeau returned the ball to the pitcher. As *Sporting Life* complained, "This exhibition of dirty work occupied nearly ten minutes."[6]

The Spiders were forging an identity, and that identity was one of aggressiveness. Captain Jay Faatz and third baseman Patsy Tebeau drew notice, much of it negative, for arguing with the umpires and quarreling with opposing players. On September 14 the Spiders played a doubleheader at Boston in which both contests degenerated into a nonstop barrage of bickering. In the first game, won by the Beaneaters, Cleveland committed seven errors and the game was reported to be "full of kicking with the umpire by Capt. Faatz and his lieutenant Tebeau."[7] Game Two brought more of the same. In the third inning, Cub Stricker tried to spin out of the way of a Kid Madden pitch, but the ball hit the bat and rolled down to second for a double play. Faatz and Tebeau became so animated in their arguments that umpire Wes Curry fined Faatz $75 and Tebeau $60 (Tebeau had also been fined in the first game). Curry ordered Faatz from the field, but the Cleveland captain refused to leave even after Curry called the park police to escort him out. Only after Faatz discussed the matter with team secretary George Howe did he consent to vacate the premises.

The Boston fans booed heartily at the scene, and when umpire Curry was fired by the league shortly afterward, *Sporting Life* laid the blame on the Spiders' doorstep:

> Whatever may have been the real reason for Umpire Curry's removal at this late period of the season, such removal may be criticised on the score of judgment, coming as it did right on the heels of the disgraceful row raised by Captain Faatz at Boston. With the unthinking mass and the unreasoning player it will be equivalent to a notice that umpires have no rights that kicking captains are bound to respect, that the law for the government of players upon the field is a dead letter, and that the League will not support its umpires when they come in conflict with the captains of potential clubs. There are perhaps good reasons for Mr. Curry's removal, but it would have been the better policy to have deferred the dismissal until the near end of the season, or at least until the disgraceful Faatz incident had been effaced from public memory.[8]

Though the Spiders finished sixth in the eight-team league in 1889, they helped decide the pennant race on the season's final weekend. Boston and New York had battled for the flag all year, and the Beaneaters came to Cleveland with a one-game lead over the Giants on October 4. Unfortunately for the Boston club, Cleveland was the "bad town" for its biggest star, Mike (King) Kelly. The many temptations of Cleveland nightlife were usually too strong for Kelly to resist, and this visit to Cleveland was no different. In his team's most important game of the year, Kelly showed up too hung over to play. Wrapped in an overcoat over his street clothes, Kelly planted himself on Cleveland's bench and kept up a running, rambling commentary on the game.

When Boston pitcher John Clarkson, seeking his 50th win of the season, gave up three runs to the Spiders in the third inning, Kelly screamed at his teammates, "You never win when I don't play!" More drunken haranguing followed, and the "King of Ballplayers," as Kelly liked to call himself, walked onto the field and confronted umpire John McQuaid. When Kelly tried to throw a punch at McQuaid, two Cleveland cops wrestled him away and ejected him from the ballpark. In the end, the Spiders scored a 7–1 victory that knocked Boston out of first place. After the game, Boston manager Jim Hart claimed that local "rogues" got Kelly drunk and set him up to be ejected, as revenge for Jay Faatz's troubles in Boston three weeks before.[9]

The next day, the Giants came to Cleveland to play the final three games of the season for both clubs. Though Boston rooters promised the Cleveland players a large amount of money—thousands of dollars, if reports are to be believed—to beat the New Yorkers, the Spiders reverted to form. They lost all three games as the Giants clinched the pennant.

Cleveland's return to the National League was an eventful one, though the Spiders wound up in sixth place with a 61–72 record. They might have made more progress in 1890 had baseball not been thrown into turmoil mere days after the close of the season. For years, major league ballplayers had been fed up with their treatment at the hands of the club owners, and in 1885 they formed a trade association called the Brotherhood of Professional Base Ball Players. In October of 1889 John Ward, shortstop of the New York Giants and president of the Brotherhood, announced that the players would quit the two major leagues *en masse* and form a circuit of their own in 1890.

4

The Players League

"Besides furnishing the best ball in the country, the players [of the Players League] will have the sympathy of the people with them. No man living that I know of feels friendly to the way the League bosses have been running things. This selling and trading of players as though they were so much cattle is all wrong and the time has come when the players must take the bull by the horns and do something for themselves."

—Will Johnson, brother of Players League organizer Al Johnson, September 1889[1]

The birth of the Players League increased the number of major league teams from 16 to 24 and set off a wild scramble for players. The Spiders roster suffered massive defections, as most of the Spider mainstays—Jimmy McAleer, Patsy Tebeau, and Jay Faatz among them—jumped to the new circuit. So did three of the team's top four pitchers (Gruber, Bakely, and O'Brien), outfielder Larry Twitchell and second baseman Cub Stricker. It was 1887 all over again, as Frank Robison faced the task of building a new team almost from scratch. He also needed a new manager, as Tom Loftus left to take the reins of the American Association team in Columbus.

To strengthen itself, the National League dropped its two weakest teams in Indianapolis and Washington and filled their spots with two clubs it stole from the American Association. Brooklyn, the Association pennant winner in 1889, and Cincinnati moved into the National League and left the Association gasping for air. To replace the Brooklyn and Cincinnati franchises, as well as a failed team in Kansas City, the Association was forced to turn to second- and third-tier cities. Syracuse, Rochester, and Toledo rounded out the roster for the crumbling Association.

Meanwhile, the Players League lined up capital, scouted locations for ballparks, and negotiated with star players in a whirlwind of activity. The new circuit created eight teams, seven of which (all except Buffalo) prepared to do battle with established National League clubs. Cleveland was one of the first cities to land a spot in the Brotherhood circuit, as the new Cleveland Players League club was incorporated on November 21, 1889. The owner of Cleveland's new club, and the moneyman behind the league itself, was the 30-year-old Albert L. Johnson, a wealthy Cleveland streetcar magnate (and now a rival of Frank Robison in more ways than one).

Al Johnson and his brother Tom, who served in Congress and later became mayor of Cleveland, had built the Nassau Railroad Company in Brooklyn, which featured a five-cent fare to Coney Island. The Johnsons sold their Brooklyn interests for more than four million dollars, making them wealthy enough to build adjoining grand mansions in that city. Al Johnson was a baseball "crank" through and through, and saw an opportunity to break the National League's stranglehold on professional baseball. Besides, the league would need eight new ballparks, which could be built on the family's streetcar lines. In Cleveland, Johnson put up a wooden park at East 55th Street and prepared to take on the National League Spiders.

Cleveland's best young player, shortstop Ed McKean, spent the winter months agonizing over where to cast his lot. He signed a contract with the Players League in October of 1889, but changed his mind and signed another contract with Robison and the Spiders in November. This angered his Brotherhood mates, who put him on their blacklist for "flip-flopping," though the shortstop returned the money that the new league had advanced to him. However, McKean waffled again when spring rolled around, and resumed negotiations with Al Johnson. Now both leagues were upset with him, and Cleveland's correspondent to *Sporting Life* condemned McKean as "the most notorious flopper in the business and should be made an example of by both sides."[2] Not until early April did McKean decide to remain with the Spiders at a salary of $2,500, a $500 raise over his 1889 figure.

Chief Zimmer also stayed with the established circuit. He, too, had signed with the new league, but a three-year contract offer from the Spiders led him to repudiate his agreement with Johnson's team and remain in Robison's employ. Zimmer was joined by pitcher Eb Beatin and outfielder Bob Gilks, but all the other key players were gone.

The new Spiders manager was Gus Schmelz, a highly respected innovator of the era. Schmelz, a red-haired, dignified, fiercely bearded man of 40, had managed Columbus and Cincinnati of the American Association during the preceding several seasons. He opened a preseason training camp for his 1884 Columbus team, and as a result some credit him with inventing spring training. He also was one of the first managers to employ the bunt as a strategic weapon, and some papers, including *Sporting Life*, used the term "the Schmelz stystem" to describe an offensive attack based on the bunt and the sacrifice.

The problem with Schmelz, in the eyes of some of his players, was that he fell in love with the bunt. He overused it, giving away outs to move runners around the bases one station at a time. Good hitters, who derided the bunt as a "baby hit," would much rather swing away with men on the bases, but Schmelz had them bunting even more than Tom Loftus had. One player complained that whenever a Spider reached first base, Schmelz would order a bunt to move him to second and another to move him to third. Then, with two outs, "the next man also sacrifices and the side is out."[3] It was an exaggeration, but perhaps not much of one.

Still, Schmelz treated his players well and was popular with most of his men. Not everyone liked him; Tony Mullane, his mercurial star pitcher in Cincinnati, walked off the team when he believed that Schmelz was

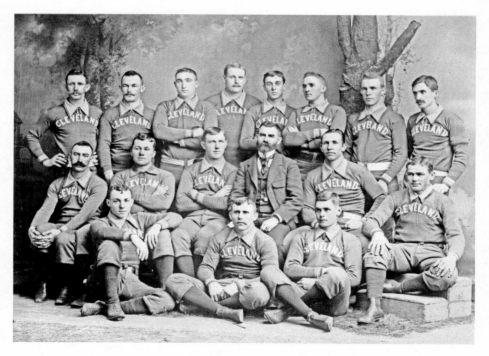

The 1890 Spiders, with bearded manager Gus Schmelz in the middle (National Baseball Library, Cooperstown, New York).

pitching him too often for the pay he received. However, Mullane was a difficult and temperamental man whose behavior could be unpredictable even in the best of times. Tim Murnane, the ex-player turned columnist for the *Boston Globe*, once stated that Schmelz "knew more about raising whiskers than good ball players."[4] But those sentiments were definitely in the minority, and Frank Robison was confident that his Spiders, with Schmelz directing the action, were well equipped to do battle with the upstart Players League team across town.

The new league was committed to providing the fans with offense, and the Cleveland entry—called the Infants due to the presence of so many young players—promised to do its part. To that end, Al Johnson signed two of baseball's top hitters to anchor his lineup. One was Pete Browning, the original "Louisville Slugger," who at age 29 was one of the greatest batters and most colorful characters the game had yet seen. Browning, a prodigious drinker and larger-than-life carouser, nonetheless posted a career average of .341, mostly for Louisville in the American Association. He suffered from mastoiditis, a bone infection that had left him nearly deaf, and was illiterate. Browning was also a notoriously awful fielder, called the Gladiator for his brave but mostly losing battles with fly balls and line drives. However, Browning hit so well that his bat (usually) drove in more runs than he booted in for the opposition.

The other star was a Cleveland boy, Ed Delahanty, who jumped from the Philadelphia Phillies to join his hometown Players League nine. Delahanty, the oldest of five ballplaying brothers, was the son of Irish immigrants who settled in Cleveland shortly after the Civil War. Ed joined the Phillies in 1888 at age 20 and showed promise, batting .293 as a part-timer in 1889. He was ready to break out, and it must have galled the Philadelphia fans to see one of the rising stars of the game reach his potential elsewhere. The strong-armed Delahanty preferred to play shortstop, though he could be erratic in the field. Nonetheless, when Ed McKean finally decided to remain with the Spiders, "Del" became the starting shortstop for the Infants.

The men in charge of the Players League knew that offensive fireworks drew more fans than tight defensive battles, so the new circuit adopted a lively baseball to boost hitting. Called the "Keefe ball," because it was designed and manufactured by star pitcher and would-be sporting goods mogul Tim Keefe, this lively ball promised to boost hitting in a game that had tilted toward the defense in recent years. In retrospect, Robison may have erred in hiring Schmelz, a station-to-station, one-run-at-a-time bunting enthusiast, while their crosstown rivals made headlines with the big bats of Delahanty, Browning, and others. It remained to be seen which team would win the hearts of the Cleveland fans.

To manage the Players League entry in Cleveland, Johnson signed Henry (Ted) Larkin, a 30-year-old first baseman who had spent the previous six years with the Philadelphia Athletics of the Association. Larkin was a solid performer and a .300 hitter who had captained the Athletics during the previous two seasons. Jay Faatz, one of John Ward's key lieutenants in organizing the Players League, expected to play first base for the Infants, but a nagging wrist injury kept him on the sidelines. Unable to play, the former captain was reduced to an advisory role with the Infants. Larkin was never much of a fielder, but his presence at first gave the Infants a passable infield with Patsy Tebeau at third, Cub Stricker at second, and Delahanty at short.

Henry (Ted) Larkin managed Cleveland's Players League entry until August, when Patsy Tebeau replaced him (Library of Congress).

The decimated Spiders, with McKean at short, Eb Beatin on the mound, and Chief Zimmer behind the plate, were strong at three positions. A fourth spot, center field, was claimed by a 19-year-old named George Stacey Davis. Davis, from Cohoes, New York, was a switch-hitting shortstop and out-fielder who had played semi-pro ball in Albany in 1889. He made the jump to the National League in 1890 and took over center field for the Spiders. Despite the fact that he had never played above the semi-pro level, Davis held his own at the bat and displayed a strong throwing arm. Opposing baserunners tested his arm all summer, and Davis compiled an incredible 35 outfield assists before they stopped challenging him. Davis was a coming star, and his arrival was an unexpected stroke of good fortune for the Spiders.

Otherwise, the team was desperately short of talent, and some of the new Spider starters were simply not of major league caliber. The first baseman, the oddly nicknamed William (Peek-a-Boo) Veach, had batted .134 for Kansas City six years before. "Peekie" bounced around the minors after that with only middling success, frustrating his managers with his drinking and nightlife escapades. Gus Schmelz found it necessary to put a temperance clause in Veach's contract, though few believed that Veach would make it through the season without going on a major bender. However, with three major leagues and 24 rosters to fill, the Peek-a-Boo Veaches of the world were able to gain employment.

Both teams needed pitching, though the Infants, with Jersey Bakely, Cinders O'Brien, and Henry Gruber, stood better in that regard. The Infants also signed a left-handed curveball specialist named Willie McGill, who had pitched a no-hitter in the Central Interstate League the year before. No one seemed to mind that McGill stood five feet and three inches tall and was only 16 years old. McGill's father chaperoned the young pitcher on road trips. The Spiders were fortunate to keep Eb Beatin, but the starters after him were a scruffy lot, and the Infants knew that they would be vulnerable to long losing streaks if Beatin faltered, slumped, or was injured.

The Infants, despite their superior talent, opened the season on the road in disastrous fashion. They lost to Buffalo by a score of 23 to 2 when starting pitcher Henry Gruber walked 16 men, tying the major league record. The Bisons swept the next three games, scoring 15, 19, and 18 runs against the shell-shocked Infants, mainly due to Cleveland's poor defense. Ed Delahanty was no shortstop—he committed nine errors in a single day during the July 4 doubleheader—but he was a local favorite, and he remained there for most of the season. By June the Infants were mired in seventh place, where they would remain until season's end.

Perhaps the most exciting thing that happened at any Cleveland ballgame all season was a lightning strike on the Brotherhood ballpark. On June 4, during the third inning of a game against last-place Buffalo, rain clouds suddenly appeared and drenched the field as the players dashed for cover. Shortly afterward, a lightning bolt shot out of the sky, struck a wooden pillar, and collapsed a section of the grandstand. Many spectators suffered electrical shocks and several female fans fainted, though no one was seriously injured. Another bolt broke the flagpole on top of the grandstand.

Incredibly, Al Johnson wanted to finish the game (lest he have to issue rain checks) when the storm abated, but umpire Bob Ferguson was in no mood to continue. Ferguson announced to the few hundred in attendance that the game was cancelled, whereupon the rain resumed harder than ever.[5]

Also, perhaps Pete Browning was not as bad a fielder as everyone thought. He could make a spectacular play every now and then, as he did on June 4 in Chicago. According to the *Cleveland Plain Dealer*:

The one act of the afternoon which stands out like a wart on a man's nose was a catch by Col. Browning in the fifth inning. Mr. Duffy, a distinguished townsman with whom it is a genuine pleasure to deal, tripped to the bat with his teeth set so hard that his jaw bones stuck out like handles on an Etruscan vase. He reached for the first ball which Mr. Bakely was good enough to land over the rubber.

The sound that followed was the same as when the slats fall down in an old-fashioned bed. The ball mounted towards the town of Jefferson until it was lost to sight. It came into view again in a few moments in the extreme left field, and then it was observed that Mr. Browning was only a few rods away.

He rattled his lengthy legs towards his heart's desire as long as possible, and then jumped in a northwesterly direction, turning four times in the air and stretching one arm for the ball in a manner of a boy after his second piece of pie.

He got it.

Then applause went up from the grandstand like an insane man experimenting with a French horn. Pete had to doff his cap a dozen times.[6]

Ed Delahanty, a Cleveland native who played shortstop for the 1890 Infants (author's collection).

The Spiders were in little better shape. They lost three of their first four contests on the road in Pittsburgh, the last a 20–12 defeat. The Spiders then returned to Cleveland and beat Cap Anson's Colts in the home opener, and pulled up to the .500 mark by mid–May before the bottom dropped out. The Spiders won only 12 of their next 52 games and, like the Infants, took possession of seventh place and stayed there all year. What's more, Gus Schmelz and his passion for bunting angered his charges, especially team captain Ed McKean. The young shortstop clashed with his manager over strategy so often that Schmelz relieved McKean of the captaincy in July, replacing him with Chief Zimmer.

The 1890 Spiders were a lost cause by mid-season, and on July 26, after a 2–14 skid solidified the team's hold on seventh place, Frank Robison fired Gus Schmelz. The bearded manager had lost his support among the players with his fanatical devotion to the bunt and his daily tinkering with the lineup. He had also grown testy as the losses mounted; as Charles W. Mears wrote in *Sporting Life*, "When a man makes an error ... he is sure to be overhauled for it and that kind of treatment makes the case worse."[7] Lacking talent, he overworked star pitcher Eb Beatin, while catcher Chief Zimmer caught every one of the 77 games Schmelz managed. Robison replaced Schmelz with Bob Leadley, former manager of the Detroit Wolverines.

The new manager was an accountant by trade, and during the 1880s served as business manager of the Detroit club of the National League. Detroit won the pennant in 1887 but stumbled in 1888, and Leadley replaced Bill Watkins as the non-playing manager for the last 38 games of the season. As Detroit was then not populous enough to support a major league club, the Wolverines dropped down to the International Association for the 1889 season, keeping Leadley in charge. He was highly regarded in Detroit; as the *Detroit Free Press* once stated, Leadley "is an educated, cultured gentleman, and ranks high in the estimation of the base ball world."[8]

Leadley, who like Schmelz managed from the bench in a suit and tie, did not lose his job in Detroit for poor performance; instead, he lost it for performing too well. One of his players remarked afterward that the Detroit club was "one of the greatest minor league teams gathered" and "won the flag so easy that fans stopped going out to see the games."[9] Leadley's Wolverines won the flag in 1889 and dominated the league so completely in 1890 that the fans lost interest, and the International Association folded in early July of that year.

Leadley put his stamp on the team. He stopped the endless lineup shuffling, putting outfielder Bob Gilks in the leadoff spot with Ed McKean behind him, and sharply curtailed the bunting. The bunt-hating McKean was so happy that he walloped two home runs in a game against Pittsburgh in mid–August. The new manager also dismissed Peek-a-Boo Veach, the incumbent first baseman, who was unreliable both in the field and at curfew time. Leadley replaced Veach with Jake Virtue, who had played for him in Detroit.

Jake Virtue was an outstanding fielder despite a crooked finger on his throwing hand. He broke it in 1889 while playing first base for Leadley's Detroit Wolverines. He remained in the lineup because the Wolverines were fighting for a pennant and had no other first baseman available. So, Jake gritted his teeth and played through the pain. Detroit won the pennant, but Virtue's finger had set itself and remained oddly bent for the rest of his life. Nonetheless, Virtue solidified the first base position and added another good bat to the lineup. The Spiders were marginally improved the rest of the season, and though they never left seventh place, Leadley earned credit for stabilizing the ballclub.

Owner of an impressive, Gay Nineties-style handlebar mustache, Virtue was a good hitter and an excellent fielding first baseman who, by all rights, should have enjoyed a long and successful career. Unfortunately, Virtue "had a huge failing," wrote historian David Nemec. "He was so short of self-confidence (some in Cleveland were unkind enough to say courage) that an error in the first inning or a strikeout in his first at bat would ruin him for the rest of the game."[10] Still, he was regarded as a coming star. The Spiders once offered to trade him to the Phillies for Ed Delahanty, a deal which would have returned both men to their home towns (Delahanty was a Cleveland native and Virtue a Philadelphian). The Phillies turned it down, but the offer shows that some put Virtue on Delahanty's level.

While the Spiders struggled, the Infants suffered setbacks of their own. Ted Larkin failed to get the best out of his men, and by mid-summer his players had tuned him out. Despite the presence of Browning, Delahanty, and other solid players, the Infants fell to seventh place in June and never left it. Larkin was not around at the end; on August 1, after a 4–3 loss to the Philadelphia Quakers left the Infants with a 34–45 record, Al Johnson fired Larkin and named Patsy Tebeau to replace him.

Jay Faatz, who captained the team the previous two seasons, was not available to take the post. In late July the Players League sent Faatz and Larry Twitchell to Buffalo in a bid to shore up the league's weakest franchise. Faatz's absence left Tebeau, the captain of the Infants, as the logical choice to succeed Larkin.

Tebeau, at age 25, now commenced a managerial career that would define Cleveland baseball for nearly a decade. Though the Infants played no better for Patsy than they had for Larkin, Tebeau nonetheless brought a dash of hustle and enthusiasm to the ballclub. He even found a way to make Pete Browning bunt, which the "Louisville Slugger" hated to do. One day, Browning told his new manager to make weak hitters like Jimmy McAleer lay down the bunts. Patsy simply threatened to tell McAleer how

Browning had insulted him. This would probably have caused a fight in the clubhouse between McAleer and Browning, so to keep the peace, Browning agreed to lay down bunts whenever Tebeau wanted them. He probably grumbled about it, but he did it anyway.

The 1890 season was a disappointing one for the Spiders, but one good thing came out of it. Davis Hawley, a prosperous Cleveland businessman who owned a minority share of the Spiders and served as the team's secretary, took to the road in midseason to find some talent for the faltering ballclub. He signed a big, rawboned, 23-year-old pitcher from Tuscarawas County, Ohio, named Denton Young, who had posted a 15–15 mark for Canton of the Tri-State League that summer. Young was a hard-throwing right-hander who had tossed a no-hitter (with 18 strike-outs) against McKeesport in late July, and on August 6 the Spiders, who paid the Canton club $500 for Young's contract, gave the Ohio farm boy his first taste of big league action against Cap Anson's Chicago Colts.

Anson and company hooted at the appearance of Young, who would soon gain the nickname "Cy." Perhaps it was because the speed of his pitches resembled that of a cyclone, or (more likely) it came from his appearance on and off the mound. Young's Cleveland uniform was a few sizes too small for him, and his rustic manner of dress off the field might have been the cause of his new moniker, as "Rube" and "Cy" were common appellations for a country bumpkin. Still, Young threw a complete game, the first of a Wednesday doubleheader, and won the contest by an 8–1 score.

The Colts won the second game, and afterward Anson approached Hawley and suggested that, though this boy Young was an incredibly raw specimen, the Chicago club might be able to make something out of him. Anson almost casually offered Hawley $1,000 for the rookie hurler.

Hawley's answer, in brief: Forget it, Anse. We'll keep the rube, too—small uniform and all.

Young almost immediately became Cleveland's number two starting pitcher behind Eb Beatin. This was admittedly not a difficult feat, as the starters behind Beatin (who won 22 games that year and lost 30) were mediocrities such as Jack Wadsworth (2–16) and Ezra Lincoln (3–11). The rookie from rural Ohio took a regular turn during August and September of 1890, posting a 9–7 log and completing all 16 of his starts. He had yet to learn the finer points of pitching, but his performance gave the Cleveland fans a glimpse of things to come.

Many years after Young's debut, Davis Hawley recalled a conversation he had with the rookie. "The night of Young's first National League game," said Hawley, "he complained to me that although he had let Anson's team down with a few hits, he had not had his usual speed." Why did Young feel that way? Because, as Young stated, "well, down in Canton the catchers could not hold me [because] I was so fast, but this man Zimmer didn't have any trouble at all, so I guess I didn't have much speed."[11]

"This man Zimmer" proved a steadying influence on Young. Chief Zimmer, unlike most of his teammates, did not drink, smoke, or swear and was widely regarded as one of baseball's gentlemen. He was also incredibly durable, catching every one of Cleveland's games in 1890 from mid–April to early September, when he left the team to care for his wife, who had been stricken with typhoid. Other catchers reportedly resented the Chief, fearing that their teams would demand a similar heavy workload from them. He did not hit much in his early years with the Spiders, but his glove work and his calming presence did wonders for the pitching staff. He and Cy Young became close friends as well as battery mates, and Zimmer caught most of the young phenom's games during most of the 1890s.

Long afterward, Young recalled his first major league game for a reporter:

> The thing that stands out most vividly … was the fact that I crossed Chief Zimmer in a pinch, handing him a curve ball when he had called for a fast one. Zimmer got the ball squarely on his bare hand. Then he started for the box. I expected to get a good call-down. In fact, I wouldn't have been surprised if Zimmer had started by swinging his right. Here I was, a green kid, pulling off a bonehead that might have laid up one of the league's star catchers. I'll remember my surprise to my dying day when Zimmer said: "Now, look here, young fellow, you must learn to watch my signs a little closer. I called for a fast one and you gave me a curve. A thing like that might have lost us the game. You're just starting in. Now, please watch what I tell you to pitch, and if you're bound to pitch something different, let me know about it. You're doing finely. Just remember and it will help you win a lot of games you'd lose otherwise." Surprised, was I? Well, slightly. And I made up my mind right there that the finest man God had ever created was my catcher, Chief Zimmer.[12]

The war continued unabated between the National and Players Leagues, but by August cracks were beginning to show in the newer circuit. The players were as determined as ever to make a success of the Players League, but the investors behind the circuit were weakening. Some had already made back-channel inquiries into selling out to the established league.

Both leagues padded their attendance figures. Albert G. Spalding, Chicago White Stockings team president, liked to tell how in June, a reporter asked Chicago team secretary Jonathan Brown for the official attendance of the day's game. "Twenty-four eighteen," chirped the secretary, though there were probably fewer than 100 people in the stands. When the reporter left, Spalding asked Brown how he could make such a statement.

"There are twenty-four on one side of the grounds and eighteen on the other," replied Brown. "If he reports twenty-four hundred and eighteen, that's a matter for his conscience, not mine."[13]

In Cleveland, the fans lost interest with both clubs near the bottom of the standings. The Spiders were kept out of last place by the utter incompetence of the Pittsburgh Pirates (who won 23 games and lost 113 that season) while the Infants avoided the cellar thanks to the horrid Buffalo Bisons (who finished at 36–96). On September 1, the two Cleveland teams lost four games in one day, with each club losing a doubleheader. At least both teams ended the season on a high note, with the Infants winning 11 of their last 15 and the Spiders winning 10 in a row in mid–September. The last two Spider wins came on October 4, the season's final day, when Cy Young won both ends of a doubleheader against the Phillies.

The Players League probably won the attendance battle with the National, but the established circuit had better negotiators. Though the baseball war left several National League teams in serious trouble, especially the New York Giants, Albert G. Spalding played a magnificent bluff, exuding such confidence in the financial health of the League that he coaxed the wary Players League investors into abject surrender. Many of the players, including Brotherhood president John Ward, were willing to carry the fight into 1891, but the moneymen behind the Players League were ready to sell out, and did, one by one. Al Johnson held out for a while, but he eventually caved as well. By the end of 1890, the Players League was dead, the American Association crippled, and the National League triumphant.

The Players League adventure had damaged the Cleveland Spiders, but not fatally. Frank Robison and his partners lost money on the season, and *The Sporting News* reported that both Cleveland teams lost a total of $50,000.[14] At least the Cleveland club never approached the brink of collapse as had the New York Giants franchise, which required a large cash infusion in July of 1890 to forestall a total breakdown. In Cleveland and in every other major league city, the players, owners, and fans looked forward to the 1891 campaign, one in which baseball would return to normal. As the *Plain Dealer* put it, "Good by, old season of 1890; may we never see such another."[15]

⫸ 5 ⫷

Patsy Takes Over

"I've had enough of it. There's more wind than money in it. Let the men who put up the capital manage the game, and let the men who do the playing get paid for it and keep still. This is all any ballplayer should ask. There is one thing certain and that is that I will not play again under the same conditions as I did this season."
—Chicago outfielder Jimmy Ryan on
the Players League adventure, 1890[1]

Bob Leadley, the Spiders manager in 1890, retained his post for the 1891 campaign, and Patsy Tebeau's brief managerial tenure in Cleveland was over, if only temporarily. Tebeau had made a positive impression on the baseball world, and though the Infants of the Players League won nine fewer games than they lost under his direction, he had displayed his talent for leadership. Many of the writers who covered Cleveland baseball for the local dailies saw Tebeau as a manager in waiting. If the newly reconstituted Spiders stumbled, or if the team got away from Leadley, the 26-year-old Patsy's time would come sooner rather than later.

With the collapse of the Players League, most of the Brotherhood men returned to their former employers. Patsy Tebeau resumed his career with the Spiders, as did Jimmy McAleer and Henry Gruber. Ed Delahanty and Ted Larkin returned to the Phillies and Athletics, respectively, while Pete Browning, the Players League batting champ, signed with Pittsburgh of the National League. Two former Spider pitchers, Cinders O'Brien and Jersey Bakely, also went elsewhere, Bakely (whom the Spiders did not want because of his drinking) going to Washington and O'Brien joining Mike Kelly's Boston Reds of the Association. Neither man lasted much longer in the major leagues, as Bakely's arm gave out, while O'Brien, who won 18 games for Boston in 1891, died of pneumonia in early 1892 at the age of 25.

Cub Stricker was another ex-Spider who cast his lot elsewhere in 1891. The second baseman was still angry with his double-play partner Ed McKean for abandoning the Players League and vowed to never play next to McKean again.[2] Stricker left Cleveland and joined O'Brien in Boston. This left a hole at second base, which the Spiders filled with one of the top young infield stars in baseball. Clarence (Cupid) Childs, who batted .345 for Syracuse of the Association in 1890, would become one of Cleveland's most dependable and popular players.

Clarence Childs was born on a farm in Maryland in 1867 as one of 11 children. His father died when Clarence was very young, and the widow Childs moved the family to Baltimore, where the country boy learned to play baseball on the city sandlots. Quick, fast, and sure-handed, Clarence rose through the semipro and minor league circuits until 1888, when the Philadelphia Quakers (soon to be known as the Phillies) gave him a two-game tryout. Clarence went hitless and failed the audition, but landed on the Syracuse team in 1890. He became a star there and when the Syracuse club failed after that turbulent season, Childs hooked on with another Association club, his hometown Orioles of Baltimore.

However, Childs knew that the Association was tottering, and that National League teams were eyeing him. When the Association made the ill-advised decision to free itself from the National League and drop out of the National Agreement, Childs broke his contract with Baltimore. He signed a deal (for more money) with the Cleveland Spiders in February of 1891, but the Orioles were not willing to let him walk. They sued the 22-year-old infielder in Baltimore City Circuit Court for breach of contract, and the case gained national attention when it was heard in April. The judge ruled in Childs' favor, freeing him to play for the Spiders. The Cleveland management could not resist celebrating its good fortune. The front office dispatched a telegraph to Oriole manager Billy Barnie that stated, "He who laughs last, laughs best."

They called him Cupid because, well, he looked like one. He was five feet and eight inches tall but carried 185 pounds on his frame, and his round face and cheeks gave the impression that he had never lost his baby fat. People who saw him play could hardly believe that such an odd-looking man, who was also called "Fatty" or "the Alderman," could hit and field so well. According to an article in a Grand Rapids, Michigan, newspaper, "Childs is the most curiously built man in the baseball business: he is about as wide as he is long and weighs about as much as [boxer Jim] Jeffries, yet there are few men in the league who can get over the ground faster than the 'dumpling.'"[3] He claimed the second base position for the

Spiders, batting a solid .281 and scoring 120 runs in 1891.

With the Players League threat out of the way, Frank Robison felt confident enough in the future of Cleveland baseball to build a new ballpark. The lease on the plot of land at Payne and Euclid expired at the end of the 1890 season, so Robison bought up properties at Dunham (now East 66th) Street and Lexington Avenue in the Hough district east of downtown Cleveland. He was not interested in the Brotherhood park at East 55th Street, partly because that site was not near his streetcar line and partly because he did not want to do any favors for Al Johnson. Robison's rival now

Clarence (Cupid) Childs, the oddly-shaped second baseman (National Baseball Library, Cooperstown, New York).

owned a ballpark with no team to play in it, so the Brotherhood site hosted Wild West shows and revival meetings in 1891.

Two homeowners and one saloon owner on Lexington refused to sell to Robison, so the new ballpark, called National League Park at its inception, went up around those properties. It had to be built quickly, as Robison did not receive a building permit until February 12, 1891, less than three months before the scheduled home opener on May 1. The new League Park was planned as a single-decked wooden structure with a pavilion supported by iron posts. It had 9,000 wooden seats and, because the park had to be built to fit into the existing street pattern in its residential neighborhood, it contained little foul ground. The fans were close enough to the action to hear the players talking, and arguing, on the field.

The left and center field areas were large, with the stands 353 feet down the line in left and 409 in straightaway center, increasing to 445 in the deepest part of center. Right field, however, was tiny, because the outfield fence, 20 feet tall, stood only 290 feet down the line (less than that before the team was able to buy out the reluctant property owners on Lexington). Best of all, as far as Robison was concerned, his Payne Avenue streetcar line stopped at the front entrance of the park. His streetcars fed the ballpark, and the ballpark provided customers for his streetcars.

Wooden ballparks could be built quickly then, and at the end of March, only six weeks after construction began, League Park was ready to be painted. Head groundskeeper Tom Lawrence planted the grass and supervised the installation of an infield made of crushed gravel topped by clay. By May 1, the new park was ready for baseball. After the Spiders took an abbreviated trip to the South and opened their season at Cincinnati and Pittsburgh, the players returned to Cleveland for their first glimpse of their new home.

Thanks to Jake Beckley, Patsy Tebeau would not be with them on that historic day. Beckley, the Pittsburgh first baseman, was notorious for tripping, hip-checking, and even slashing at baserunners, and in late April Beckley set his sights on Tebeau. On a play at first, Beckley spiked Tebeau in the ankle, causing an injury so severe that the Spider captain was confined to bed by the team physician. This was dirty pool, even by the standards of the era, and Tebeau carried a grudge against the Pirate first sacker for years. "Beckley has injured more men on the diamond that any three players," Tebeau said a few years later. "He put me out of the game for three months in 1891, and the same injury has kept me on the bench from two to six weeks a season ever since."[4] Actually, Patsy returned in early July, but the injury bothered him for the rest of his career.

The Spiders were impressed with League Park. They found the big lockers, hot showers, and spacious clubhouse a huge improvement over the Payne Avenue venue. The Cleveland fans reacted positively as well, and on May 1, 1891, more than 9,000 people crowded into the new structure to see the Spiders face the Cincinnati Reds (managed by former Cleveland field boss Tom Loftus). The afternoon began with a parade from the Hollenden House downtown to League Park, with the Spiders and Reds accompanied by a 16-piece brass band. The game was set to begin at 3:45 p.m., but the crush of people made long lines at the two ticket windows. Not until after 4 did the game begin, with Cy Young on the mound for the Spiders.

Tebeau, still laid up in bed, was not in the lineup that day, but the Spiders christened their new home with an easy 12–3 win over the Reds. More than 4,000 fans came the next day to see their team lose to Cincinnati, but the Spiders won the next two to take a share of first place with a record of 8–4. That was the high point of the season, as the Spiders then lost three of four at Chicago and suffered a four-game sweep at home against the Phillies in mid–May. They fought their way back to second place, but a Decoration Day doubleheader loss at New York started a 2–10 skid that knocked Leadley's club all the way down to sixth position.

Eb Beatin, who threw 474 innings for the Spiders in 1890, pitched only 29 in 1891. His arm was worn out, and after posting an 0–3 mark for the 1891 Spiders, his career was finished at the age of 24. Cy Young, still learning the finer points of major league pitching, took over as Cleveland's number one starter with Henry Gruber and ex-Cincinnati Red Lee Viau in the next two rotation slots. Viau, who joined the Spiders late in the 1890 season, was a character. He won 27 games as a rookie for Cincinnati in 1888 and 22 more in 1889, but his many alcohol-fueled escapades turned the local fans against him. He refused to pitch on Sunday for religious reasons, though he usually spent the Sabbath drinking and getting into trouble. Still, he had talent, and the Spiders needed more of it.

Viau was indirectly responsible for the emergence of John McGraw, who became the Cleveland team's biggest enemy later in the decade. On March 25, while the Spiders trained in Jacksonville, Viau pitched against a team of youthful "all-stars" who had recently returned from a tour of Cuba. The shortstop of that team was a 17-year-old from Truxton, New York, who weighed only 120 pounds. That teenager, John McGraw, belted three doubles off Viau (who was more concerned with getting his arm in shape than in getting batters out) and the young man's performance made the pages of *Sporting Life* and *The Sporting News*. The resulting national attention brought several offers to McGraw, who signed with Cedar Rapids, Iowa, of the Central League. Before the year was out McGraw was a Baltimore Oriole, and his Hall of Fame career began.

The Spiders hovered around the .500 mark under Bob Leadley, but there was little excitement around the team. The main problem with the Spiders was the absence of captain Patsy Tebeau. He had established himself as the spiritual and emotional leader of the team, and the players responded to his aggressive leadership much more than they did to Bob Leadley's laid-back style. "I want [Tebeau] back in the team," said shortstop Ed McKean. "I know there is nobody in the country that can see a fine point as quickly and we need such a man now."[5] The Spiders were mired in mediocrity, so the local papers started boosting Tebeau at Leadley's expense. Glowing accounts of Tebeau's leadership skills and his personal attributes appeared with regularity; one such article described a scene in which Patsy rescued a man from drowning. The unfortunate individual had fallen into a fountain at the Kennard House, a downtown hotel, and

Tebeau pulled him out of the water and saved his life. It appeared as if the main Cleveland papers were engaged in an all-out campaign to dismiss Leadley and replace him with Tebeau.

The two biggest crowds of the season came to League Park to cheer the Spiders in a doubleheader (with separate admissions) on the Fourth of July, but a poor showing on that day cost Leadley his job. Seven thousand fans saw the Spiders enter the ninth inning of the first game with an 11–4 lead, and when Cleveland scored four more runs in the top of the ninth, the contest seemed well in hand. Pitcher Lee Viau then fell apart as the Phillies scored ten times in the bottom of the ninth. Leadley rushed George Davis in from the outfield to put out the fire, and Cleveland escaped with a 15–14 win. The Spiders then fell behind early in Game Two, as Philadelphia pitcher Kid Gleason dominated the Spiders and cruised to an easy 9–1 win. Ten thousand fans went home disappointed, and one week later, Frank Robison fired Leadley and made Patsy Tebeau his manager.

The history of the Cleveland Spiders really began on that day. Tebeau, who had rejoined the Cleveland lineup on July 4 after ten weeks on the sidelines, had a plan—to turn the Spiders into a scrappy, fighting ballclub. This was the style of baseball he knew, having learned it in Goose Hill and the Kerry Patch. Patsy wanted a team of fighters, and he was determined to have it. "My instructions to my players are to win games, and I want them to be aggressive. A milk and water, goody-goody player can't wear a Cleveland uniform," remarked Tebeau to a reporter.[6] This highly aggressive attitude would define the Spiders, for good or ill, for the rest of the decade.

In 1882, when Patsy Tebeau was 18 years old, the American Association emerged as a rival to the six-year-old National League. The new Association moved into cities that William Hulbert, founder and president of the League, had driven from its ranks. Those cities included Cincinnati, expelled in 1880 for selling beer at its ballpark; New York and Philadelphia, dismissed for failing to complete their schedules in 1876; and Louisville, which collapsed after a gambling scandal in 1877. Hulbert was a brilliant organizer, but a strict moralist as well, and his rigidity had left some of the nation's largest baseball markets open (rejecting New York and Philadelphia while placing teams in Syracuse, Troy, and Providence). The Association sought to fill that void.

St. Louis, Patsy Tebeau's home town, hosted a National League team in 1876 and 1877, but the club went bankrupt and dropped out of the circuit. Part of the problem was that amateur ball in the Mound City was so popular that a professional nine found it difficult to gain traction. Still, the city was growing so quickly and producing so many outstanding athletes that it was only a matter of time. A German-born local beer baron named Christopher von der Ahe assembled a team and placed it in the new Association. Von der Ahe knew little about baseball, so he gave the reins of the new Brown Stockings, or Browns, to a series of failed managers (including the future Cleveland boss Jimmy Williams). In late 1884 he found the right man, an Irishman from Chicago named Charlie Comiskey.

In Comiskey, Patsy found a template for his future management style. Comiskey's Browns brought the barely controlled aggression of Goose Hill and the Kerry Patch to the Association. The Browns not only intimidated their opponents, but also made the umpires' lives a living hell. Any decision against the Browns on the home grounds would be the spark that set off a riotous argument, with the St. Louis fans joining in the fun by throwing bottles or even storming the field. The umpire—the Association used only one per game in those days—often needed a police escort to and from the ballpark for his own safety. Few arbiters could stand up to the constant abuse, and the Browns enjoyed a huge home field advantage as a result. They won nearly 77 percent of their home games between 1885 and 1888, their glory years.

The other Association teams hated playing in St. Louis. Shortstop Bill Gleason was an expert at what would later be called "bench jockeying," directing a never-ending stream of hostile language at the opposing batters, fielders, and baserunners. "Comiskey and Bill Gleason," wrote Comiskey's biographer G.

CHARLES COMISKEY.
ALLEN & GINTER'S
RICHMOND. Cigarettes. VIRGINIA.

St. Louis Browns manager Charlie Comiskey was a role model for Patsy Tebeau (Library of Congress).

W. Axelson, "used to plant themselves on each side of the visiting catcher and comment on his breeding, personal habits, skill as a receiver, or rather lack of it, until the unlucky backstop was unable to tell whether one or half a dozen balls were coming his way."[7] The umpires were too cowed to stop them, so in 1886 the circuit instituted the first coaching boxes in foul territory near first and third bases. This cut down the interference, but not much. In 1885, *Sporting Life* magazine offered the opinion that "if [Gleason] should someday break a limb or his neck, not a ball player in the American Association would feel the slightest regret."[8]

The Browns played this way because it worked. They won four Association pennants in a row beginning in 1885 as fans streamed into von der Ahe's ballpark. Their success made professional baseball popular in St. Louis and broke the dominance that amateur play had enjoyed in the Mound City for more than a decade. Comiskey's men played dirty, but they won, and that was all that mattered. "First place is the only subject of conversation," Comiskey once said. "Everybody chokes up before they get as far as second."[9]

Tebeau and Comiskey, five years apart in age, shared some personality traits. Both were outstanding fielders at the first base sack (though Comiskey was reputed to be one of the greatest ever), and both were mediocre hitters who made up for their middling offense with leadership and personality. Tebeau also considered himself an innovator like Comiskey, who revolutionized first base play by ranging far off the bag and designing plays for the pitcher to cover the base. Both men were Irish-American, Comiskey by birth and Tebeau by choice. Most importantly, Tebeau and Comiskey shared an insatiable will to win at all costs. Bill Gleason once said that Comiskey "never went to sleep at night until he had figured out how he was going to win the game the next day,"[10] and the same description could be applied to Tebeau as well.

A secondary role model for Patsy Tebeau was Cap Anson, the long-time batting star and manager of the Chicago White Stockings. Though Anson had dismissed Patsy after a 20-game tryout in 1887, the younger man nonetheless admired the Chicago field boss and absorbed some of his methods and tactics. Anson, like Patsy a first baseman, was known far and wide as the "King of Kickers" for his constant arguments with the umpires, and though the White Stockings did not play as dirty a game as the Browns—perhaps no team could—Anson made himself the focus of every game with his battling nature and foghorn voice. Anson, like Comiskey, was highly successful. The Chicago club won the National League pennant five times in seven years during the 1880s under Anson's direction, and Tebeau no doubt took a few mental notes during his short stay with the club.

With these examples (and that of the always-combative Jay Faatz, his captain in 1889) to guide him, Patsy took over the Spiders on July 11, 1891. He immediately dismissed some of Leadley's favorites; as Jack Doyle remarked years later, the new manager "set to housekeeping by weeding out the lobsters who were being toted around the country by his theoretical and cloud-pushing predecessor."[11] He already had some of the pieces of a contending team in place, with Cy Young on the mound, Chief Zimmer behind the plate, Jimmy McAleer in center, and himself at third base. Tebeau went to work assembling the rest of the puzzle, and perhaps it should not have surprised anyone when he filled out his roster with his favorite kind of player, the rough-and-tumble Irishman.

Patsy also knew the rule book. While nursing a lead with two on and one out against the Chicago Colts, Patsy ordered Ralph Johnson, out of the lineup that day with an injury, to bat for pitcher Lee Viau. Tebeau knew that a new rule, which took effect at the beginning of the 1891 season, allowed a team unlimited one-way substitutions. Chicago manager Cap Anson, who had led the Chicago club since 1879, did not. Anson confronted Tebeau. "Hold on, you can't do that," bellowed Anson.

"Can't I?" asked Tebeau. "I'll bet $100 I can. Don't the rules allow me to substitute a player at any stage of the game?"

Anson discussed the matter with the umpire, who assured him that the new Cleveland manager was correct. "All right, all right," sighed Anson, "go ahead. He can't hit [pitcher Pat] Luby, anyway."[12] The move eventually failed, as relief pitcher George Davis gave up four runs in the ninth and lost the game. Still, Patsy had to be proud that he outfoxed his first major league manager.

The National League saw the Spiders' new attitude in a riotous game in Cincinnati that August. The Reds, enraged by umpire Phil Powers' bad call that led to five Cleveland runs in the eighth inning, took their anger out on the Spiders, with infielder Arlie Latham blocking Jimmy McAleer off third base. This angered McAleer, who kicked Latham twice and received a hard punch on the jaw in return. McAleer grabbed a bat and chased Latham around the field, with the rest of the Spiders and Reds either chasing the combatants or brawling with each other. The fans, not wanting to be left out, poured out of the stands and attacked the Spiders until the local police intervened. The Cincinnati cops pulled four Spiders off Latham, saving the Reds captain from serious injury, then herded the visitors to safety.

Tebeau expected every man on his team to join in whenever a fight broke out, and that included star pitcher Cy Young. Cy stayed close to the bench while his teammates brawled with the Reds, and Patsy was so angry that he took Cy out of the starting rotation for a while. Young made three relief appearances during the next 11 days as punishment, and did not start again until August 28, losing a 9–4 decision to Boston. He broke a personal five-game losing streak on September 1, defeating Brooklyn by a score of 7 to 1. Cy was streaky, alternating short winning and losing skeins, but once he made his way back into Tebeau's good graces, his status as Cleveland's top pitcher was assured. He closed the 1891 campaign with six wins in a row to boost his record to 27–22.

One National League manager who noticed Young's success was Cap Anson, who had offered Davis Hawley $1,000 for the Ohio farmer-turned-pitcher the year before. Anson described the experience of batting against Young to a reporter from *Sporting Life*:

Cy Young

It seems to me, in spite of the fact that I am a tolerably good sized man, as though the ball was shooting down from the hands of a giant. If it comes very close it makes you draw back in spite of yourself, for it appears to accumulate speed as it goes along. Some of the boys on my team who don't reach up as far in the world as I do in a bodily sense declare that they get the same notion and that they always feel when Young lets the ball go as though he were about to push it down upon their unprotected heads. If I had Young I'd win the championship in a walk.[13]

Cy Young in 1892, the year he won 36 games in his second full season (author's collection).

While Cy Young was making a name for himself in Cleveland, another future Spider struggled to make the grade in New York. Jesse Burkett was a 22-year-old left-handed pitcher from West Virginia who stood only five feet and eight inches tall.

Burkett was much too small for a major league moundsman even in that day and age, but the New York Giants of the National League had lost most of their key performers to the Brotherhood circuit, and they were starved for talent. The Giants gave Jesse 14 starts and seven relief appearances, and put him in left field on his non-pitching days. He went 3–10 on the mound, ending his pitching career almost before it began, but his .309 batting average showed promise. However, when the Players League collapsed and the ex-Giants returned to the team, Jesse had no position to play. The Giants sent him to Lincoln, Nebraska, where he gave up pitching and concentrated on the outfield. The Spiders bought his contract in August of 1891, and in 1892 Jesse claimed left field on a permanent basis.

Jesse, who was born in 1868, grew up in Wheeling, a tough industrial town on the Ohio River. When Jesse was 12 years old, he was swimming in the river when he saw a young girl drowning. While other people froze in fear, Jesse frantically searched for the child under the surface. "I crawled about the bottom," he said many years later, "but I couldn't see anything. Finally one of my hands touched her and I brought her to the surface. Her heart was still beating but they couldn't bring her to."[14] The girl died on the beach, and Jesse was haunted by his failure to save her for the rest of his life. Even as an old man, he could not describe the long-ago tragedy without dissolving into tears.

Jesse hid his emotions behind a personality so irascible that his nickname, "Crab," was well earned. He learned his baseball in the rough and tumble Wheeling industrial league, and he was tough enough to handle the inevitable volleys of insults and challenges offered by bigger and more experienced players. He was a master of the cutting insult, and, when the teasing flared out of control, he was quick to settle the matter with his fists. "Jesse is one of the most constant and one of the rankest kidders in the business," said *The Sporting News* in 1903. "That would be alright if he could take a kid himself, but the moment that somebody comes back at him with a few facts stated in sarcastic words he goes wild and wants to fight."[15] To Jesse Burkett, this was simply a part of the game as it was played during the 1890s. "You got to be a battler," he once explained. "If you don't they'll walk all over you. After you lick three or four of them they don't show up any more looking for a fight."[16]

Perhaps Jesse was embittered by an embarrassing fielding miscue that he committed in a game against Boston in September 1890. He dove for a ground ball in deep right field, missed it, and tore the foul flag (which marked the boundary between fair and foul territory) out of the ground in so doing. He could not locate the ball, so he assumed that the ball rolled into the hole where he had torn the flag out of the ground. An unidentified newspaper clip from the Baseball Hall of Fame described the aftermath with the headline "Jesse Burkett's Brief Engagement as a Star Comedian":

> Burkett wheeled around several times with the flag in his hands, as if he were hunting for a place to plant it. Then he threw it down and began to dig up dirt in great handsful. A Scotch terrier in the quest of a chipmunk could not have made the dust fly more furiously. All at once it dawned upon the spectators that Jesse was digging for the ball and a roar of laughter went up all around, the players on both sides joining in. Jesse, however, dug the harder and only ceased after Whistler had recovered the ball and Hines and Hardie had both got home.
>
> The crowd had a great deal of sport with Burkett after this little incident. Next time he started to the field some one yelled "Here's a shovel, Jesse." When he went to bat he was advised to knock it into the hole where he had dug out the other. Still another was unkind enough to yell "Rats!" and "Sic 'em Towser."[17]

The New York papers had a lot of fun at Jesse's expense due to this play, and Jesse ever after had no use for sportswriters. "You could hit the (expletive) out of the ball and no newspaperman would say a word about it," complained Jesse. "They're all alike."[18]

Patsy Tebeau, however, cared little about Jesse's outfield troubles in New York. In August of 1891 the manager released Ralph Johnson, one of Bob Leadley's acquisitions, and installed Burkett in left field. He also instructed Jimmy McAleer to teach the newcomer the finer points of playing the outfield. McAleer was a great teacher. "I couldn't catch a medicine ball with a net," Burkett admitted long afterward, "but I went to school with Jim McAleer. He would coach me during a game when the ball came my way ... and the schooling with Jim soon took the awkward edges off my fielding."[19] The Crab would never become a great outfielder, but he was good enough to play left field for Cleveland for the rest of the decade.

The 1891 season ended with the Spiders in fifth place with a 65–74 record. Patsy Tebeau had led the Cleveland ballclub to 31 wins and 40 losses during his tenure, but he had given the Spiders an identity as a scrappy, battling crew. The Spiders, after three seasons in the National League, were no longer an expansion team. They were a ballclub on the rise, and it remained to be seen how far Patsy Tebeau and his aggressive style of play would take them.

⅙ 6 ⅙

Half a Pennant

"All the credit I want for the magnificent work of the Clevelands this season is that I insisted on keeping Tebeau in the team when the others were not in favor of retaining him. Now his position is assured as long as he wants to keep it. Among the officials of the club he has no enemies. Tebeau's word in the club policy in a playing way is law. We all know that he understands the business better than we do, and there is not, nor will there be, any interference with him in the management of his men. He is a jewel, and the Cleveland club officials know it."
—Davis Hawley, Cleveland club secretary, October 1892[1]

The National League had vanquished the Players League in 1890, and a year later the reeling American Association surrendered as well. The Association had a bad habit of losing its strongest markets (Brooklyn, Cincinnati, and Cleveland, to name a few) to the National League, and the so-called "Beer and Whiskey League" was ready to collapse by the end of the 1891 campaign. In early 1892 the National League absorbed four Association teams (Louisville, St. Louis, Baltimore, and Washington) and bought out the other four. The result was a 12-team amalgam officially titled the "National League and American Association of Professional Base Ball Clubs," but almost no one used the unwieldy moniker. It was the National League, and it now owned a monopoly on major league baseball.

The league needed money to pay for the buyout of the rival league, so the magnates agreed to stage a 154-game season, the longest in baseball history up to that time. To add interest to the pennant chase, the league divided the 1892 season in half. The first half was set to end on July 13, and the first place team on that date would gain a pass into a post-season matchup against the winner of the second half. This October match between the first and second half winners, titled the "League Championship Series," would crown the official National League champion of 1892.

By this time, the core of the Cleveland team had taken shape. Cy Young on the mound, Chief Zimmer at catcher, Burkett and McAleer in the outfield, and the infield of Tebeau, Childs, and McKean were fixtures in Cleveland and would remain so almost to the end of the decade. Others would come and go, but these seven men would define the Cleveland Spiders for years to come.

The regular starting eight was solid enough, with Jake Virtue holding down the first sack and George Davis manning right field. However, pitching was always in short supply, and with Henry Gruber fading and Eb Beatin and Lee Viau nursing sore arms, Tebeau looked for a reliable second starter. He found one in the person of a right-hander from Indiana named George "Nig" Cuppy.

George Cuppy was born with the last name of Koppe, courtesy of his Bavarian-born parents. However, George owned a dark complexion of the type usually described as "swarthy." For this reason, he gained the nickname "Nig," as darker-skinned ballplayers sometimes did in that day and age. In an era that saw deaf players like Cincinnati's Bill Hoy commonly referred to as "Dummy," a name like Nig raised no protests, and there is no evidence that George Cuppy ever took offense at the moniker. Nig he was, and Nig he was destined to remain.

The 22-year-old Cuppy had spent the 1890 season with Dayton of the Tri-State League, then moved to the New York-Penn League in 1891. While splitting his time among four different teams that year, he won 21 games and played 17 contests in the outfield. He hit well for a pitcher, too.

Cuppy, despite his small stature, found success for one simple reason. He was, by far, the slowest-working pitcher in baseball. His dawdling on the mound frustrated batters and caused some of the games he pitched to last for a then-unthinkable two hours or more. Even a newspaper in Logansport, Indiana, his home state, could not help but comment on the mound antics of its favorite son. "It is really amusing," wrote a Logansport reporter, "to those in the stands to witness the maneuvers of this little twirler with the swarthy complexion and pearly teeth. He fondles the ball, rubs it on the back of his neck, grins at the batsman, and then stops to adjust his cap and hitch up his trousers. He does all this several more times before he delivers the ball to the batsman."[2]

As if the Spiders were not despised enough in other National League cities, Cuppy's pitching made them even more so. Batters hated facing him, fans hated watching him, and umpires hated working the plate when he pitched. Cuppy appeared not to care, because his act was a successful one. One report described his pitching style as follows: "[Cuppy] stood holding the ball, and holding it, and holding it some more. The maddened batsmen fumed and fretted and smote the plate with their sticks; the umpires barked and threatened; the fans counted and counted, often up to 56 or 59—and then Cuppy let go of the ball. By this time the batter, if at all nervous or excitable, was so sore that he slammed wildly at the pitch, and seldom hit it."[3]

Another addition to the Spider cast of characters in 1892 was Jack O'Connor, known far and wide as "Rowdy Jack." He was a childhood friend of Tebeau's in St. Louis, where they honed their baseball (and fighting) skills with the Peach Pies of that city. O'Connor, a first baseman, catcher, and occasional outfielder, got to the major leagues first with the Cincinnati Reds in 1887, but his hard-drinking, bullying ways incensed opponents and teammates alike. He was dismissed from the Reds by manager Gus Schmelz after a clubhouse brawl. He played in an outlaw league for a while, then landed on the American Association club in Columbus in 1889. He performed well for three years, but his days were numbered in Columbus when Schmelz took over as manager, and O'Connor was soon out of a job again. As the Spalding baseball guide for 1892 reported, "On July 3, President Kramer of the American Association expelled John O'Connor of the Columbus club from the Association, for habitual drunkenness, disorderly conduct and insubordination. He was suspended by the club the day before without pay, for disgraceful conduct."[4] Fortunately for the now unemployed ballplayer, Patsy Tebeau needed a utility player, lieutenant, and enforcer, a role that Rowdy Jack was born to play. O'Connor became the Cleveland team's assistant manager, running the club on the field when Tebeau was absent due to injury, ejection, or suspension.

George (Nig) Cuppy, the slowest-working pitcher in the National League (author's collection).

At least "Rowdy Jack" was not "Dirty Jack." That nickname was reserved for another rough, tough Spider named Jack Doyle, who joined the Cleveland team in 1891. Doyle had played with O'Connor in Columbus and cut a swath through the Association with fists and spikes. Born in Ireland in 1869, Jack Doyle grew up in Holyoke, Massachusetts, where he learned to treat baseball as a blood sport and opponents as fair game.

Doyle was undersized—five feet and nine inches tall and about 155 pounds—and he made up for his lack of size with an aggressiveness that made him stand out even in that rough and tough era. He trampled opposing fielders like a football running back and often left his spike marks on their feet and ankles. "I was a hard base-runner," he admitted long afterward. "You had to be those days. It wasn't a matter of being rough or dirty. With the dead ball, games were won by very small margins. As a result, a stolen base meant more than it does today. It often meant the difference between victory and defeat. And my base-running was for just one purpose: to win."[5] Doyle always looked for any edge he could find. When he caught, he liked to drop pebbles into the batter's shoes to make their subsequent attempts at baserunning more difficult. Doyle earned a reprimand from the National League for that stunt.

The other National League teams could not help but notice that Patsy Tebeau was filling his roster with the kind of player he valued most—the battling, hard-charging Irishman. McKean, Burkett, O'Connor, Doyle, and McAleer were Irish to the core, while Tebeau himself was as Irish in outlook and attitude as one could be. More Irish-American players would come and go during the next several years, and the team was so rich in Irishmen that the papers called the team the "Hibernian Spiders."

Perhaps the Cleveland manager was consciously following the blueprint set by Charlie Comiskey, the St. Louis Browns manager who won four pennants during the 1880s with a largely Irish-American cast. Or, maybe Tebeau simply felt comfortable with those players who shared his aggressive makeup. At any rate, the Irish were the largest single ethnic group represented in the National League at the time, with more than 40 percent of major league players during the early 1890s claiming Irish descent. Due to their success, the Irish gained a reputation for being quick-thinking, intelligent ballplayers and natural leaders. As "Scrappy Bill" Joyce, a longtime National Leaguer and a graduate of the same Goose Hill enclave of St. Louis that produced Tebeau and many other ballplayers, once put it:

Give me a good Irish infield and I will show you a good team. I don't mean that it is necessary to have them all Irish, but you want two or three quick-thinking sons of

Celt to keep the Germans and others moving. Now you take a German, you can tell him what to do and he will do it. Take an Irishman and tell him what to do, and he is liable to give you an argument. He has his own ideas. So I have figured it out this way. Get an Irishman to do the scheming. Let him tell the Germans what to do and then you will have a great combination.[6]

Chief Zimmer, one of Cleveland's most valuable players, angered club management before the season began. In January of that year the club sent contracts to all its players with new, more restrictive language approved by the National League. One new provision that the players hated was the "reserve" clause, which gave the team the rights to a player's services for the following year into perpetuity. This clause was designed to bring player movement to a halt, and because the National League now owned a monopoly on major league baseball, the circuit could impose such a rule with little or no opposition. Zimmer, an experienced business-man who knew a thing or two about contracts, saw no reason to sign, as his three-year deal from 1890 had one more year to run. The Chief thought about it for a while, and then signed the contract and sent it back—with all the objectionable clauses crossed out.

Charles (Chief) Zimmer, catcher and businessman (National Baseball Library, Cooperstown, New York).

Davis Hawley, the Cleveland team secre-tary, said, "Zimmer will sign a contract just as we want or he will not play ball next sea-son. If we waived the reservation clause on him, we would have to do it with others, and that we don't propose to do." *Sporting Life*, too, criticized the Cleveland catcher and claimed that he was making "an unreason-able kick." Said the paper, "All cannot be paid the same salaries, but all should sign the same form of contract. There must be no exemption or favorite-playing if satisfaction and harmony is to be as prevalent among players as it now is among club owners."[7] Eventually, Zimmer signed the contract with the new clauses intact.

Zimmer's maturity served him well in dealing with his unpredictable teammates. According to umpire Tim Hurst, Rowdy Jack O'Connor fumed with resentment one morning when he read a Pittsburgh newspaper article that referred to Zimmer as Cleveland's "star catcher." That afternoon, he was sitting on one end of the Spider bench with Zimmer, bat in hand, at the other. O'Connor snarled at the Chief, "If you didn't have that stick in your hand I'd knock your head off."

Ed McKean yanked the bat out of Zimmer's hands. "He hasn't got the stick in his hands now, Jack," said the big shortstop. "Go ahead and knock his head off—if you can."

Said Hurst, "Rowdy Jack started to get up, settled back on the bench and began to cry like a child. A little later he and Chief were shaking hands, and the prospective fight ended in the establishment of a friendship that has never since been disturbed."[8]

Zimmer was also an innovator. In 1891 he devised a mechanical game, called "Zimmer's Base Ball Game." As *Sporting Life* described it,

> Charley Zimmer, the good-natured and gentlemanly catcher of the Cleveland Club has invented and patented an indoor game of base ball that ought to make him a little fortune. It promises to become one of the greatest toys of the age. A regular game can be played. The ball is pitched from an ingenious device and goes straight over the plate. If a hit isn't made or the ball struck at all the "catcher" gets it. All the "players" are in position, and there are regular catches in the outfield and pick-ups in the infield. The bat is a curious contrivance, and it takes good judgment to operate it. A fast or slow ball can be pitched, and the batter is liable to be "fooled" by changes of pace. Nothing like it was ever seen before in toy games. The invention is to be shown in Hudson's window after Thanksgiving, and will surely attract great attention.[9]

The game board featured a diamond with pictures of most of the stars of the day, and many of Zimmer's Spider teammates too. Zimmer sold thousands of the games during the next few years, providing him with a secondary source of income to supplement his baseball salary.

Zimmer was not the only Spider with off-the-field interests. Jack O'Connor played semipro football during the fall months, Cupid Childs showed interest in an acting career, and Ed McKean wrestled in the Greco-Roman style, competing in matches in and around Cleveland and drawing crowds that often included his Spider teammates. He also wrote columns for local newspapers, even trying his hand at poetry every now and then (one of his efforts was titled "The Short Stop's Reverie"). McKean was not yet 30 years old but was already fighting his weight every winter. One report said that during the winter of 1891, McKean's weight increased to 207 pounds and he needed to lose 30 or more before the new season began. McKean slimmed down successfully, but his weight problems would become a recurring theme as the decade progressed.

The Spiders started the 1892 season well. They lost two of their first three games on the road, then returned to Cleveland and took two of three from Cincinnati and swept three more contests against the Chicago Colts. Tebeau and his men were brimming with confidence on the morning of Friday, April 29, while preparing to face the New York Giants that afternoon.

That's when Jake Virtue decided to bring a gun into the clubhouse.

Ed McKean saw the pistol in Virtue's locker and picked it up. Perhaps he wondered if it was loaded.

It was. The gun discharged and tore away part of McKean's right index finger. McKean was out of the lineup for nearly four weeks, and the injury affected his hitting for the rest of the season. He drove in a career high 93 runs, but his average in 1892 was the lowest of his career with the Spiders, and he hit no home runs for the only time in his career.

McKean's freakish injury rattled the Spiders, who defeated the Giants but then lost their next five games to fall below the .500 mark. They played erratically in the shortstop's absence, winning six in a row, then losing four in a row, and alternating short winning and losing streaks through May. McKean returned to the lineup on May 25 in Pittsburgh, but went 0 for 5 at the plate and committed two costly errors in a 9–7 defeat. Tebeau could have put George Davis at short and placed McKean in the outfield while his finger healed, but Patsy stuck with his star shortstop, and by late June McKean was back to playing like his old self, or close to it.

The split season format was a godsend to the Spiders. The injury to McKean could well have scuttled their season; indeed, McKean's troubles upon his return to the lineup contributed to a 1–8 skid that dropped Cleveland to eighth position in the now 12-team league. Patsy Tebeau knew not to panic. The first-half title may have been out of reach, but the second half would begin on July 15. If McKean and other Spiders regained their footing, Tebeau's ballclub would make some noise in the second pennant race.

Patsy was nothing if not innovative. He understood the value of pinch hitting earlier than many of his contemporaries, as seen on June 7 in Brooklyn. With the Spiders behind by one run in the ninth inning, the manager called pitcher George Davies back to the bench and sent Jack

Doyle to hit in his place. Doyle was the second pinch hitter in Cleveland Spiders history, and one of the first few in the National League. Pinch hitters had been allowed by baseball rules beginning in 1891, but few teams had yet availed themselves of the opportunity. Doyle singled, though the Spiders failed to score and lost the game by a 2–1 count. Doyle boasted for the rest of his long life that he was, in fact, baseball's first pinch hitter, and that his single won the game that day. Neither of these statements is true, though one still finds books on baseball history that credit Doyle with being the first.

Tebeau was also an early devotee of the intentional walk. Pitching around the opposing team's best hitter was sharply criticized in many circles; as Chicago Colts pitcher Clark Griffith put it, "The pitcher who is afraid of any batter ought to quit the business."[10] The move drew boos from the fans, even in Cleveland, but it worked often enough that other managers began to use it as well. By the mid–1890s, the intentional walk had become an accepted part of managerial strategy, though calls to ban or modify the practice continue to this day.

The first half of the 1892 season ended on June 13 with Boston, at 52–22, in first place and the Spiders in fifth at 40–33. Brooklyn, Philadelphia, and Cincinnati held the second, third, and fourth positions. After a one-day break, the National League would resume play from scratch, with every team at 0–0. The Beaneaters were assured of a spot in the October post-season championship series, and the winners of the second half-season (if not Boston) would gain the second slot.

McKean's hand still bothered him, but he slowly rounded into shape, though an incident in mid–July was a distraction that the club did not need. At the end of the first half, the shortstop "went on a drunk" and missed a game, though the contest was subsequently rained out anyway. Tebeau, knowing that his injured shortstop had played through pain to help the team, downplayed the problem. The first half flag was out of reach anyway, and the Cleveland manager trusted his star shortstop to be ready when the new half-season began.

The Spiders had, in large measure, righted the ship after the injury to McKean. They had, after a slow start, fought their way to seven games above the break-even point, and *Sporting Life* praised Tebeau's team as "one of the best-balanced teams in the League, being equally strong in batting, fielding and base-running, well-handled and aggressive."[11] Tebeau believed that his team was as likely as any to win the second half, but he had some holes to fill. Lee Viau, an 18-game winner the year before, suffered from a sore arm and made one disastrous start for Cleveland in which he failed to survive the second inning. Viau, a notorious drinker, was unreliable even when healthy, so the Spiders released him in May. Fellow moundsman George Davies was mediocre at best, losing more games than he won, and although Cy Young and Nig Cuppy gave the team a one-two starting tandem that only Boston could match, the Spiders desperately needed a third starter.

Young, who won 27 games in 1891, made a major leap to stardom in 1892. Incredibly, Cy had made 62 starts during his first two major league campaigns, winning 36 of them, and had not yet pitched a shutout. It was starting to bother him. "It seems absolutely impossible for me to shut a team out," he told a Cleveland reporter. "Sometimes we'll have 'em ten to nothing in the eighth, and then they'll go in and get a run or two just to keep my record intact. Some people think I let down, but if you ever see me let an opposing club make a run on purpose, even if we have beaten them 100 to 0, you can kick me off the field. My arm never gets lame and I would be foolish to let a batter fatten up his average off me on purpose."[12]

He rectified that omission on April 15 at Cincinnati, holding the Reds to four hits and no runs. He would throw eight more shutouts in 1892. He had become such a recognizable star that it seemed as if Cy had been around forever; the papers called him "Old Cy Young" though he was still only 25 years old and pitching in his third major league season.

At the end of the first half, major league teams cut player salaries. The owners, who resented the fact that they were still paying the big-money deals that they agreed to during the Players League challenge two years earlier, demanded that the players agree to salary reductions, some by as much as 30 percent. The owners met with their players and put it to them bluntly: take a significant cut in pay or be released. The standard player contract allowed management to terminate a contract on ten days' notice, so a magnate could simply use the ten-day rule to drop a contract at any time.

Most observers figured that this would happen. The failure of the Players League stripped major leaguers of their negotiating power, and the death of the American Association in late 1891 gave the National League complete dominance over the highest level of professional baseball. It was inevitable that the magnates would plead poverty and demand salary relief. Still, it was a shock to see the abrupt dismissals of some of the game's biggest names, mostly veterans over 30 years of age on the downside of their careers. Several stars, including catcher Deacon McGuire and pitchers Charlie Buffinton and Tony Mullane, refused to take pay cuts and were unceremoniously cast adrift.

John Clarkson, regarded by many as the greatest pitcher of the 19th century, was the most prominent of those released. Clarkson, a 31-year-old right-hander from Cambridge, Massachusetts, had compiled an incredible record since joining the Chicago White Stockings late in the 1884 season. His 53–16 record in 1885 and 36–17 in 1886 helped Chicago to consecutive pennants, and at the close of the 1887 campaign the Boston club bought his contract for the then-record amount of $10,000. His 49 wins in 1889 almost brought a championship to Boston, and he won 34 games in 1891. In only eight full seasons of National League play, Clarkson had compiled nearly 300 wins. He could hit a little, too, belting 24 homers during his career.

Still, Clarkson was slowing down. He had walked more men than he struck out in each of the previous two seasons, and in early 1892 he was unable to pitch due to a sore arm. The Boston club, with young stars Kid Nichols and Jack Stivetts in its rotation, saw a chance to get out from under Clarkson's high salary. The pitcher had used the Players League as a wedge to pry an unprecedented 3-year contract for $25,000 from Boston's owners in 1890, and ever after players like to joke that if they had "one of those Johnny Clarkson contracts," they would be perfectly happy. Clarkson's deal was nearly at its end, but arm woes and 8–6 record made it inevitable that he would be booted from the club. Besides, the Beaneaters had already clinched the first half championship, so the season was already a success with or without their veteran star hurler.

Several teams expressed interest in signing Clarkson (at a much lower salary), but Cleveland won the day. In late June, Clarkson signed on with the Spiders as the third starter behind Cy Young and Nig Cuppy. This move was a good one for Cleveland, as Clarkson recovered to make 28 solid starts for the Spiders. He filled the hole in the rotation and gave the team a boost heading into the second half of the split season. However, several members of Frank Robison's ownership group criticized the outlay of money for Clarkson. Robison had signed the pitcher to a two-year deal for $2,500 per year, making the new arrival the highest paid man on the roster. This did not sit well with some of the team directors, and their irritation would cause a showdown in the near future.

Perhaps the directors opposed the signing because they knew how difficult Clarkson could be. Clarkson came from a prosperous family in Cambridge, where his father owned a thriving jewelry and watchmaking firm. John had trained as a jeweler during his teenage years, and would sometimes threaten to quit baseball and join his father in business. He was sensitive to criticism and would sulk if he thought his efforts were not appreciated. Cap Anson, his manager in Chicago, said of Clarkson, "Many regard him as the greatest, but not many know of his peculiar temperament and the amount of encouragement needed to keep him going. Scold him, find fault with him, and he could not pitch at all." However, said Anson, "praise him and he was unbeatable. In knowing exactly what kind of ball a batter could not hit and in his ability to serve up just that kind of a ball, I don't think I have ever seen the equal of Clarkson."[13]

Clarkson was also unpopular with many of his fellow players due to his actions during the Players League adventure. He had attended some of the Brotherhood's early meetings and voted in them as well, but when the Boston management offered him a large sum of money to stay loyal to the National League, Clarkson not only quit the rebel circuit, but helped the established club sign players to fill the spots of those who left. In December of 1889 the Players League formally expelled Clarkson and several other "turncoats," and some of the radicals in the organization accused the pitcher of being a National League spy. Clarkson insisted that he acted in good faith, but players had long memories, and it remained to be seen if Clarkson's presence on the Cleveland club would be a distraction to a team fighting for a pennant.

Jack Doyle left the Spiders in July. Some say that Doyle's aggressive playing style was so violent that not even Tebeau could abide it; more likely, Doyle and Jack O'Connor were very similar players, and the cost-conscious club needed only one man to fill the super-sub role. "Dirty Jack" drew his release (he later claimed that he had requested it) and continued his career with the New York Giants. Doyle, who played for ten different major league teams in a career that lasted until 1905, would battle the Spiders many times during the remainder of the decade.

The addition of Clarkson stabilized the rotation, and the Spiders started the second half well. Boston stumbled out of the gate while Cleveland, Brooklyn, Philadelphia, and Cincinnati fought for the lead. Perhaps the Beaneaters were rattled after management released popular veterans such as Clarkson and Mike "King" Kelly, or maybe the Bostons let down with a post-season berth already assured. In their first game of the second half, the Beaneaters lost to the St. Louis Browns by a 20–3 score. In the meantime, the Cleveland Spiders dropped their first game to Washington, then reeled off a streak of wins and grabbed first place. On August 1, the Spiders held the top position by a game over Boston.

That first loss of the second half was filled with bickering between Tebeau and umpire Charlie Mitchell, an arbiter who had clashed with the Spiders earlier that year. A heavy rain turned the field in Washington to a sea of mud, but Mitchell refused to call the game off. John Clarkson, Jake Virtue, and Cupid Childs all made wild throws with the wet, slippery ball, leading to two unearned runs in the fourth that gave the Senators the lead. The subsequent arguments resulted in a $10 fine for Virtue and a $50 fine for Tebeau. Mitchell also ejected the Cleveland manager.

Pitching made the difference for the Spiders. Injuries to Childs, Tebeau, and Burkett could have derailed the Cleveland ballclub in the second half, but the starting trio of Young, Cuppy, and Clarkson kept the team afloat. Tebeau's aggressive leadership played an important role as well. On September 21, Pittsburgh starting pitcher Adonis Terry allowed the Spiders only one hit in the first eight innings, but Tebeau's kicking kept his team in the game. With Pittsburgh leading by a 2–1 score after eight, Umpire John Gaffney tried to call the game on account of darkness, but Tebeau bullied the umpire into continuing play, hinting darkly at what the home fans might do if the game did not proceed. In the ninth, Terry walked two men, a sacrifice moved them to second and third, and a walk-off single by Ed McKean won the game for the Spiders. It also gave John Clarkson the 300th win of his career.

Cleveland built their lead to seven and a half games by early October. The Beaneaters put on a furious charge, winning 14 of their final 16 games, but the Spiders held on and clinched the second-half pennant when Boston lost the second game of a doubleheader against Chicago on October 11. It was only half a pennant, but it was Cleveland's first championship of any kind in the National League.

Though the pitching of Cy Young (36–12), Nig Cuppy (28–13) and John Clarkson (17–10), and the outstanding hitting of Childs, McKean, and Burkett helped bring the flag to Cleveland, the lion's share of the credit went to Patsy Tebeau. As *The Sporting News* put it at season's end, "As a base ball general [Tebeau] stands second to no person. As a controller of men he is more of a success than any man now upon the base ball diamond. Where he learned his remarkable methods of keeping players under control is not known. He simply has that knack.... The result is plain to be seen. It is shown in the work of the men that he manages."[14]

With the half-pennant clinched, the Spiders could afford to forfeit a game, which they did in Pittsburgh on October 12. The previous day's contest against the Pirates, Pittsburgh's last scheduled home game of the season, had been stopped due to darkness with the teams tied at 4. Pittsburgh management scheduled a makeup game for the following day. The Spiders, however, had planned a benefit game for their players in Cleveland on that date, and Patsy Tebeau had no intention of giving it up. The Spiders were to play a local amateur squad from the Cleveland Athletic Club, with the proceeds to be split evenly among the players. Most teams in that era played games of this type to give their men a nice payday at season's end.

"We have a benefit game arranged at Cleveland tomorrow," said Tebeau. "The benefit is for the players, and if we don't get home tomorrow we will not get the benefit. We are willing to allow the Pittsburgh Club to have the game as a victory. There is no rule to fine us, and we will go home." The Spiders played their benefit, winning by a score of 13 to 1 and raising about $100 per man.[15]

The Spiders looked forward to playing Boston, the first-half winners, for the championship, but the Beaneaters were not especially keen on the idea. When Boston manager Frank Selee suggested that the mid–October weather in New England would not be conducive to good baseball, it appeared that his club was trying to get out of playing the post-season series. Tebeau was having none of it. "If the weather in Boston is likely to prove too chilly for base ball," said the manager, "we can contest the majority of games on the Cleveland and some neutral grounds to be determined by the authorities of both clubs. I know that the Cleveland people will turn out to see the championship games if they have to wear ear-laps and snow shoes. I am heartily sorry for the stand taken by the Boston Club and so are the Cleveland players."[16]

The 1892 Spiders, half-pennant winners. Top row: Young, Davis, Roettger, Shearon, Doyle, McAleer, O'Connor, Davies. Bottom row: Virtue, Williams, Cuppy, Childs, Tebeau, Viau, Burkett, McKean (author's collection).

The Boston players, who posted a 102–48 record to Cleveland's 93–56 during the full season, may have considered themselves the champions with or without a postseason series, but the public wanted to see the matchup, and the public won out. In early October, the Bostonians agreed to play the Spiders in a nine-game set beginning on October 22 in Cleveland. The first three contests were scheduled at League Park, the next three at the South End Grounds in Boston, and the final three, if needed, at neutral sites, including New York, to be determined later. Remarkably, most observers regarded the Spiders as the favorites, mainly due to the presence of Cy Young, whose 36 wins led the league and had established the big pitcher, in his second full National League season, as the best hurler in the game. Cleveland also had the momentum, as the Beaneaters had relaxed after clinching their first-half flag and allowed Cleveland to pass them.

Boston, however, had strengths of its own, beginning with its two top pitchers. Kid Nichols and Jack Stivetts had nearly matched Young, each posting 35 wins. Left fielder Hugh Duffy and center fielder Tommy McCarthy, the "Heavenly Twins," were wizards at strategy, refining the hit-and-run to a science and finding new ways to win games, while Frank Selee had established himself as one of the top managers in the league. Boston was solid at every position, while Cleveland was stronger at some and weaker at others. In the end, the Beaneaters may have decided to play because some of the nation's more cynical sportswriters hinted darkly that Boston had deliberately lost the second half to make post-season play, and the extra money it would bring, possible. That accusation, and Tebeau's suggestion that "the Beaneaters fear the humiliation of possible defeat," gave Boston more than enough incentive to play, and to win.[17]

The first contest, played on October 17 at League Park, was one of the greatest games of the 19th century. With 6,000 fans in the seats on a Monday afternoon, starting pitchers Cy Young and Jack Stivetts put zeroes on the board in inning after inning. Young gave up six hits and Stivetts four, and with only one error (by Cleveland's Chief Zimmer) in the game, neither side could land a blow on the other. Cleveland came close to winning the game in the ninth when Jesse Burkett tried to score from third on an infield grounder, but was thrown out at the plate by Boston's Joe Quinn. After eleven innings, the Spiders and Beaneaters were still scoreless when umpires Pop Snyder (the former Cleveland Blues catcher) and Bob Emslie decided that it was too dark to continue. The first game of the series had ended in a tie, treating the fans to perhaps the best pitching duel yet seen in the National League.

Game 2 on Tuesday was a different story. Hugh Duffy whacked two triples and a double off Cleveland's John Clarkson, and though the Spiders belted 10 hits off Boston's Harry Staley (they were saving Kid Nichols for the games in Boston), superior Boston fielding made the difference. Boston won the second game 4 to 3. Tebeau sent Cy Young to the hill again in Game 3, but the Beaneaters won a close one behind Stivetts, 3 to 2. Now the Spiders were down three games to none, with a fully rested Kid Nichols, the Boston ace, ready to face them in Game 4.

Selee's decision to save Nichols was the right one, as the Kid scattered seven hits in a 4–0 shutout win over Nig Cuppy. Tebeau sent Clarkson to the mound for the fifth game on Saturday, and for a while it looked as if the Spiders would finally win a game. Clarkson belted a three-run homer in the second inning, and at the end of the third he enjoyed a six-run lead. But the Beaneaters were no quitters, and they pounded their ex-teammate for 12 runs in the next four innings. Boston, behind Stivetts, won by a 12–7 score and put themselves one win away from the championship.

The final game was played before only 2,000 fans in Boston, and the Spiders took an early 3–0 lead before Cy Young faltered, giving up four in the fourth. Boston won 8 to 3 and clinched the title without losing a game. Tebeau's men played hard, with Ed McKean (.440) and Cupid Childs (.409) walloping the ball, but Tebeau went 0 for 18, Jack O'Connor 3 for 22, and Jake Virtue 3 for 24. It was a bad time for a slump, and as *Sporting Life* remarked, "Tebeau's fielding was all right, but this was the year he could not hit a balloon with a shotgun."[18] Despite their pre-series status as the favorites, the Spiders had to recognize

Veteran hurler John Clarkson, who joined the Spiders in the middle of the 1892 season (author's collection).

that Boston was simply a better, more balanced team. "The Clevelands put up a stiff game and fought every inch," said *Sporting Life*, "but they [played] against a team that has proved their superiors in all the points of the national game."[19]

Boston dominated the Spiders so thoroughly that some in the national press raised new suspicions of their play. *The Sporting News*, the six-year-old weekly from St. Louis that was already becoming known as the "Bible of Baseball," opined in late October that the series "proves to all that after the first season's flag [Boston] did not try for the succeeding empty honor, but let it go, by default as it were, and saved itself for the more glorious struggle, if such it may be called, that came later."[20] Though the Beaneaters earned only $76.92 per man for winning the series (while the losing Spiders received nothing), such accusations soured the public on the whole concept. The attendance, which totaled about 32,000 for six games, was disappointing, and in November the National League owners met in Chicago and dropped the split-season format.

Because many teams lost money, or claimed that they did, the magnates also reduced the upcoming season to 132 games and vowed to enact even more pay cuts. As the 1893 *Reach Guide* stated, ""The clubs have this year acknowledged their error in both the double championship and the lengthened season by abolishing both. This year [1893] there will be one continuing season beginning late in April and ending about the first of October."[21]

The 1893 season would also see Frank Robison and Patsy Tebeau take near-total command of the Spiders. There was friction between Robison and the other members of his investment circle; some did not want Tebeau promoted to the manager's job in mid–1891, and some objected to the signing of an aging John Clarkson in July of 1892. This friction led Robison to buy his partners out. The streetcar magnate was sufficiently optimistic about the future of baseball in Cleveland, and in his selection of Patsy Tebeau as his manager, that he and his brother Stanley spent an undisclosed sum to gain full control of the franchise. Frank H. Brunell had sold out a few years earlier when he left Cleveland to become sports editor of the *Chicago Tribune*. Davis Hawley, George W. Howe, and the remaining smaller investors sold their stock in the team to Robison, though Hawley remained in his post as club secretary and Howe stayed on as treasurer.

⊯ 7 ⊯

The Battling Spiders

Cleveland audiences are the hardest losers of any in the League. Let the club win a game 10 to 0, due, perhaps, to the rotten errors of the other side, and it will be denominated a brilliant game. Let them lose a brilliant contest of, say 3 to 2, full of brilliant fielding and fine base-running, and it will be termed a shiftless game. Cleveland patrons stick by a club really well, but three-quarters of them are mad all over unless the club wins six games a week.
—*Sporting Life*, July 1893[1]

The 1893 season marked a turning point in major league baseball. In that year, the National League introduced the most significant rule change in the game's history; the circuit also saw the continuation of a trend, long in the making, that intensified that season and would continue to do so throughout the decade.

The rule change came about because National League moguls were worried by a drop in offense. In 1889, National League teams as a whole batted .266 and scored 5.84 runs per game. By 1892, the average of runs per game was down to 5.10 and the league batting average had fallen to .245. Power pitchers had taken over the game, and their fastballs were faster than ever. Cy Young was the prototype of the 1890s pitcher, a big, muscular farm boy with a strong right arm who could throw fastballs all day long. Young and New York's Amos Rusie threw their pitches so hard that batters complained of being overmatched. On their best days, Young and Rusie, among others, could be nearly unhittable.

To stop the slide in offense, the National League owners voted to change the configuration of the pitching area. Before 1893, the pitcher stood in a rectangular box, the front line of which was 50 feet from home plate and the back line 55½ feet. The pitcher was required to start his motion with his foot on the back line, and was allowed to take one step forward in his delivery. The magnates decreed that beginning in 1893, the box would be replaced by a slab of rubber 60½ feet from the plate. They also decided that the pitcher must keep one foot on the rubber during his delivery, eliminating the step forward. This added five feet of pitching distance, they hoped, would benefit the offense and bring more hitting into the game.

This new pitching distance was not only the last major rule change in baseball history (save for the introduction of the designated hitter in 1973), but also the most significant. By moving the pitcher back by a mere five feet, the National League owners set in motion an offensive explosion that changed the game far more than they could have imagined. The game would never be the same, and only the teams that adapted to the new field configuration successfully would win pennants during the rest of the decade.

The other feature of 1893 was a rise in player misbehavior, both on and off the field. Umpire-baiting, protracted arguments, and fan interference had troubled the sport for years, but the 1893 season saw more of this behavior than ever before.

Historian David Nemec, who has written extensively about 19th-century baseball, states that the players, as a whole, were an angry lot. The Players League failure had put the magnates firmly in charge again, and the collapse of the American Association left the National League with no competition on the major league level. The moguls used their new monopoly power to slash salaries in mid–1892, wiping out the gains that the players had made during the Players League adventure. The owners now could, and did, bleed more profits out of their players by filling the Sundays and off days on their schedules with exhibition games in minor league towns. Some league owners went further, humiliating their employees by charging them rent for their uniforms, squeezing every nickel on their meal money, and making them take tickets and count turnstiles—in full uniform—on game days. Low salaries and poor working conditions drove some players out of the game, especially the educated ones. Their exodus left the field open for a rougher, tougher type of ballplayer.

So the players, powerless in their dealings with their employers, took out their frustrations on the field.

The Cleveland Spiders looked to the 1893 campaign with optimism. Yes, they had suffered a sweep at the hands of the Boston Beaneaters in the post-season championship series, but their second-half pennant gave them hope. It also added to Patsy Tebeau's reputation as a field general; indeed, the *Cleveland Leader* called him "Young Napoleon" and exulted, "Tebeau is the youngest captain who has ever won a championship in the

National League, and is generally regarded among ball players as being one of the shrewdest men who ever stepped upon the diamond. It is a fact that Pittsburg once offered $10,000 for his services."[2]

That optimism was sorely tested when Frank Robison made a trade with the New York Giants that stripped the Spiders of one of their best young players. In early March, Robison announced that he had traded the 22-year-old infielder George Davis to New York in exchange for Buck Ewing, the 34-year-old catcher and outfielder.

Why would the Spiders trade an up-and-coming young star like George Davis for the much older, declining Buck Ewing? Perhaps, some reasoned, they saw no place for Davis on Cleveland's infield, with Childs at second and McKean at shortstop going strong. Possibly Ewing, whose catching days were at an end due to a lame arm, could finally fill the team's nagging weakness in right field (Ewing had moved to the outfield on a

Buck Ewing on an Allen and Ginter card, 1888 (Library of Congress).

permanent basis, and was still a .300 hitter). Davis had slumped in 1892, batting only .241 while playing four different positions. Still, Tebeau knew that his young star had battled injuries in 1892. He was solidly in Davis' corner, if his statements to the press can be believed. "Transfer Davis?" he said. "I wouldn't give George Davis for the whole New York team."[3]

However, the trade was not Tebeau's doing. It was made by Robison, who owed Giants magnate John B. Day a favor and repaid it by giving the Giants one of the best young players in the game.

Specifically, when Cleveland joined the National League in 1889, road teams were granted as little as 15% of the gate. Robison successfully lobbied for an even split of receipts between home and road teams, a policy which boosted Cleveland's bottom line immensely. The more successful and established Eastern clubs were loath to cut their profits in such a way, but John B. Day used his influence, and that of the team in the nation's largest city, to push for the even split. The grateful Robison promised to return the favor and help the Giants if they needed it in the future, and by early 1893 that day had arrived.

The Giants franchise had fallen on hard times. Champions of the National League in 1888 and 1889, the team was hit hard by defections to the Players League and almost collapsed in August of 1890. Only an infusion of capital from the other National League owners enabled the Giants to finish their season. They finished fourth in 1891 but dropped to eighth place in 1892, with attendance at the Polo Grounds in Manhattan falling by more than 40 percent. The other magnates, including Frank Robison, knew that a strong New York franchise was good for the league as a whole, so Robison, to repay the Giants for their support in the gate receipt matter several years before, offered to send a star player to New York. Said Robison to *The Sporting News*, "I went to New York to endeavor to help the New York club get on its feet again."[4]

Giants manager John Ward first asked for Patsy Tebeau. "I wanted Tebeau here—the greatest captain living," said Ward to *The Sporting News*. "Failing in that I asked for Davis. McKean would have come here but for a big local demand for his services in Cleveland. There is no more reliable hitter."[5] To complete the deal, the Giants agreed to send one of baseball's most famous players, Buck Ewing, to Cleveland. Ewing, a superstar of the 1880s whom *Total Baseball* described as the greatest all-around player of the 19th century, had served as the Giants' captain during their glory years, but he and shortstop John Ward had never gotten along. With Ward taking over as manager, Ewing was no longer welcome in New York. Besides, though Ewing could still hit, his throwing arm was nearly useless due to an accumulation of injuries.

Spider fans were stunned to lose one of the rising young stars of baseball, but Robison stood firm. "The New York club begged me to give them Davis," he said. "Now the New York club is in hard straits, and as Cleveland had benefitted by the legislation passed and had succeeded in getting together a strong club, they thought that turnabout was fair play and we ought to help them out." Cleveland writer Charles W. Mears blasted the trade. "There can be no comparison between the two men," wrote Mears, "and if Davis goes to New York it will not be a trade, but an act of charity on Cleveland's part instead."[6] No one disagreed.

To make matters more difficult, Ewing, despite his status as one of the game's most recognizable stars, was a hugely unpopular addition to the Cleveland club due to simmering resentments from the Players League adventure. Ewing was an officer in the Brotherhood and the captain of the New York Players League club, but in July of 1890 he told the papers that he had been offered $8,000 to desert the new league and manage his hometown team, the Cincinnati Reds. He turned the offer down, but the National League kept after him, and in August he was seen in intense conversation with Chicago owner Albert Spalding and Cincinnati magnate John T. Brush. It appeared to Ewing's Brotherhood mates that he was looking to jump back to the League, and only the public revelation of his apparent perfidy kept him from doing so. Ewing always denied any evil intent, but many embittered Brotherhood men saw him as a traitor, and the charge followed Ewing for the rest of his career.

After a spring

George Davis, traded to New York for an aging Buck Ewing, was elected to the Baseball Hall of Fame in 1998 (Library of Congress).

training swing through the South, the Spiders opened the 1893 season in Pittsburgh with a 7–2 win by Cy Young that featured a fourth inning home run by Cupid Childs. John Clarkson beat the Pirates the next day, and after a series of rainouts the club went to Cincinnati and beat the Reds for Young's second win of the season. The Spiders lost a 17–12 contest the next day, then traveled to Cleveland for the home opener against Chicago on May 4. This contest, played in bitter cold, saw Young on the mound for the third time in five games. On the hill for Chicago was Willie McGill, the teenage sensation of the 1890 Cleveland Players League team. Still only 19 years old, McGill had already built a reputation as a drinker and carouser, but on this day he defeated his old team by a score of 5 to 3.

Chicago manager Cap Anson outsmarted himself on the next after-noon at League Park. His Colts were leading 6 to 1 in the sixth inning on another cold day with rain and fog blowing in off Lake Erie. Umpire Tom Lynch wanted to call the game, but Anson refused to quit. He said that the fans—those who remained, anyway—deserved to see a full nine innings. The game resumed, and the Spiders scored eight unanswered runs to win the game 9 to 6.

Bad weather throughout the country played havoc with the schedule, and the Spiders played only two games in an 11-day stretch in early May. But when they played, the Cleveland offense produced runs in bunches. The beat the Browns in St. Louis 19 to 3 on May 12, then returned to Cleveland and sat through several days of weather-related idleness. When the skies cleared, Tebeau's men defeated the Reds at League Park by scores of 21 to 4 and 19 to 5. Their offensive fireworks, keyed by Ed McKean and a revitalized Buck Ewing, pushed the Spiders into first place by late May.

By 1893, McKean and Cupid Childs had established themselves as two of the most valuable players in the game. No other team could boast two such offensive weapons at second base and shortstop. McKean still made errors, though not as many as he had in his first few seasons with the Blues. His range was good if not spectacular, and his 90-error seasons were now a thing of the past. Tebeau did not mind errors much, anyway. The Cleveland manager believed that aggressive players made more errors than passive ones, and infielders who rarely made errors did so because they covered little ground. McKean was no Arlie Latham, the longtime St. Louis third baseman who let hard liners shoot by him; the players said that a fielder who jumped out of harm's way when a hot drive came near him had "Arlie Lathamed" it.

"Fatty" Childs, too, was a star at bat and in the field. Childs had dis-covered the value of the walk, and used his outstanding batting eye to walk more than 100 times per season while rarely striking out. Childs averaged well over a run scored per game and his range was among the best in the league at second base. With Childs leading off, Burkett batting second and McKean third, the Spiders batted .300 as a team in 1893.

Once again, the first Eastern trip of the season brought the Spiders back to earth. Consigned to the road for more than three weeks, the Spiders won nine of 22 games to fall back to sixth position. They recovered with six wins in a row at League Park against the Pirates and Senators to crawl back up to fourth, but the defending champions from Boston claimed first place and threatened to run away with the pennant race. During June and July, the Spiders remained locked into fourth position, unable to mount a long enough winning streak to move up the National League ladder.

Dirty play abounded in 1893. On July 12 in Cleveland, Tommy Tucker, first baseman of the visiting Boston Beaneaters, slammed so hard into Chief Zimmer in a close play at first that he broke Zimmer's collarbone. (Some reports say that Tucker spiked Zimmer as well.) The Cleveland catcher did not return to the lineup until late September, and the injury forced the Spiders to put Jack O'Connor behind the plate for two months. The Beaneaters won the game by a 17–7 score, so it was not as if the play happened as part of a close, competitive contest. Tucker was known as a dirty player, and plays like this helped to cement his bad reputation.

That game degenerated into a constant series of arguments after Zimmer's injury. In the third inning, the Spiders had runners on first and second when O'Connor hit a dribbler down the third base line. O'Connor shouted, "Foul!" Third baseman Billy Nash, thinking that umpire John Gaffney had made the call, relaxed as Rowdy Jack hustled to first. Nash, alerted by his fellow infielders, quickly stepped on third for a forceout and threw to Tucker to nip O'Connor at first. Tucker then trapped Buck Ewing between first and second, and Bobby Lowe tagged him to complete a triple play. Gaffney, who claimed he did not see Lowe tag Ewing, changed his call to a double play and sent Ewing to second base. That set off the Beaneaters, who convinced the umpire to award the triple play, but Tebeau yelled at Gaffney and argued until he reinstated the original double play decision. The Boston club then demanded to know how Ewing could be put on second when he never reached it in the rundown. Gaffney was considered one of the league's better umpires, but his flip-flopping made nobody happy and disgusted the Cleveland fans, who booed loudly the rest of the afternoon.

Zimmer's misfortune was one of many for Cleveland. Both Cupid

Childs and Ed McKean missed some time with illness, so Patsy put Buck Ewing on the infield for a few games. Jimmy McAleer's chronic leg problems limited him to only 91 games, leaving a hole in center field that Tebeau tried all year to fill. He wound up using Jake Virtue as a super-sub, the same role Jack O'Connor filled before Zimmer's injury made Rowdy Jack an everyday player. Virtue's hitting fell off from 1892, but he showed his versatility by playing six different positions in 1893. Later that summer, the Cleveland manager used pitchers Nig Cuppy and John Clarkson in the outfield.

Patsy Tebeau's combative managerial style had changed not a bit from the year before. He was convinced that his take-no-prisoners mode of play had brought the Spiders the half-pennant in 1892, and so Tebeau, if anything, doubled down on the verbal, and sometimes physical, abuse of umpires and opponents. The Spiders had their defenders, who praised Tebeau's enthusiasm and passion for winning, but many more observers were offended by his violent language in the heat of competition. Patsy merely stated that he was not the only one. "I am in favor of something that will put a stop to bad language on the field," he said. "But we are not the only offenders. I have heard the New Yorks say things in Cleveland that wouldn't grace the columns of *The Sun*. If we are worse than the Pittsburgs then I'll keel right over."[7]

Tebeau's constant razzing, echoed by the other Spiders, affected some players more than others. Frank Killen was a talented left-handed pitcher who won 36 games for Pittsburgh in 1893. He was one of the top pitchers in the league, but he was emotional and easily rattled. As Pirate manager Al Buckenberger explained, "Killen hates pitching in Cleveland because of Tebeau's calling him names. He gets mad and can't pitch."[8] Buckenberger came up with a solution. He had his star pitcher stuff his ears with cotton before his next game at League Park. Killen did not respond to Tebeau's stream of insults, and Patsy grew more annoyed as the afternoon wore on. "Is he deaf?" demanded the Cleveland manager. When Tebeau finally discovered the cotton in Killen's ears, the enraged manager grabbed Killen by the arm and pulled him close to yell at him.

Sometimes, the Cleveland manager pulled stunts that came totally out of the blue. In Brooklyn, Patsy called out to center fielder Dave Foutz, the opposing manager, "Hey, Foutz, one of your men has my bat." Tebeau picked up every bat in Brooklyn's rack and inspected it, delaying the game and annoying both the Bridegrooms and their fans. He didn't find the missing bat, but at game's end he made off with a bat belonging to Harry Stovey. The veteran Stovey, reported the *Brooklyn Eagle*, was "madder than a hornet, but he did not get his bat." The Spiders lost that game anyway, but at least Patsy gained a new bat that day.[9]

On July 25 in Cincinnati, the fans watched both the Reds and the Spiders make a farce of the game. Umpire Jack McQuaid was ill and unable to appear, so the team captains chose Jimmy McAleer of the Spiders (still nursing his leg injury) to rule on the bases and Frank Dwyer of the Reds to call balls and strikes. There were no major problems in this close contest until the bottom of the ninth inning. With the score tied, Cincinnati's Jim Canavan walked, and then Elmer Smith bunted toward first base. Patsy Tebeau fielded the ball and tagged Smith so hard that the ball came loose and dribbled away, with Canavan advancing to third and Smith taking second. McAleer, however, called Smith out and sent Canavan back to second. The Reds howled in protest, but McAleer's decision stood.

Dwyer retaliated in kind. He called every one of Cy Young's next eight pitches a ball, loading the bases. That's when Tebeau had an idea. He ordered Young to throw to third baseman Chippy McGarr, who tagged Canavan despite the fact that Canavan was standing with both feet on the base. "You're out!" cried McAleer. As the fans booed, Young threw to first, where Tebeau tagged Cincinnati's Tom Sullivan, who also stood on the bag. McAleer called Sullivan out too, and the Spiders ran off the field.

This was sheer robbery, and to forestall a riot, the Spiders returned to the diamond and resumed the inning with Canavan and Sullivan still on third and first. Two batters later, Arlie Latham deliberately took a pitch from Cy Young in the back, forcing Canavan home with the winning run. Though the Reds emerged with the win, local writer Paul Chamberlain called the game "a disgraceful travesty on base ball, disgusting to the public and hurtful to the national sport." Not only that, but "there was a flow of Billingsgate throughout the first two games with Cleveland that would have made a fish-woman sick with envy."[10]

Sometimes, using two players as umpires worked well. On July 29 in St. Louis, Browns team owner Chris von der Ahe, angry at umpire Tom Lynch for a call he made in the first game of a twin bill, refused to allow the arbiter to work the second contest. Instead, the Spiders selected John Clarkson to officiate, and the Browns chose pitcher Arthur (Dad) Clarkson, John's younger brother. The Clarksons always refused to pitch against each other, but they made a great umpiring team, and the 3–2 Cleveland win was remarkably free of arguments.

In past years, though players battled with all their might on the field, most of them respected each other. Patsy Tebeau liked to tell of an unexpected display of kindness by one of the game's roughest customers,

Boston's Mike Kelly. In July of 1890, Patsy bunted at a pitch and fouled it back into his own face. The blow knocked him unconscious and broke his nose, though Kelly, the opposing catcher, wondered aloud if Tebeau was pulling one of his tricks. The flow of blood convinced Kelly otherwise as Patsy was bundled off to the hospital. The next morning, Tebeau was surprised to see Kelly walk into his room with a huge fruit basket. "I tell you," said Tebeau, "the way that man treated me brought tears to my eyes."[11]

However, it appeared that such mutual respect was fast becoming a thing of the past. Tebeau's style of nasty, highly belligerent play, pioneered by Charlie Comiskey and the St. Louis Browns in the 1880s, had paid off for Cleveland with a half-pennant in 1892. The Spiders were no longer a doormat of the National League, and other teams copied their strategies. Most notably, Ned Hanlon, the new manager of the Baltimore Orioles, was busily assembling a roster full of hard-charging, aggressive players. Most of these new men, with names like McGraw, Kelley, Jennings, Gleason, and the rest, were of Irish descent, as was Hanlon, who seemed to be building the "Hibernian Orioles" as Tebeau had assembled his "Hibernian Spiders." The Orioles, who finished last in 1892, were not yet ready to contend in 1893, but their day would arrive sooner than most people could have expected.

Cleveland's never-ending spate of injuries forced Patsy Tebeau to shift his men around. With McAleer and Zimmer out for long periods, he sent Jake Virtue to center field and moved Jack O'Connor behind the plate. On the Fourth of July, in the first game of a doubleheader against Brooklyn, Patsy hurt his knee again in a slide and put himself out of the lineup for several weeks. Billy Alvord, who had played 13 games for the Spiders two years before, covered third base for a few days, but hit poorly. To fill the hole at third, Tebeau signed a 31-year-old veteran, James "Chippy" McGarr, from Savannah of the Southern Association.

Chippy McGarr was Patsy's kind of player. A son of Irish immigrants, McGarr grew up in Worcester, Massachusetts, and played for several American Association teams during the 1880s. He manned third base for the Boston Beaneaters in 1890, but batted only .236 and fell back to the minors. While playing for Denver in 1891, he was suspended for hitting an umpire in the back with a baseball during an argument. He was also adept at tripping enemy baserunners when the umpire wasn't looking. McGarr was not much of a hitter, but he was a good glove man, with a knack for handling bunts. Besides, as one report stated, he "had the heart of a *lion* and was as fearless as any player of his time."[12] McGarr, who earned his nickname with his quick fists, fit right in, and kept the third base job for the rest of the 1893 season.

One man who remained healthy all year was Jesse Burkett, who took a large step forward in 1893. He had claimed the left field spot in 1892 and batted a solid .275 in his first full Cleveland season. Now, with the pitchers throwing from five feet farther away, Burkett jumped his average to .348 and scored 145 runs. He was also one of the game's expert bunters. Cy Young turned in another great season with 34 wins against 16 losses, but Nig Cuppy, a 28-game winner in 1892, fell to 17–10 while John Clarkson's final log was 16–17. The Spiders hoped that their second and third starters merely needed a season to adjust to the new pitching distance. The Cleveland hitters weren't complaining, though, as the team as a whole batted .300.

Buck Ewing, thought to be washed up when Cleveland acquired him, was a bright spot for the Spiders. His .344 batting average, 122 runs batted in, and 117 runs scored set career highs despite a late-season injury that kept him out of the lineup for part of September. He also solidified the right field position, and despite his arm miseries, threw well enough from League Park's shallow right field to compile 17 outfield assists. Still, many of the Spiders resented his presence. Jesse Burkett was the most vocal, and the Crab was never one to hide his opinions. He hated Ewing and let everyone know it.

One wonders why Burkett despised Ewing so much, as Burkett was never in the Players League. He had spent the 1890 campaign as a pitcher and outfielder with the National League's Giants. Apparently, complaining about anything and everything was Jesse's default setting. They didn't call him the Crab for nothing, and though his batting skill was a welcome addition to the Cleveland lineup, his personality was not. He was a tantrum thrower, and one newspaper reported a classic, obscenity-filled Burkett tirade as follows: "Why you blank, blankety blank, do you know what I think of you? I think you are the blankest blank blank that ever came out of the blank blankest town in the blank blank land. You ought to be put in a museum."[13]

Burkett wasn't the only offender. Other teams objected to the Spiders' behavior, especially at League Park. A report in *Sporting Life* in early September detailed the complaints made by Pittsburgh manager Al Buckenberger:

> Buckenberger says that the language used by the Cleveland players at home is so vile that visiting teams are insulted. He says [pitcher Frank] Killen stuffed his ears full of cotton during one game in Cleveland, so that he could not hear the dirty

epithets that were hurled at him from the coaching lines. "Buck" further states that the Cleveland players threw bats and boots at his men while they were passing through the Cleveland dressing-room, and that Cleveland curses and oaths filled the air until it was a pale blue.... Dirty ball playing is not the cause for the general complaint, but foul language and the "what t' 'ell" demeanor of the men from the Forest City. The Pittsburgs, with their noisy coaching and queer tactics, were tin gods compared to the Ohio hoodlums.[14]

The behavioral low point of the season for the Spiders came in August during a three-game series with the Giants in New York. Mired in a nine-game losing streak, Tebeau's men took their frustrations out on umpire John Gaffney. In the first game, on Friday, August 18, the Giants scored four runs in the eighth to beat the Spiders in a 12–9 slugfest. The second contest saw New York ace Amos Rusie dominate the Clevelanders, allowing only two hits (both by Jesse Burkett) in a 2–0 shutout. After an off day on Sunday, the Spiders and Giants closed the series on Monday, August 21. The series was already a chippy, argument-filled affair, but Monday is when the fireworks started.

Nig Cuppy pitched for Cleveland, while Charlie Petty started for the Giants. In the fourth inning, with the Spiders down by two runs, Tebeau came to the plate. Gaffney called the first pitch a strike, which brought the usual stream of insults and foul language from the mouth of the Spider captain. When Gaffney ruled Petty's second pitch a strike as well, Tebeau exploded in rage. He screamed obscenities, which could be heard clearly all over the Polo Grounds, at the umpire, who ordered him off the grounds. The game was already a lost cause, even before the Giants scored seven runs in the eighth for a 13–3 win.

The New York writers were disgusted by what they saw. Said Joe Vila, New York, correspondent for *Sporting Life*,

> Speaking of the Clevelands reminds me that no "dirtier" ball team has been seen here in years. The actions of Tebeau and his players were simply disgraceful. Not content with kicking at every ball or strike called by Umpire Gaffney, they resorted to rowdyism and toughness that disgusted fair-minded persons. Tebeau himself showed that he was a rowdy of the lowest type. He made a scene in Monday's game when Gaffney called a strike on him, and used the vilest language imaginable within hearing of the spectators. He applied the foulest epithets to Gaffney, shook his fist in his face and swore like a trooper. Gaffney finally, out of respect for himself and in the name of decency, fined this man $35 and put him out of the game. Tebeau was hissed and hooted by the crowd and walked to the dressing-rooms like a typical Bowery tough mug.[15]

It could not have escaped Tebeau's notice that former Spider George Davis went eight for 14 in the three-game series. Were Davis still with the Spiders, the injury bug might not have derailed Cleveland's pennant hopes.

For the rest of the decade, the Spiders always appeared to be one star player short of winning a pennant. George Davis might well have been that player.

Despite another bad Eastern swing, the Spiders held onto fourth place at the end of August, and remained a threat to pass the Phillies for third. Tebeau believed that the rash of injuries kept his team from the top. "The Cleveland club has made a very creditable showing thus far this season," he said. "Nearly every player on the club has been compelled at one time or another to retire from play on account of injuries. McAleer, Ewing, Zimmer, O'Connor, McKean, and I have been on the hospital list and still the club kept on winning. Boston would not be so far ahead had we not been thus handicapped."[16]

Frank Robison was satisfied with his manager's performance. When a reporter asked the Cleveland owner about Tebeau's status for the following season, Robison did not hesitate. "Tebeau in '94?" he said. "Well, if anybody gets him away from me he'll have to give up big coin. Why Patsy Tebeau knows every phase of base ball. He's all right and you can bet that he will be on my pay-roll for a long time to come." He also seconded the manager's assessment of the pennant race. "I do believe that if our team had been intact all season we'd have won the pennant."[17]

Perhaps he was right, for Cleveland played its best ball of the season in September, winning 10 of its last 13 games to finish the year in third place behind Boston and Pittsburgh. One of those 10 wins was a forfeit at home against the Orioles, once one of the pushovers of the league but assembling the talent that would make them a contender for the rest of the decade. The Spiders and Orioles were tied at 11 runs apiece after seven innings, but the Spiders (who batted first that day) scored in the top of the eighth to take the lead. That's when a rainstorm blew in off Lake Erie, with fog that made the ball almost invisible. The Orioles wanted the game called, with the score reverting to the last completed inning and the contest ending in an 11–11 tie. Umpire Tim Hurst told the Orioles to play on, so Baltimore stalled for time. With Childs and Burkett on base, Tebeau hit a fly to left that John McGraw refused to field, so Patsy and both runners scored. Jack O'Connor then hit a bouncer to left that also went for a homer, and the Spiders had a 15–11 lead.

The Orioles figured that if they never retired a Cleveland batter, the inning could not be completed, but Hurst was wise to this scheme. After O'Connor's homer, catcher Wilbert Robison refused even to toss the ball back to the pitcher. That's when Hurst forfeited the game to the Spiders.

The Orioles finished in eighth place in 1893, but they were on the rise. Baltimore's 20-year-old utility man John McGraw had already emerged as the emotional leader of the Orioles, and led his team in using the same tactics that Patsy Tebeau had made famous, or infamous, with the Spiders. Baseball was a war for McGraw as it was for Tebeau, and when the Baltimore star (who played mostly in the outfield that year, but eventually took over third base) snarled at his teammates, "Get at 'em!" a pitched battle usually followed. McGraw, the son of Irish immigrants, and Tebeau, who identified with the Irish-Americans, became bitter enemies, as did the teams they led, and their many conflicts would help define the sport in the last decade of the 19th century.

8

Team Turmoil

Tame base ball is relished by very few. The kicking, however, must be genuine. None of the thin stage business, simply for effect, but red and green fire flashing from the eyes of the players. Earnest protest gives the impression that the game is being played for all it is worth and that both teams are out to win.... Mechanical ball is losing ball. Head work and body work form a combination that leads on to victory. The absence of one is fatal and the presence of both means triumph. A team under a diplomatic hold often defeats one showing greater skill, and your true diplomat is one who knows his rights and fights for them. That's why we love our Pat.

— *The Sporting News*, January 1894[1]

In November of 1893, Frank Robison dropped a bombshell on the Cleveland fans.

He wanted to sell the team.

The Panic of 1893, which caused one of the most serious and long-lasting economic depressions in American history, had hit the nation hard. It began early in the year, when the Philadelphia and Reading Railroad was found to have greatly overextended itself due to overbuilding and shaky financing. The Philadelphia and Reading went into receivership, and many of the banks that had loaned large sums to it and other railroads soon collapsed. This disaster sent the stock market tumbling and caused runs on banks nationwide. Some 500 banks and more than 15,000 businesses, large and small, failed as a result.

Industrial states, including Ohio, were walloped by the depression. Unemployment, which rose to around 25 percent across the nation, surpassed the 50 percent mark for industrial workers in Ohio.[2] Cleveland, the very epitome of a blue-collar factory town, suffered greatly, and Robison laid off scores of his own conductors, workmen, and other employees from his streetcar lines. Perhaps the Cleveland owner was overextended financially, or perhaps he was afraid that the economic downturn would soon sink the baseball business too. In any case, Robison set a price of $45,000 for the Spiders franchise and declared his intention to sell.

Within days, two of Robison's former partners, and one former enemy, put together a coalition to buy the Spiders. George W. Howe, one-time treasurer of the club, teamed with ex-secretary Davis Hawley and Robison's bitter streetcar rival Al Johnson, the money man behind the Players League entry in Cleveland, to raise the necessary cash. Though interested parties from Detroit and Buffalo looked into purchasing the team and moving it out of the city, these three men were determined to keep the Spiders in Cleveland. For a while, it looked as if the sale would proceed smoothly with little disruption.

Complications soon arose. The National League did not want the team to leave Cleveland and much preferred to let the local trio buy the club. However, Johnson, Hawley, and Howe feared that Robison would sell off some of his star players before completing a sale; already, rumors that Cy Young was headed to New York and Ed McKean to Boston were floating around. The league formed an emergency committee to oversee the "Cleveland situation," and the other magnates reportedly agreed among themselves not to buy any players from the Spiders until the sale was complete. With uncertainty in the air, the three would-be buyers lowered their bid to a reported $38,000.

Robison was a stubborn individual. He would sell for $45,000 and not one penny less, as he made clear in an angry statement to *Sporting Life* in early December:

> As a sort of ultimatum to Cleveland people, I will be open to offers from them until next Saturday [December 9]. After that, if they do not agree to my terms, Cleveland will know the team no more. Not one dollar less than $45,000 will buy it, and it cost me much more, notwithstanding the reports to the contrary by those who want to beat me out of it. I paid cash for my franchise, and by law I can sell it for cash to whomsoever I see fit. The agreement of National League franchise owners, requiring an individual owner to obtain the consent of his colleagues to sell his property is public sentiment and not law. One week will determine whether the club stays in Cleveland or goes to Detroit, and $45,000 is the pin on which the deal hangs, but it is final and unalterable.[3]

The deadline came and went with no sale. For several weeks, sportswriters speculated on the fate of the Spiders; some predicted that the team would play the 1894 season in Buffalo or Detroit, while others believed that the National League would rather take over the team and operate it rather than abandon the Cleveland market. To further confuse matters, John T. Brush, the ambitious owner of the Indianapolis Hoosiers of the Western

League, offered to take Cleveland's place on the National League schedule.

In the end, all the worry, speculation, and rumors were for nothing. In late January, the Cleveland magnate declared that, since no one had met his price for the Spiders, he had decided to keep the team. However, Robison announced several changes in policy:

1. The club would pass out no more free tickets except for newspapermen. Robison was "determined to curtail the horde of dead-heads who have made his life a burden and his base ball investment profitless, even at the risk of having his railroad interests attacked." Apparently many people in Cleveland, including union officials representing the streetcar line workers, had come to regard free Spiders tickets as their due.
2. The Spiders were now willing to play Sunday games in other cities. The Cleveland club had not played at home on Sunday since they rejoined the National League in 1889, but the politically powerful Cleveland Ministers Association was not satisfied. The ministers also objected to Spider participation in Sunday games anywhere, even out of state.
3. The team would carry only 14 players instead of the 18 men it employed in 1893.
4. The Spiders would hold spring training in Cleveland.[4]

Robison also tried to persuade several Spiders to accept pay cuts. This went over poorly with the veterans, especially after *Sporting Life* correspondent Elmer Bates printed the salaries of the individual Cleveland players in the March 24 edition. The maximum allowed salary of the National League at the time was $2,400, but stars such as Burkett and McKean were playing on the cheap, each earning only $1,800. Cy Young, the best pitcher in baseball, was at $2,300, but the deeply unpopular Buck Ewing and John Clarkson received $2,400 and $2,500, respectively. Burkett, Young, Childs, and McKean held out and did not sign their contracts until nearly the end of March, by which time many other teams had been practicing together for weeks. Childs, who was nicknamed "Fatty" as it was, reported to the team noticeably overweight even for him.

While the "Cleveland situation," as the papers put it, festered, the Spiders' style of play remained a subject of controversy. Criticism of Tebeau and the Spiders came from many quarters of the national press, but the most pointed censure came from the pen of Henry Chadwick, the veteran journalist known far and wide as "Father Chadwick." The British-born

Chadwick was employed as a columnist on cricket, his native country's sport, for the *New York Times* in 1858 when he discovered baseball. Chadwick fell in love with the game and did more than any other man to popularize the new American sport. During the game's phenomenal growth in the 1860s Chadwick produced the first true baseball guide, invented the box score, and was the first to tabulate hits, home runs, and total bases. He was not the first baseball writer, but he was the first important one, and the sport may not have attained the heights it did without his prolific pen. Chadwick, still an active commentator on the baseball scene as he approached his 70th birthday, was the most honored and respected man in the sport, richly deserving the title "Father of Baseball."

And the Father of Baseball did not like what he saw.

Chadwick had lived long enough to see the game evolve from a "gentlemen's sport" to something much more coarse and distasteful, in his view. No longer a mere pastime, baseball was now a war, thanks to managers such as Patsy Tebeau. Chadwick was especially upset at Tebeau's oft-quoted statement to a St. Louis reporter during the fall of 1893. Tebeau said, "My instructions to the players are to win games, and I want to go on record as saying that it takes aggressive hustlers to do that. A milk-and-water, goody-goody player can't wear a Cleveland uniform. There is the truth of the whole matter. We stick up for our rights, and are called names and abused for it."[5]

Chadwick regarded "aggressive hustlers" as "a new name for rowdy, kicking ball players." He scored the Spiders for their "disgraceful scene enacted on the Polo Ground last fall" and remarked that "Tebeau's allusion to milk-and-water, goody-goody players is simply his notion of players who are an honor to their club and the professional fraternity at large, from their manly and honorable methods as the 'aggressive hustlers' are a disgrace to the game."[6]

Charles Mears of *The Sporting News*, the main rival of *Sporting Life*, cared little for the views of Father Chadwick. Mears, a vocal supporter of Tebeau and the battling Spiders, retorted, "And 'Chad' is getting real old too" and "Chadwick goes into a spasm every time he hears Pat Tebeau's name mentioned."[7]

Patsy, who had moved his family from St. Louis to live in Cleveland on a full-time basis, found trouble even before spring training started. On March 3, a few days before the Spiders were scheduled to report to the Cleveland Athletic Club for practice, Tebeau and a friend decided to pay a visit to a local brothel, identified in the papers as "Nettie Strong's house of ill fame" on Bond and Lake streets downtown. Tebeau, a married man with children, later claimed that it was all the friend's idea, but the evening went badly from the start. Perhaps Ms. Strong tried to extort money from the famous ballplayer, but whatever the reason, the Cleveland manager traded punches with the muscular bouncers who kept order at the establishment. The cops arrived, broke up the fight, and hauled Patsy down to the station.[8]

Tebeau got much the worst of it, but wound up paying $250 to drop the matter. The case went no further, and some of the Cleveland papers barely mentioned it (though the Cincinnati writers, who detested Patsy, certainly did). Still, the incident was a serious lapse of judgment on Tebeau's part. He was a heavy drinker, and one wonders if an excess of alcohol played a part in his flawed decision-making process that evening.

Nonetheless, Tebeau's arrest was old news by March 12, when the Spiders gathered in Cleveland for spring practice. The team, after the holdouts signed their contracts and reported, looked solid, and the oft-injured Spiders of the year before, including McAleer, Ewing, and Zimmer, appeared to be healthy. Jesse Burkett, who joined the club after ending his holdout, was his usual crabby self, too; as *The Sporting News* reported, "Burkett is still kicking against everything in general. He must have a grudge against himself."[9] Since the Crab seemed to play his best when his mood was the worst, even his constant complaining was treated as a hopeful sign.

Perhaps Jesse was upset with a recent rule change which may have been aimed at him personally. The National League had already banned the flat-sided bat, an invaluable aid to bunting, and now decreed that, beginning in 1894, foul bunts would be counted as strikes. Burkett, who was used to fouling off one bunt after another down the baselines until he placed one where he wanted, now had a smaller margin of error. He was still the top bunter in the game, but would have to change his approach in the new season.

Burkett was only one of the many Spiders who gave the Spiders cause for hope. Cy Young, Nig Cuppy, and John Clarkson comprised a talented starting rotation, while Cupid Childs and Ed McKean gave the Spiders a keystone combo that few teams could match, either offensively or defensively. Jimmy McAleer was still the best in the league defensively in center field, and with Burkett in left and Buck Ewing in right, the team could afford to carry McAleer's weak bat. If everyone remained relatively healthy, Jack O'Connor could resume his role as a substitute in the outfield, at first base, or behind the plate, where Chief Zimmer was as solid as ever.

First baseman Jake Virtue, however, was fading. Some say that he became gun-shy (pardon the expression) in the field in 1892 after a collision with catcher Chief Zimmer during the 11-inning post-season battle between Cy Young and Boston's Jack Stivetts. As Virtue and Zimmer chased a popup down the first base line, Mike Kelly of the Beaneaters called for Jake to take it though Zimmer was already camped under it. Thanks to Kelly, Virtue and Zimmer slammed into each other. The impact knocked both men to the ground, and the batter was safe at first. The collision had a noticeable effect on Virtue, who was less active and covered less ground at first base in 1893. Also, though almost every hitter in the National League saw his batting and slugging average rise sharply after the pitching distance increased, Virtue was an exception. He struggled at the plate all year, and though he was not yet 30, his production declined sharply. With Chippy McGarr at third, Tebeau took over at first and relegated Virtue to the bench.

The season started well, with the Spiders winning seven of nine games on their opening road trip despite the absence of Cupid Childs, who was ill. Jake Virtue played second base in the opener and Buck Ewing took over there a few days later. Childs returned in a 1–0 win at Cincinnati, and then the Spiders won five games at home against Louisville and Chicago. They lost two of three in Pittsburgh, but went to St. Louis and won three in a row to raise their record to 17–4. The Spiders held first place by two and half games on May 19 before losing five of their next six and dropping to second behind Pittsburgh.

As usual, the national press complained about the foul language and

Jesse Burkett, the irascible but hard-hitting outfielder (author's collection).

objectionable behavior of Tebeau and his men. A loss at Pittsburgh on May 12 lasted for an incredible three hours and five minutes because Tebeau and his Spiders bickered on nearly every call in an attempt to intimidate umpire Jack McQuaid. However, the Spider style of play proved a winning one, at least early on. By May 16 Cuppy's record stood at 6–0, with Clarkson at 6–1 and Young at 5–3. In early June Tebeau told the press, "There's not a weak spot on the team that I can see."[10]

Cleveland fans—many of them, anyway—took their cues from Tebeau's behavior. On May 25, with the Pirates leading the Spiders at League Park by nine runs in the bottom of the ninth, a crowd of 9,000—the largest of the season—grew restless and began pelting the players on the field with seat cushions. As umpire Bob Emslie tried to restore order, the capacity crowd stormed the field amid another barrage of flying seat cushions. The Spiders were trying to bat, but the crowd apparently figured that the game was lost, so they might as well end it themselves. Emslie forfeited the game to the Pirates, and *The Sporting News* called the scene "a stain on the fair name of Cleveland patrons of the game that will be hard to wipe out" and "the most disgraceful affair that has ever marred the history of the national game."[11]

Eighty years later, in 1974, Ten-Cent Beer Night at Cleveland Municipal Stadium ended in eerily similar fashion. Unruly fans stormed the field in the ninth inning, the umpires were unable to control them, and Cleveland lost the game by forfeit.

Despite the forfeit loss, Cleveland entered June in first place. On June 1 Cy Young's 22–8 win in Boston against the defending champion Beaneaters kept the Spiders in a virtual tie for the lead with Pittsburgh and the suddenly surging Baltimore Orioles. Philadelphia and Boston stood only half a game back in the tightest pennant race the league had seen up to that time. With five teams less than a game out of first place, any stumble could prove fatal.

That's when the bottom dropped out for Cleveland. Once again, an Eastern road trip crushed the Spider pennant hopes, as nine losses in 15 games dropped the team to fifth. Jimmy McAleer suffered a severely sprained ankle in Brooklyn that kept him out of the lineup for weeks, while injuries to Ewing, Cuppy, and others unsettled the lineup. When the Spiders started losing, the fans tuned them out. The July 4 doubleheader against the Giants at League Park drew only 3,000 people while crowds of 10,000 or more filled the stands in other cities. The Cleveland city officials had chosen that day for the grand opening of the Soldiers and Sailors Monument in Public Square downtown, and most of the streetcars were idle. The fans that made it to League Park saw the Spiders lose both games.

By early July, reality had set in. The Spiders opened the month in sixth place, but six consecutive losses at home to Boston and New York knocked Tebeau's club out of the first division. McAleer was hurt, Burkett wanted to be traded, Ewing could neither hit nor throw, Clarkson suddenly started losing game after game, Young was overworked, and Cuppy's fragile arm caused him to miss a few starts. Patsy tried out several young pitchers, but neither Frank Griffith, nor Frank Knauss, nor John Lyton, nor Chauncey Fisher were ready to pitch major league ball. On July 5, Boston came to town and scored 11 runs off Clarkson in the third inning alone. Patsy was so desperate that he put Jake Virtue on the mound for three innings and Jesse Burkett for two. Burkett, who gave up only two runs, was the only bright spot in a 22–7 loss.

The next two games against Boston were even more disastrous. On July 6, Burkett muffed two easy flies in the first inning as the Beaneaters scored eight runs off Nig Cuppy. By the third the score was 15–0, and though Cuppy pitched a complete game, the visitors walked off with a 19–6 win. The next day saw Boston reach double figures again in a 16–10 victory. Cleveland had given up 69 runs in only four games, and this loss dropped the Spiders to the .500 mark at 29–29. After the Beaneaters left town, the Spiders rallied with three home wins against the awful Washington club (one a 23–4 stomping that may have been the easiest win of Cy Young's career) but crowds in the hundreds rather than the thousands had become the rule, not the exception, by mid-summer.

A new outfielder, one whom Patsy knew very well, joined the club in July. George "White Wings" Tebeau was Patsy's older brother and was cut from the same mold. George was a scrappy, combative outfielder, sarcastically called "White Wings" because he bore no resemblance to the "white winged dove of peace." George, like Patsy a good fielder, a mediocre hitter, and a natural leader, played left field in Cincinnati for three seasons in the late 1880s, then moved to Toledo of the American Association in 1890. In Toledo, he feuded with manager Charlie Morton, and after he "spoke words to Morton that cannot be found in the Bible,"[12] the team let him go.

George spent the next few years in the minors but emerged as Washington's Opening Day left fielder in 1894. He hit poorly in Washington, and when he requested his release to join his brother in Cleveland, the Senators readily agreed. George Tebeau took over in center field, and while he was no Jimmy McAleer with the glove, he was a slightly better hitter. The elder Tebeau filled the position pending McAleer's return.

The injured center fielder, fighting a recurring battle with charley horses in his legs, was not with the team, but he was not idle. Frank Robison appeared at McAleer's apartment one day, thrust a wad of cash and a fistful of train tickets into his hand, and ordered him to hit the road and find some new players. In early July McAleer, who would later prove himself a good judge of talent, signed Harry Blake, an outfielder from Atlanta of the Southern Association. Blake, only 20 years old, was a younger version of McAleer. He was an Ohio native (Blake was from Portsmouth, McAleer from Youngstown), a below-average hitter, and an outstanding fielder with a great throwing arm. Blake joined the Spiders on July 7 and claimed the center field slot, moving George Tebeau to right. When McAleer returned, Blake shifted to right and put White Wings on the bench.

As the losses mounted in early July, John Clarkson neared the end, and the end for this 300-game winner was not a pretty one. He was only 32 years old, but had spent a decade pitching over 500, and twice more than 600, innings per season. His pitching arm was worn out, and the high-strung pitcher's fragile mental state was starting to deteriorate. He won seven of his first eight decisions in 1894, but then started losing with regularity. The frustrated pitcher convinced himself that he was not to blame; instead, his teammates were losing games deliberately.

He may have had a point. Clarkson won only one of his final nine decisions, but on three separate occasions the Spiders fell behind with him on the mound and rallied to win after he left. Those three games occurred in a 12-day stretch in July, and the last was one in which Clarkson left a game against the Phillies with a 10–7 deficit, only to see the Spiders win by a 20–10 score. The Spiders were winning, but not for him. On the other hand, Clarkson, once friendly with the umpires, now criticized and complained about their calls on a regular basis. With no one on base, the lone umpire stood just behind the pitcher to call balls and strikes, so the pitcher and the umpire spent a lot of time together. Clarkson sabotaged his own efforts by mistreating the arbiters.

By mid-season, John had concluded that some of the Spiders were not giving their best efforts when he was on the mound. He complained to Patsy Tebeau that one of the outfielders was trying his utmost to make the Spiders lose when he pitched. The offending player, claimed Clarkson, "would throw me down at critical stages of games whenever he had the opportunity. He would dodge flies under the pretext that the sun was in his eyes, and in this way lost many a game, which, of course, was always charged up to me."[13]

One would assume that the outfielder in question was Jesse Burkett, who had been so vocal in his hatred for Buck Ewing. Jimmy McAleer, a staunch Players League supporter, was out of the lineup in early July with his leg injury, while George Tebeau and Harry Blake (neither of whom was in the Players League) were both new to the team. On the other hand, left field in League Park was perhaps the most difficult sun field in the league, and it was easy for any left fielder to lose a fly ball. One can never say with confidence if Clarkson's complaints were valid, or the rationalizations of an athlete whose career was ending poorly.

With Clarkson's penchant for blaming his teammates, many of whom still resented his dealings in the Players League enterprise, Tebeau realized that Clarkson's presence was a detriment to the chemistry of his ballclub. In July, Tebeau traded Clarkson to the Baltimore Orioles for pitcher Tony Mullane, though the veteran right-hander later claimed that he left the team of his own volition. "I grew disgusted," stated Clarkson, "and one day told Tebeau that I guessed it was no use for me to pitch any longer, and so I packed my baggage and skipped."[14] Clarkson refused to report to Baltimore, and with that his career was over.

Mullane, like Clarkson a National League veteran who had pitched tons of innings since the early 1880s, was 35 and nearing the finish line as well. He appeared in only four games for the Spiders and quit the team in late July. Neither Clarkson nor Mullane, who won more than 600 major league games between them, ever pitched in the big leagues again. Their defections left Tebeau with few options in the rotation behind Cy Young and Nig Cuppy.

Late July saw the departure of another once-great veteran ballplayer. Buck Ewing crashed to earth after his fine 1893 campaign; at mid-season of 1894, his .251 batting average stood as one of the lowest in the league. He battled injuries all year, and at the age of 34 it appeared that Ewing, who began his big league career in 1880, had finally reached the end. The Spiders released him on July 18, the day after Clarkson left. In 1895, Ewing signed on as manager of his hometown team, the Cincinnati Reds, with whom he would battle Patsy Tebeau and the Spiders many times during the next several seasons.

After hitting the .500 mark on July 7, the Spiders righted the ship and won 14 of their next 16, mainly by overworking Young and Cuppy. The hot streak vaulted Cleveland to fourth place, but a 9–15 record in August dropped the team to sixth. They were out of the chase by Labor Day, and the home crowds grew smaller as the end of the season approached.

In early August, perhaps the ugliest game of the season occurred in

Pittsburgh. The Pirates and Spiders hated each other, a feeling that only intensified on May 24 when Jimmy McAleer's spikes sliced open catcher Connie Mack's knee in a play at the plate. This injury virtually ended Mack's playing career. The next day, during the game at League Park that was forfeited to Pittsburgh when unruly fans threw seat cushions, Pirate first baseman Jake Beckley camped under a foul pop-up when a dog, belonging to a Cleveland fan, charged out of the stands and attacked him. Beckley eluded the dog and caught the ball, but waited for a chance to get revenge. He got it on August 8 when he tripped Cupid Childs and sent him tumbling down the first base line. The Spiders feared that Childs' collarbone was broken; it most likely was not, but the Cleveland infielder suffered a shoulder injury that put him out of the lineup for two weeks.

An enraged Patsy then turned his venom on rookie umpire Willard Hoagland, bickering and threatening the arbiter all day. The Spiders lost by a 10–3 score, and at game's end, Patsy challenged the umpire to fight under the stands afterwards. Hoagland accepted the challenge; perhaps Tebeau did not know that Hoagland was an experienced boxer. The umpire removed his coat and made ready to fight, but *The Sporting News* described what happened next. "Once under the stand, Tebeau grabbed a bat. Hoagland pulled off his coat and squared. Tebeau, seeing he was up against it, dropped his bat and ran out into the stand into the arms of the crowd which was waiting for him."[15] Tebeau later explained that the Spiders had to rush to catch a train, though it looked like he would rather take his chances with the enemy fans than face a real fighter. Still, Hoagland quit about three weeks later, leaving league president Nick Young to search the country for a replacement.

Tebeau and his National League imitators drove many umpires from their jobs during the 1890s. One columnist, frustrated by the poor quality of game officials during the era, demanded to know why, in a nation of 70 million people, the National League could not find six decent umpires to control its games. The reason was that Patsy Tebeau, John McGraw, and a host of other baseball rowdies had made the umpire's life a nightmare, and few men wanted the job. Umpires of the 1890s saw themselves much as inner-city teachers in failing school districts see themselves in modern times. They felt unappreciated, constantly abused, poorly paid, and utterly expendable.

Ed McKean, as usual, was a bright spot in a disappointing season. At age 30, the Cleveland shortstop was at the peak of his game, batting .357 and leading the club in runs batted in with 128. His double-play partner, Cupid Childs, put together his best season, scoring 143 runs and belting the ball at a .353 clip. Even Tebeau, a mediocre hitter, posted a .302 average and stayed healthy for once, missing only five games. The main Cleveland starters, Cy Young (26–21) and Nig Cuppy (24–15) were solid; the problem lay with the lack of pitching behind the top two. Tebeau was so strapped for hurlers that he used 14 pitchers in 1894, 11 of whom started at least one game.

Tebeau, perhaps unwittingly, came up with an innovation in pitching strategy. In 1894 Nig Cuppy started 33 games, and Tebeau also used him 10 times in relief. Cuppy proved highly successful in the hybrid role. He finished all 10 of the games in which he relieved, earning eight of his 24 wins in those contests. During the next several years, Tebeau employed Cuppy as his emergency game-finisher, a role that is known today, more than 120 years later, as a "closer."

With Clarkson gone, Mullane quitting, and the Spiders well out of the pennant race, Tebeau brought in some more new pitchers for auditions in September of 1894. One of those pitchers was a 19-year-old from the Pittsburgh area named Rhoderick John Wallace.

Roddy Wallace, like Nig Cuppy (and Jesse Burkett in his debut with the Giants several years before), was small for a pitcher. A right-hander who stood only five feet and eight inches tall, he dreamed of playing for his hometown Pittsburgh Pirates, but manager Connie Mack turned him away without giving him a tryout. However, his fine pitching for an independent team in Franklin, Pennsylvania, that summer led the Spiders, who had nothing to lose by giving him a look, to sign him.

Wallace reported to the Spiders on September 13, 1894, and received two pieces of information from manager Tebeau. First, the rookie would make his major league debut against the defending league champion Boston club two days hence. That was a shock, but the second item was even more stunning. Roddy, Tebeau said, was no name for a ballplayer. From now on, we're going to call you Bobby.

The newly named Bobby Wallace lost his debut, giving up 13 hits and seven runs in a contest ended by rain after six innings. He won his next two decisions, however, and showed that, for a pitcher, he was an outstanding athlete, with quick feet and sure hands. Wallace, still a teenager, appeared to have potential, and performed well enough to earn another look at spring practice in 1895.

The season ended on a high note, with Cleveland sweeping three games in late September against the Phillies; one was a 26–4 win for Cy Young, who had suffered through a seven-game losing streak a few weeks before. On September 30 the Spiders closed the 1894 campaign with a bizarre game in Cincinnati in which neither side appeared to be trying very hard. The Reds walloped Nig Cuppy for 12 runs in the first three innings, but the Spiders answered with 11 in the seventh. Cleveland tied the game at 16 with runs in the eighth and ninth, and nearly won the game with two outs in the final frame. Jack O'Connor, the runner at third, tried one of his old tricks, slapping the ball out of third baseman Bill Merritt's hands and dashing across the plate, but umpire Jack McQuaid ruled O'Connor out for interference. McQuaid then avoided an ugly argument by declaring the game a tie, which seemed to suit everybody just fine.

The Spiders finished in sixth place, 21 and a half games behind Baltimore. The Orioles, long one of the league's sad-sack clubs, had assembled a team of battlers and fighters that rivaled Tebeau's Spiders for dirty play and umpire abuse. By winning the pennant, the Orioles proved that rowdy baseball was winning baseball, and the National League would see much more umpire abuse, foul language, and fan violence during the coming years.

9

The Temple Cup

"Tebeau is an earnest worker, no doubt, but if he is to be the manager of a National League team he should be able to curb his tongue and temper and behave as other managers do. I think this universal cry against the behavior of the Clevelands has served to keep the Forest City boys in check a bit, and will ultimately redound to the credit of the League."

—Joe Vila, August 1893[1]

The Cleveland Spiders of the mid–1890s were one of the National League's top road attractions, but home attendance was another story. The Spiders drew only 82,000 fans to League Park in 1894, the worst turnout in the circuit save for the last-place Louisville club. By way of contrast, the Spiders played before 24,500 people in New York during the second game of the Decoration Day doubleheader in May. The Cleveland team also drew 20,400 to Baltimore's Union Park on Labor Day. Frank Robison must have wondered what the Spiders had to do to reach such attractive, and profitable, attendance figures.

The 1894 team held spring practice in chilly Cleveland instead of the South, but the 1895 Spiders tuned up for the season with a trip through the warmer states. This may not have been a good idea, as both Nig Cuppy and Cy Young fell ill, and Harry Blake suffered a serious abdominal injury that kept him out of the lineup until late June. Players generally liked the warm weather, but unfamiliar food, rough playing fields, and frequent rainstorms could wear down even the healthiest athlete. Nonetheless, the team showed promise on the trip, which ended when the Spiders played in Fort Wayne, Indiana, against the local Western League team, which Frank Robison also owned. The Spiders defeated the minor leaguers by a score of 32 to 1, then headed to Cincinnati to open the season.

The two Ohio teams were fierce rivals, and the Spiders and Reds had staged many tough battles in previous years. Now, with former Spider Buck Ewing managing the Reds, the rivalry took on new intensity. Patsy Tebeau, who never warmed to Ewing's presence on the Spiders, was his usual confident self. "Beat them? Why, the boys say they will simply smother the Reds," he boasted. "Honestly, I'm sorry in advance for Ewing, for he'll be awfully roasted by the Cincinnati papers for losing games to Cleveland."[2]

Two days later, with Cuppy and Young still recovering, Mike Sullivan started for the Spiders in the season opener. The Reds beat Sullivan 10–8, and after a rainout Bobby Wallace lost the second game by a score of 14 to 2. A third loss in Cincinnati and one in St. Louis left the Spiders at 0–4 and at the bottom of the National League. It was not time to panic, but the Spiders were off to a slow start.

To make matters worse, "Fatty" Childs was not happy with his contract and jumped the team. He stated that he would return if Robison increased his salary by $300, but the Cleveland owner would not budge. "[Childs] made a demand for more salary," said Robison, "but I refused to give it to him. If he has quit, he will stay out until I get ready to take him back at my terms."[3] Childs sat out for three days, then capitulated. He returned on April 24 with four hits in a 12–3 win at St. Louis, Cleveland's first victory of the season.

As the pennant race heated up, other teams looked covetously at Cleveland's stars and tempted Frank Robison with large amounts of money. Andrew Freedman, a Tammany Hall politician and a powerful figure in the national Democratic Party, had recently bought the New York Giants and believed that he could build a winning team by writing a few large checks. Freedman made headlines when he offered to buy the entire Cleveland club in September of the previous year; now, he publicly offered Robison $6,000 in cash for Jesse Burkett and Ed McKean, a sale that would have ended Cleveland's pennant chances. Robison, who already had a standing offer of $10,000 from Chicago's Cap Anson for the services of Cupid Childs and Cy Young, was not interested in the least. He believed that his team had a strong chance to win the pennant, and he would not tear it apart in mid-season.

Jesse Burkett caught wind of New York's interest in him and, as the *Washington Post* reported, strolled up to Tebeau in early June. "Say, Cap," he said, "New York will pay you a pretty good price for me just now. Do you want to sell?"

"Sell, nothing!" replied the manager. "I wouldn't exchange you for the three best men on their team."[4]

The Spiders suffered the usual rash of injuries during the early months of the season. Harry Blake's injury brought George Tebeau off the bench to play right field, and an attack of tonsillitis put Patsy Tebeau on the sidelines for nearly two weeks in May. On May 22 Cupid Childs caught a throw in the groin and rode the bench for three weeks. The manager suffered the team's most serious injury; a strained muscle in his leg, a remnant of the spiking that Jake Beckley inflicted in 1891, put Patsy on the bench from late June to the second week of August. However, the Spiders managed their injuries much better than they had the year before, and the internal bickering of 1894 was now a thing of the past. Even with Patsy out of the lineup, the Spiders won 14 games in a row at home in July and roared into first place.

Jack O'Connor, catching in place of Chief Zimmer, saved a win on June 3 with a clever, if dishonest, new trick. Bobby Wallace carried a 4–1 lead into the eighth inning in Baltimore, but the Orioles rallied for three runs to tie the score. Seeing that the young pitcher was rattled, O'Connor wanted to give him time to compose himself. Ed McKean usually did so by calling time and untying and retying his shoes as slowly as possible, but O'Connor found a new way to delay a game. The catcher fainted dead away at home plate. It was all an act, of course, but the players milled around for a good ten minutes before Rowdy Jack pronounced himself fit to continue. Umpire William Betts ejected him for his stunt, but Wallace calmed down and got out of the inning with no further damage. The Spiders scored five times in the ninth, while the Orioles touched up Wallace for four runs before Nig Cuppy came in to get the last out.

Patsy Tebeau liked to use a little trickery too. Chief Zimmer was nicked in the arm by a pitch one day and trotted down to first. However, umpire Tom Lynch did not see the ball hit Zimmer and called him back to the plate. When Zimmer hesitated, Lynch threatened to fine him ten dollars. Tebeau, coaching at first, ordered Zimmer to stay put. "If you don't come down here [to first]," roared Tebeau, "I'll fine you $20. Who are you going to listen to, me or Lynch?"

Tebeau then had a flash of inspiration. He pinched Zimmer's upper arm as hard as he could, then said, "Go back to bat and show Lynch where the ball hit you." Zimmer showed the painful bruise to Lynch, who apologized. "Sorry to have doubted you, Chief," said the arbiter. "Take first."[5]

Baltimore was now the Cleveland team's fiercest rival, and Patsy Tebeau showed nothing but disdain for the Oriole fans. In Baltimore one afternoon, Cupid Childs, a native of that city, was greeted at the plate in the sixth inning by a delegation of his friends and admirers, who presented

him with a large floral horseshoe. Tebeau muttered under his breath—
such a scene would never have been tolerated on Goose Hill back home
in St. Louis—but, because the Spiders owned a six-run lead at the time,
the manager let the ceremony proceed. Unfortunately for the local hero,
he booted a couple of grounders in the very next inning, leading to an
eight-run outburst by the Orioles.

Patsy could stand it no more. He grabbed the floral display, ripped it
to pieces, and hurled the remains into the grandstand in the general direction of Childs' friends. "There's your flowers," he screamed, "and the next
bunch of (blankety-blank) that give flowers to one of me players, I'll fire
the player off me club and his damn friends can keep him if they like him
so well."[6]

Another Tebeau joined the club in July, but this one was not related
to Patsy and George. Charles Alston Tebeau, called "Pussy" because his
initials spelled "CAT," grew up in Worcester, Massachusetts, and played
second base and the outfield for Lowell of the New England Association,
an independent minor league. When the league collapsed in June of 1895,
Tebeau drew interest from Cleveland and also from Portland of the New
England League. He signed with Portland, then changed his mind and
joined the Spiders.

Some cynics imagined that Patsy hired a third Tebeau to confuse his
opponents; he could simply put the name Tebeau on his lineup card three
times and have them bat in whatever order he wanted depending on the
situation. Of course, that trick would only work on the first pass through
the lineup. Anyway, Pussy Tebeau played only two games for the Spiders.
He thought he was a free agent, but Portland owned his contract and was
surprised to see his name on Cleveland's roster. Portland put in a claim
for his services, the National League upheld it, and the Spiders were forced
to release Pussy Tebeau. Patsy, in a sour grapes type of mood, remarked
that the third Tebeau was not very good anyway.

With pitching at a premium in the National League, Tebeau tried to
fill his rotation behind his dependable top two starters, Cy Young and Nig
Cuppy. Bobby Wallace was a serviceable third starter, making 28 starts
and winning about half of his games, but the fourth slot was wide open.
Phil Knell, a 30-year-old left-hander, had been released by Louisville after
posting a 7–21 log in 1894 and losing all six of his decisions in early 1895.
Patsy, who had no lefty in his staff, gave Knell a tryout, and the veteran
won seven of 12 decisions but posted an earned run average of 5.40.
Another candidate for the fourth slot was once one of the brightest pitching stars in baseball, a man who had won 32 games for St. Louis six years

before and had won 20 or more in a season on two other occasions. His name was Elton "Icebox" Chamberlain.

Chamberlain, called Icebox because of his coolness in tight games, was an odd duck. He could, and sometimes did, pitch with either hand, and though he was primarily a righty he sometimes picked inattentive runners off first with a lefty throw. He was a star in St. Louis, but the team let him go because "[he] is of a sullen, sulky disposition and is very hard to manage."[7] Perhaps that was why the Players League, which tried its best to sign the stars of the other two leagues, showed no interest in Chamberlain. The ambidextrous pitcher was a skilled ventriloquist who enjoyed using his talent to get his teammates in trouble, and the Reds had suspected him of throwing games in 1893 in league with a local gambler who frequented the Cincinnati ballpark. On the other hand, he had thrown a seven-inning no-hitter against the champion Boston club in one of his last appearances for the Reds, and had won 157 major league games before his 27th birthday. If "Icebox" could get back on track, the Spiders would have another top-rank starter to go with Cuppy and Young.

In early 1895, Chamberlain agreed to join the Spiders, boasting to *Sporting Life*,

> I am giving it to you straight that I never felt better in my life and have taken off 13 pounds. Nothing ever pleased me better than my release from the Cincinnatis and if ever I played ball in my life I'll play it this year. Some people may have their own ideas about my work last season with the Reds, but I'll tell you truly it was that bum atmosphere coupled with the rankest water in the universe that kept me down. But I'll tell you once more this is going to be my base ball year and no mistake. I feel out of sight.[8]

Chamberlain, who in Cincinnati and Louisville had been accused of caring more about the racehorses he owned than his pitching, could be a frustrating individual. He promised to join the Spiders "soon," but put off Tebeau with one excuse after another. For one thing, he demanded a percentage of the money the Spiders paid for him and refused to report until he got it. Though "Icebox" had been a star and was still a young man, *Sporting Life* commented in July, "Chamberlain is not such a good pitcher that he can afford to antagonize the Cleveland Club, and unless there is a speedy coming to terms the indifferent man may find his base ball career cut short, and he will then be able to devote all his time to his string of two trotters."[9] In the end, Chamberlain never did report to the Spiders in 1895. Perhaps he was stalling the Spiders because his arm was not in shape, but he would not join the club until the following spring.

Perhaps the Spiders did not need Chamberlain anyway. Cy Young, after a slow start, put together one of his finest seasons, winning 35 games and losing only 10. Nig Cuppy chipped in with 26 wins and Bobby Wallace added 12. After using 14 pitchers in 1894, Cleveland employed only six in 1895, mainly because Tebeau used both Young and Cuppy in relief roles. Each of Cleveland's top two pitchers made 40 starts and seven relief appearances, and both men pitched more than 350 innings. The Spider strategy appeared to be simple. Patsy would work Young and Cuppy like rented mules as long as their arms held out.

The Spiders retained their hold on first place in mid–August, but their on-field behavior was often as nasty as ever. In a hard-fought game in Cleveland against the Reds on August 15, umpire Hank O'Day took abuse from both Tebeau and Jack O'Connor after a series of close plays went against the Spiders. O'Day, an ex-pitcher in his first full season as an umpire, ejected Tebeau and fined O'Connor $100 (in escalating $25 installments) for their vile language. The enraged O'Connor then warned the arbiter not to show up at League Park the next day. If he did, Rowdy Jack promised not only to attack him, but also to set the notoriously ill-tempered Cleveland fans against him too.

O'Day reported this threat to the league and refused to officiate the next day's game unless Frank Robison personally guaranteed his safety. Perhaps the owner did so, because O'Day worked the game, a 5–2 Cleveland win that proceeded uneventfully. O'Day proved that he could not be intimidated, and his 1895 season was the first of a career that lasted until 1927 and landed him in the Hall of Fame in 2014.

Later that same week, a game between the Spiders and Senators in Washington turned into a riot, and it was not even Cleveland's fault this time. Once again, Hank O'Day was the umpire, and a long game stretched into the late afternoon as the sun set. The field became darker by the minute, and the leading Senators wanted the game ended, but O'Day ordered the teams to continue play. O'Day did not stop the contest until Cleveland took the lead and the win in the eighth inning. The Washington fans were so outraged that they swarmed the field and mobbed the umpire, who fled to the clubhouse and hid as the local police kept the angry mob at bay.

Ninety minutes later, when O'Day emerged from his hiding place, the mob charged at him again. Police called for reinforcements, and a pitched battle ensued on the streets of Washington. Eventually, the cops hustled O'Day to safety and arrested several of the rioters. The next day, O'Day proved his courage once again, umpiring a doubleheader as if nothing had happened the day before.

One of the few umpires who could stand up to Tebeau and the battling Spiders was Tim Hurst, an Irishman from Pennsylvania who spent his youth working, and fighting, in the coal mines. Hurst spoke in an Irish brogue that was so rich and thick that some players deliberately picked arguments with him just to hear his entertaining voice. He was so skilled with his fists that in 1897, four Pittsburgh Pirates jumped him after a game one afternoon. Hurst fought all four at once and whipped them all.

Hurst knew, as many umpires did not, that an arbiter needed to head off trouble before it could start. One day in 1897, Hurst sidled up to an abusive player and, said the *Boston Record*,

> put his mouth close to the player's ear and said coolly, "Now you're getting a bit chesty, I see you've made a couple of good stops, knocked out a couple of hits and you think you're solid with the crowd. Well, I'll just tell you something. I'll give you the key to my room at the hotel, where everything is nice and quiet, and when we get in there alone I'll break that jaw of yours so you can't kick for the rest of the season. I'll see that you get out quietly so you can explain your injury by saying you fell down somewhere."[10]

One day, a large crowd filled Cleveland's League Park to see the Spiders play the hated Orioles. The mass of humanity was so large that hundreds of spectators stood in the outfield behind flimsy rope barriers. Cleveland crowds were always on edge anyway when Baltimore came to town, so Patsy figured that a well-placed threat could influence umpire Hurst to call things his way. In the pre-game meeting, Tebeau warned Hurst that if any close calls went against the Spiders, he would cut the ropes and send the crowd charging at the umpire.

Hurst, however, loved just such a challenge. Early in the game, he called Tebeau out at third on a play that the manager had definitely beaten. Patsy charged at Hurst, but the umpire was ready for him with his fists ready for action. "Yer out, you (blankety-blank)!" shouted the umpire. "Ye may have beat the throw, but I called yez out! Now go cut them ropes—and if ye as much as turn yer face to that crowd, I'll kill yez dead where ye stand!"[11] Tebeau took Hurst at his word and realized that he was licked. The manager meekly trotted back to the bench, and the crowd accepted the decision without protest.

A veteran team like the Spiders did not enjoy many opportunities to haze a rookie, so they made those rare occasions count. Eddie O'Meara was a 22-year-old catcher who looked forward to some playing time when he joined the team, but Tebeau assigned him to warm up pitchers and to play in exhibition games to save wear and tear on the regulars, Zimmer and O'Connor. O'Meara had never been to New York, and one day, as the

Spiders rode back to their hotel after a game in Brooklyn, the veterans shoved O'Meara out of the carriage and galloped off. The players assured O'Meara that their hotel on Broadway was nearby and easy to find. Problem was, they dropped the rookie off in Brooklyn, not Manhattan. O'Meara, carrying his catching gear and too embarrassed to ask for directions, wandered the streets for hours before he finally made it back to the hotel.[12]

Cleveland dropped out of the first position when the defending champion Orioles roared past them with 23 wins in 25 games, all but one of them at home. On September 7, the Spiders arrived in Baltimore for a three-game set, the last meeting of the two clubs in the regular season. Cleveland won the first contest to pull within one game of the lead, but Baltimore took the final two to leave Tebeau's men three games back. The Spiders closed their season with a flourish, winning ten in a row in mid–September, but the Orioles won 14 of their final 18 and clinched the pennant on the final weekend. Cleveland finished a close second, three games out, for their best finish yet in the National League. Their finish qualified Cleveland for the post-season for the second time in four years, as they prepared to battle the Orioles for the Temple Cup.

The Temple Cup was the creation of William Chase Temple, a wealthy Pennsylvania lumber and coal baron who became the owner and president of the Pittsburgh Pirates in 1891. His Pirates had finished the 1893 season in second place, and Temple believed that they deserved a shot at the pennant winners in a post-season series. Accordingly, Temple commissioned a large silver trophy at a cost of $800 and donated it to the National League. The Temple Cup series, the first of which would take place in October of 1894, was planned as a seven-game set. The winning team, decreed the trophy's namesake, would receive a 65 percent share of the players' proceeds from the series, with the losers receiving 35 percent. In addition, the first team to win the Temple Cup three years in a row would take permanent possession of it.

Temple's brainchild may have sounded like a good idea, but it failed in its execution. The Baltimore Orioles won the 1894 pennant by three games over the New York Giants in a hard-fought race, and saw no reason to play the Giants again. Accordingly, the Orioles regarded the pennant itself as the true league championship and treated the Temple Cup as a mere series of exhibition games. Players on both teams chafed over the division of proceeds, but because the league refused to alter Temple's directive, the Orioles and Giants took matters into their own hands. They simply paired up and made their own agreements to split their winnings on a 50–50 basis. This action removed any incentive for the players, especially the Orioles, to win.

Though the attendance was good—more than 20,000 fans swarmed the Polo Grounds in New York for the third game on a Saturday—the result was a listless, poorly-played series plagued by player indifference. The Giants won in four straight games, with pitchers Amos Rusie and Jouett Meekin winning twice apiece. As one Baltimore paper reported with disdain, "They [the Orioles] could not have beaten Towsontown or Hoboken in those games. They were not in condition to beat anybody."[13] To make matters worse, all but one of the Giants reportedly reneged on their agreements to split their money with the Orioles. Rusie handed his Baltimore partner, outfielder Joe Kelley, $204 after the last game to even things between them, but none of the other Orioles saw any extra money. This led to rancor between the two clubs for years afterward, and Temple, disgusted by the whole affair, sold his interest in the Pirates a year later. He was through with baseball, though the National League retained the Temple Cup and plowed ahead with plans for another series in 1895.

By early September, it was clear that Baltimore and Cleveland would finish one-two in the National League race, but not that they would meet for the Cup. The Giants, reigning Temple Cup champions, demanded the right to defend their title, though the New Yorkers had faded badly in mid-season and dropped to ninth place. The league, after some controversy, rejected the Giants' arguments and retained the original format.

The Orioles, winners of their second consecutive pennant, may not have had much more incentive to win than they had the year before, but the Spiders certainly did. Cleveland had been represented, off and on, in the National League (and the National Association before that) since 1871 without yet winning a championship. Their half a flag in the second part of the 1892 split season was their only claim to success, and if the National League regarded the Temple Cup series as a championship match (though few fans around the country agreed) then the Spiders would play with their usual energy and enthusiasm. Accordingly, they rejected all overtures from the Orioles to split their winnings. Tebeau and his men hated the Orioles and made it known that they were out for blood.

The first game of the series was played in Cleveland on October 2, a Friday, and the 8,000 fans in attendance at League Park lived up (or down) to their bad reputation. The city assigned a few policemen to patrol the park, as on any other game day, but a few local cops were no match for the Spider fans in this contest against the despised Orioles. The Clevelanders pelted the opposing players with fruit and vegetables, even when the game was in progress, and chanted abusive slogans, especially at Tebeau's enemy John McGraw. Somehow, the game began despite the riotous atmosphere, with Cy Young facing Baltimore's Sadie McMahon, a veteran right-hander.

The first contest was the best of the series. Young and McMahon kept the game scoreless until the fifth inning, when Chippy McGarr singled to left, Young beat out a bunt, and Jesse Burkett sacrificed the runners to second and third. Ed McKean then popped out to Kid Gleason behind second base, and McGarr dashed home with the first run of the game. Both teams scored in the sixth, but two Baltimore tallies in the eighth gave the visitors a 3–2 lead. The Spiders tied it on a double by Tebeau and a single by Harry Blake, but McGraw and Wilbert Robinson whacked back-to-back doubles in the top of the ninth to go ahead by a 4–3 count.

In the bottom of the ninth, Burkett doubled to lead off the inning. With darkness approaching, Ed McKean appeared to be fooled by a pitch from McMahon, but got his bat on it and drove it to right field for a single. Burkett scored, and the game was now tied. Cupid Childs singled, and Jimmy McAleer tried to move the runners over with a sacrifice bunt. Instead, he beat the throw to first and loaded the bases with no outs. Baltimore brought the infield in and cut down McKean at the plate on Tebeau's grounder.

Chief Zimmer then bounced a perfect double-play ball to second baseman Kid Gleason, who stepped on second to force Tebeau and threw to first. Somehow, the slow-footed catcher beat the throw as Childs crossed the plate with the winning run. This play may have been the high point of Zimmer's long career, as it won the first game of the series by a 5–4 score.

The second contest on Saturday brought more of the same fan behavior, as some of the 10,000 spectators rained vegetables, seat cushions, and soda bottles on the peeved Orioles. Baltimore's sensational right-hander Bill Hoffer, a 31-game winner in his rookie season, stumbled against the Spiders, who scored three times in the first. Burkett led off with a single and took second on a wild pitch. McKean singled him home, and after a sacrifice by Childs, McAleer was hit by a pitch. Tebeau's fly ball scored McKean, and a double by Zimmer scored Tebeau for a 3–0 Cleveland lead. There the score remained as the giddy Cleveland fans blew whistles and horns, and "bells large enough for a fire engine house, but the greatest musical instrument was an invention of the tin horn species that was fully eight feet long and had a dozen tubes attached through which as many fans blew at once."[14]

The Spiders never trailed in the game. They scored one in the fifth, two in the sixth, and one in the seventh as Nig Cuppy cruised to a 7–2 win. Monday's crowd for the third game was a better-behaved bunch, though quite possibly a louder one. This time, the fans brought some new noise-making accessories to League Park. Said the *Plain Dealer*, "There were gongs large enough and loud enough to equip an electric railroad; monster rattles made after the pattern used in the nursery and filled with rocks; there were the remnants of a dozen defunct brass bands, and, in fact, everything that could make noise without exploding."[15]

Fan enthusiasm was at an all-time high after the first two wins against the Orioles, and more than 15,000 people—the largest crowd to attend a ballgame in Cleveland up to that time—crowded into League Park, with people balancing themselves on ledges, teetering on the tops of fences, and hanging precariously on and around the scoreboard. Those who could not get into the park filled the roofs and crowded the windows of nearby buildings, and even climbed trees to see the action. Reported the *Plain Dealer*, "The cross-trees on the telegraph poles held all that could perch upon them, while the climbing braces were occupied wherever they were high enough to admit of a glance into the grounds."[16] Before the game started, the fans were treated to the sight of Nig Cuppy, the previous day's winning pitcher, receiving the present of a shotgun from his admirers. Cuppy celebrated the gift by firing two blasts into the air, to the delight of the assembled throng.

Cy Young retired the Orioles in the first, while Cleveland scored three runs in the bottom of the inning. Burkett singled and was forced by McKean at second. Singles by Childs and McAleer brought McKean across the plate, and a groundout by Tebeau scored Childs. McAleer stole third and came home on a grounder by Zimmer.

Baltimore pitcher Sadie McMahon settled down and blanked the Spiders until the seventh, when Cleveland erupted for three more runs. A double by Harry Blake and singles by McGarr and Young scored one run, and McKean, after a group of fans interrupted the game to present the shortstop with a diamond stud, lifted a sacrifice fly to score McGarr. Left fielder Joe Kelley's off-target throw to the plate scored Young, and the Spiders led 6–0. Young gave up one run in the eighth, but scattered seven hits for a 7–1 win that put Cleveland one game away from the championship. At game's end, the fans poured onto the field and marched around the diamond blowing their horns and shaking their noisemakers, but the Baltimore players left the park unmolested this time. As one reporter put it, "With all the crowd and all the noise nothing occurred that need be regretted by the audience or the management."[17]

Despite the relatively peaceful third game, the people of Baltimore were outraged by press reports of the riotous scenes at the first two contests. They were determined to answer in kind, so the fourth contest featured a fan riot that began before the first pitch was thrown. When the Cleveland team arrived at the park that afternoon, Baltimore rooters pelted the Spiders with garbage, bottles, and other missiles on their way into the park. Though a cordon of Baltimore police tried to protect the visiting players, it seemed to take forever for the Spiders to transit the 15 feet or so from their carriages to the safety of the players' entrance. Once the players made it onto the field, the crowd was so uncontrollable that the game was only able to commence after a dozen of the most unruly fans had been arrested and hauled away for disorderly conduct.

Finally, the game began. Perhaps the riotous scene outside Union Park, and the 9,000 or so booing, threatening Oriole fans inside it, kept the Spiders from playing their usual game. Baltimore pitcher Duke Esper held the Spiders to five hits, while Baltimore scored five times off Nig Cuppy. The first run came in the second on a single by Steve Brodie and a double by George Carey. In the third, John McGraw, Willie Keeler, and Hugh Jennings all singled to bring in one run. After Joe Kelley walked, Brodie's sacrifice fly scored Keeler. That was all the Orioles needed, though they scored two more in the late innings. The Orioles won 5–0 to keep their slim chances alive.

That's when the worst rioting of the day commenced. About 1,500 Oriole rooters attacked the Spiders again as they ran for their carriages. The cops tried to beat back the mob, but failed, and the Cleveland ballplayers took cover as the rioters threw bricks, rocks, and chunks of dirt at them. Somehow the carriage driver was able to whip the horses to a gallop and pull the players to safety, though Cupid Childs suffered a gash in the head from a flying missile.

Patsy, once he and the Spiders had reached the safety of their hotel, professed himself unconcerned. "One swallow don't make a summer," he said. "And we'll get that Cup for they have to face Cy Young again tomorrow."[18]

Perhaps the Baltimore fans knew that defeat was imminent, for only 4,200 people came to see Young face Bill Hoffer in the fifth game. The weather was cold and the crowd was a docile one, compared to the day before, and the contest proceeded without any major pre-game incidents. The two pitchers matched zeroes for six innings, but in the seventh the Spiders broke through. Young doubled to the fence in left center, and Burkett singled to right with Young taking third. Childs lofted a fly to

Joe Kelley in left, but Kelley dropped it and brought Young home with the first run of the game. Singles by McAleer and Tebeau drove Burkett and Childs in for a 3–0 lead. Baltimore scored once in the bottom of the inning, but Cleveland put up two more runs in the eighth to go up 5 to 1.

Patsy Tebeau owned a volcanic temper, but he kept it under wraps with victory close at hand. In the bottom of the seventh Baltimore pitcher Bill Hoffer smacked a grounder to Childs at second. When Tebeau dove off the bag to take Childs' off-target throw, he collided with Hoffer and tripped him. The collision was probably not intentional on Tebeau's part, but the angry Hoffer tackled the Cleveland manager and threw him to the ground. Patsy, however, kept his cool and defused the potentially danger-ous confrontation. Hoffer was out at first, though the Orioles argued unsuccessfully that Patsy's foot never touched the bag.

John McGraw knew that the series was as good as lost, but he got one last shot in at his sworn enemy Tebeau. Patsy led off the ninth with

The 1895 Cleveland Spiders, Temple Cup champions. Top row: O'Meara, Blake, McAleer, Young, Zimmer, O'Connor, Childs. Middle row: McGarr, Frank Robi-son, Patsy Tebeau, Davis Hawley. Bottom row: Cuppy, Knell, Burkett, Wallace, George Tebeau, McKean (National Baseball Library, Cooperstown, New York).

a fly ball to right, but Willie Keeler dropped it and Tebeau was safe. Chief Zimmer followed with a single, but Patsy was out trying to reach third. There, McGraw applied a hard tag to Patsy's face, leaving the Cleveland manager with a bloody lip. The fans—the ones that were left, anyway—cheered heartily, but once again Patsy refused to take the bait. He ignored McGraw and walked off the field.

The Orioles scored once in the ninth and loaded the bases with two out, but when Steve Brodie grounded out to pitcher Cy Young to end the game, the Spiders claimed the Temple Cup. Fittingly, the last out came on Young's throw to Patsy Tebeau at first base. Immediately afterward, the Spiders made a dash for their clubhouse to avoid a crowd of angry, defeated Baltimore fans. This time, the cops kept the mob under control, and the Spiders made it safely out of Baltimore that evening. They would soon enjoy a nice payday, especially as the Spiders had turned down all offers to split their winnings with their opponents. Each Spider (even Eddie O'Meara, the bullpen catcher who saw action in only one game all year) received $516 for winning the series, while each Oriole took home $316 for losing it. *The Sporting News* proclaimed O'Meara "the luckiest man on earth."

The people of Cleveland rejoiced in their first National League championship, and the local Elks Club held a banquet for the Spiders upon their return to the city. Each table featured a centerpiece in the shape of a baseball diamond. There was a menacing black spider on each base and on the pitcher's mound, and at home plate was an oyster, representing Baltimore. The oyster was being devoured by four more black spiders. Toasts were made, speeches were delivered, and William Temple, patron of the Cup itself, sent a congratulatory telegram as well.[19]

Patsy Tebeau in 1895 at the height of his success (Library of Congress).

Patsy Tebeau's stock had never been higher, and he even received a cable from New York Giants owner Andrew Freedman. Freedman, who hated the Orioles with a passion, wrote Tebeau, "You have clearly demonstrated that you are the base ball general of the season. The pennant winners have simply won through a fluke. Accept congratulations."[20]

⫿ 10 ⫿

A Riotous Season

"I will pay almost any sum in reason for a heavy batting outfielder and infielder. This may seem strange when you consider we have twenty-five men under contract, but Mr. Robison has instructed me to win the pennant this year at all hazards, and I am determined to do it. He absolutely restricts me in no way whatever. There is no player on the team, not even my brother, who would not be displaced if a stronger man could be secured for the same position."
—Patsy Tebeau, February 1896[1]

One wonders, with the benefit of hindsight, why the unwieldy 12-team league did not simply split into two divisions, East and West, as the American and National Leagues did in 1969 when the circuits expanded to 12 teams each. (As American League president Joe Cronin reportedly said at the time in support of divisional play, "You can't sell a 12th place club.") The National League, bloated to 12 teams with the absorption of Louisville, Washington, St. Louis, and Baltimore from the defunct American Association in 1892, could have been split neatly along an East–West axis as follows:

East: Boston, New York, Brooklyn, Washington, Philadelphia, Baltimore.
West: St. Louis, Chicago, Louisville, Cleveland, Cincinnati, Pittsburgh.

The two divisional winners could have met each fall in a true "World's Series" in contrast to the anticlimactic Temple Cup matchup, which was taken less than seriously by the players and largely ignored by the fans. Eventual expansion—to cities such as Minneapolis, Detroit, Milwaukee, Kansas City, or second teams in Chicago and New York, among other possibilities—might have stabilized the league and preempted any ambitious competitors.

Such planning would have required National League team owners to have vision, an attribute that was sorely lacking in the baseball magnates of the 1890s. They were a group of mostly self-made, strong-willed men with an aversion to helping each other; most of the owners took the attitude that so long as his own team turned a profit, he could not care less whether any of his competitors succeeded or failed. Some of them out-and-out hated each other, as shown in early 1899 when a league meeting erupted into fisticuffs between Chicago's Jim Hart and Philadelphia's John I. Rogers. Nick Young, the league president, held his post for 18 years almost solely due to his inoffensive and retiring manner. A true visionary such as Albert G. Spalding, a great pitcher and Chicago team executive who built a sporting goods empire that prospers to this day, would have been unacceptable to the warring teams.

All the while, a man named Byron Bancroft (Ban) Johnson watched and waited. Johnson, a former Cincinnati sportswriter, had founded the Western League in 1894 and was determined not to repeat the mistakes of the more established circuit. With eight teams in larger Midwestern cities such as Detroit, Indianapolis, Milwaukee, and Kansas City, Johnson punished rowdy ballplayers, supported his umpires, and catered to the fans, things that the National League had utterly failed to do. Ambitious, forward-thinking baseball men (St. Paul's Charlie Comiskey, Milwaukee's Connie Mack, and others) who were frustrated with the National League gravitated to the Western. Johnson continued to build his league as the 1890s progressed, waiting for the right time to challenge the National and establish his circuit as an equal.

In retrospect, the Spiders of the middle 1890s were an oddly-constructed team. On the positive side, Cleveland enjoyed outstanding offensive contributions from Cupid Childs at second, Ed McKean at short, and Jesse Burkett in left field. Burkett won his first batting title in 1895 with a .405 mark, while McKean enjoyed one of his greatest seasons with a .341 average and 131 runs scored. Burkett scored 153 runs and stole 41 bases, while Childs, though his batting average fell to .288, scored 96 runs and drove in 90. The catching position was also solid, as Chief Zimmer was a dependable hitter and a durable, good-fielding receiver. At the same time, the positions that traditionally provide offense were manned by hitters who proved mediocre at best. Patsy Tebeau at first base and Chippy McGarr at third were only fair hitters, while Jimmy McAleer in center field and Harry Blake in right were downright poor. McAleer and Blake were sensational fielders, and remained in the starting eight because Tebeau valued a strong defense. The problem was that their presence left two black holes in the lineup. The top three lineup spots, held by Burkett, Childs, and McKean in that order, were as strong and productive as any in baseball. The next five slots were among the weakest.

Frank Robison recognized the problem, even if Tebeau did not, and his attempts to upgrade the offense at third base and right field led to some friction between the owner and his manager. In early 1896 Robison signed Tom Delahanty, a 22-year-old third baseman who had played for Detroit in 1895, and John Shearon, a 25-year-old right fielder from Buffalo of the Eastern League. Delahanty was a Cleveland boy, the younger brother of Phillies star Ed Delahanty and the second oldest of the five Delahanty brothers who played major league ball. Tom Delahanty was several inches shorter than his brother Ed, but resembled him otherwise, and Robison believed that a local lad might draw fans to League Park. Shearon had played for the Spiders briefly in 1891, then returned to the minors and built a solid resume, batting .346 at Buffalo in 1895. Delahanty and Shearon both excelled in spring practice and opened the 1896 season in the lineup. McGarr rode the bench, and Robison sent Blake, over Tebeau's objections, to Fort Wayne of the Interstate League.

Robison also owned the club in Fort Wayne, where the ballpark sat next to one of his streetcar lines, and hired a Patsy Tebeau clone to direct the team on the field. The new manager was none other than George Tebeau. George had performed well for the Spiders in 1895, batting .326 in a utility role, but at age 34 he was ready to start his own managing career. He led Fort Wayne to a second-place finish in 1896 with the same combative style that his brother had made famous. Later that season, George started a fracas in Toledo and choked an umpire. This attack turned into a fan riot and only ended when the local cops dragged George off the field. Patsy would have been proud.

The Cleveland starting rotation was one of the best in baseball. Most National League pitchers struggled to adapt to the increased pitching distance after 1892, but Cy Young may have been helped by it. He could still throw his powerful fastball past batters, and the extra five feet gave his curve more space to break away from the plate. Nig Cuppy, too, saw his curveball improve, though his dawdling on the mound still drove everyone crazy. Zeke Wilson held down the third spot; a right-hander from Alabama, Wilson had failed in a trial with Boston in early 1895, but then signed with Cleveland and won three of his four decisions. The fourth starter was Bobby Wallace, who made 16 starts while seeing increased playing time in the outfield. Wallace was only a fair pitcher (though he dominated the Brooklyn club nearly every time he faced it), but Tebeau recognized his all-around athletic talent and believed that the diminutive Scotsman might be more valuable as a position player.

Elton "Icebox" Chamberlain, however, was a washout. After putting off the Spiders for a whole year, Icebox finally consented to join the team. He boasted to the press that he was "good for another five seasons," but it quickly became obvious that Chamberlain's arm was as sore as ever. He made two unsuccessful starts for Cleveland before drawing his release in May, and at age 28 his career was finished. It was a disappointing end after all the trouble he put the Spiders through.

Cleveland's pennant chances in 1896 looked better than ever as the season opened. The Spiders had finished only three games behind Baltimore the year before, and now the Orioles were crippled by the absence of John McGraw, their third baseman and chief instigator. McGraw, whose bout with malaria in 1895 had limited him to 96 games, contracted typhoid fever during the spring of 1896. He nearly died, and his weight dropped to 118 pounds before he began to recover. McGraw would stay on the sidelines until late August, and the Orioles would have to get along without their emotional leader.

At the same time, Frank Robison was deeply concerned about attendance at League Park. The 1895 team had finished a strong second and won the Temple Cup, but the Spiders drew only 143,000 to League Park. Cleveland's fan turnout was much improved from 1894 but still ranked 11th in the

John McGraw, Baltimore Oriole third baseman and Patsy Tebeau's bitter enemy (author's collection).

league, as only Louisville drew fewer people. The lack of Sunday ball was a big factor in the team's attendance woes, so Robison tried a new tack. He announced that the Spiders would schedule no Sunday games in other cities during the upcoming season. "We will play no Sunday games," he said to *Sporting Life*, "unless we are absolutely obliged to, to meet salaries and expenses."[2] Robison hoped that his stance would curry favor to the powerful anti–Sunday forces in Cleveland. Some of the more radical local ministers had urged their parishioners to boycott Spider games because they played on Sundays in other cities. Now, the churchgoing public had no reason not to attend.

Stanley Robison, the team vice president, elaborated.

> A Sunday game in Cincinnati, Chicago or St. Louis, early in the season would mean a crowd of 12,000 or 15,000, perhaps 20,000 people. Now, we will give that up and play only on week days. If these people who have stayed away from our home games because of the fact that we played Sunday ball will come out and make this good we will be happy and will play no more Sunday games…. I hope the people of Cleveland will appreciate our sacrifice and patronize our splendid club.[3]

The team also declared that it would not play Sunday games, or hold Sunday workouts, on the spring training trip to Hot Springs, Arkansas.

Their "sacrifice" made little difference. Bad weather in Cleveland in early May held attendance down, but turnout remained disappointingly low even as the weather improved. The Robisons could only look on helplessly as the league's other Ohio-based team, the Cincinnati Reds, cheerfully ignored the state ban on Sunday baseball and drew crowds of 20,000 or more on the Sabbath. Cincinnati's Protestant ministers were not nearly as powerful as those in Cleveland, and the local political boss, George B. Cox, was a sports fan who allowed Sunday ballgames.

Nonetheless, the Spiders jumped into the 1896 pennant race with confidence. They opened the season on the road, winning four of nine games, and opened in Cleveland on May 2 against the Reds. Cy Young pitched the Spiders to a 2–1 win in that game and started a 14–4 run that lifted Tebeau's men into first place. The league was tightly bunched early on, and in late May Washington, in eighth position, stood only four and a half games out of the lead.

However, neither of Robison's two new additions to the lineup lasted long. Tom Delahanty, Robison's favorite, looked overmatched against major league competition, batting .232 and making 11 errors in the 16 games he played. Robison's other selection, right fielder John Shearon, was even worse, hitting .172 in 16 games. Both men were released in May, as Chippy McGarr regained the third base job and Harry Blake returned from Fort Wayne to take over in right field. Patsy now had his team back the way he wanted it.

The Spiders retained their lead in a wild game in Boston on May 29. The Beaneaters led by a score of 4–2 in the eighth when a previously quiet game turned nasty. After a foul ball was lost in the stands, umpire Tim Keefe put a new ball into the game. However, the Spiders were batting, and Boston liked to slip an old, "punky" baseball into the game when the other team was at the bat. Tebeau, wise to all of Boston's tricks, grabbed the ball, tore up the cover with his spikes, and fired it over the grandstand and out of the park.

Tim Keefe was once one of baseball's greatest pitchers, but to Patsy Tebeau he was merely another umpire to be intimidated. Keefe ordered Tebeau to the bench, but Patsy answered with language so vile that the umpire thumbed the manager out of the game. Now the scene grew dangerous, as Tebeau refused to leave and Burkett, McAleer, and O'Connor— what one paper called the "Indignation Committee"—surrounded the outnumbered Keefe and showered him with insults in all four directions at once. Keefe eventually restored order, but the Spiders deliberately made a farce of the game, as McAleer trampled Boston catcher Marty Bergen in a play at the plate and O'Connor acted "like a crazy man" on the bases. It was "one of the most disgraceful scenes ever seen at the South End Grounds,"[4] wrote Boston columnist Tim Murnane.

The Beaneaters scored three times in the ninth to put the game away, or so they thought. The Spiders, brought back to life by the near-riot of the previous inning, scored five times to tie the score. The teams played scoreless ball into the 12th, when Keefe once again tried to put new balls in the game, only to have Burkett and O'Connor spike two of them and throw them away. Somehow they completed the 12th inning, Keefe declared the game over due to darkness, and Cleveland retained first place with a 7–7 tie. The Boston papers expressed their disgust with the visitors' behavior; one paper stated that "Patsy Tebeau and his companions participated in the most rowdyish proceedings ever seen at a ball game in Boston." Boston management not only increased the police presence for the next day's game, but also charged the Spiders $1.25 for the ball Tebeau threw out of the ballpark. They deducted the charge from Cleveland's share of the gate receipts. As for Keefe, the former pitching star resigned his post in disgust a few weeks later.

The Spiders were riding high in June of 1896, but Tebeau and his men embarrassed the National League with a series of troubling incidents. On June 19, the Spiders and Chicago Colts played a Friday afternoon contest in Cleveland. The Spiders could do little with Chicago pitcher Clark Griffith, who allowed only five hits, and in the eighth inning Tebeau's temper boiled over. With two out, two men on, and the Colts leading by a 7–3 score, catcher Jack O'Connor caught Chicago's Fred Pfeffer leaning too far off first base. O'Connor pegged a quick throw to Tebeau, who tagged Pfeffer. Umpire Tom Lynch, who had been calling games in the league since 1888, ruled Pfeffer out, and the Spiders ran off the field.

Lynch, however, changed his mind and called Pfeffer safe, claiming that Tebeau had illegally blocked the runner off the bag. Patsy, O'Connor and several other Spiders charged at the umpire. While the Spiders screamed abuse at Lynch, Chicago's George Decker, the runner at second base, scampered home. Lynch had not called time, so Decker's run put the Colts ahead 8 to 3.

TIMOTHY KEEFE.
ALLEN & GINTER'S
RICHMOND. Cigarettes. VIRGINIA.

Tim Keefe, once one of baseball's greatest pitchers, quit his umpiring job after a quarrel with the Spiders in May of 1896 (Library of Congress).

That was the last straw for Patsy. He called Lynch a series of obscene names, and reportedly threatened to "wipe the earth" with the arbiter. This statement set off Lynch, who not only ordered Patsy out of the game, but removed his chest protector and his coat and offered to fight Tebeau on the spot. The two men prepared to do battle, but other players on both teams, assisted by the local police, separated the would-be combatants. The fans were in an ugly mood already, and the cops acted lest a riot break out.

Umpire Lynch refused to continue. He stormed off the field under police protection and returned to his hotel, leaving two players to umpire the rest of the game. Chicago manager Cap Anson, incensed because Tebeau refused to leave the game despite having been ejected by Lynch, protested the game but dropped his complaint when the Colts won the contest anyway. The loss dropped Cleveland out of first place and into second, half a game behind

Baltimore. On the next afternoon, a Saturday, Lynch did not appear. He wanted nothing to do with Tebeau, the Spiders, and their rowdy fans, so the players umpired that game too, a 12–6 Cleveland win.

Afterward, the thoroughly disgusted Lynch told a reporter, "I suppose I should not have permitted my indignation to get the better of me, but after all there are things that pass human endurance, and one of them surely is to be called vile names."[5] Lynch refused to work in Cleveland after that, and stayed away from League Park until 1898.

This fracas, unpleasant as it was, was nothing compared to what happened in Louisville seven days later.

The first game of a three-game set in Louisville on Thursday, June 25 set the tone for the series. The Spiders freely man-

Umpire Tom Lynch challenged Patsy Tebeau to a fistfight on the field in 1896. In 1910, long after Tebeau had left the game, Lynch was elected president of the National League (author's collection).

handled umpire George (Stump) Weidman, a former pitcher in his first season as an arbiter. Jesse Burkett, apoplectic at one of Weidman's decisions, grabbed the umpire by the arm and "shook him like a rat," while Jack O'Connor rammed into him with his shoulder. (It was illegal under league rules to punch an umpire, but apparently not to abuse him in other ways.) Weidman, thoroughly cowed, did not eject either man. Cleveland won by an 8–3 score, and Louisville captain Fred Clarke fumed with anger after the game. Clarke figured that the way to defeat the second-place Spiders was to employ similar tactics. He decided to try a little umpire abuse of his own.

On Friday, a close contest was marred by constant bickering and arguing from both sides. Both Clarke and Tebeau tormented the overmatched Weidman as the Louisville fans roared their disapproval at the scene on the field. The game was tied after 9 innings, which took more than three hours to play due to the frequent breaks in the action (and also because Nig Cuppy, the slowest worker in the National League, was pitching for Cleveland that day). In the tenth, with darkness approaching, Cleveland pushed four runs across the plate, and Clarke instructed his Colonels to stall for time as the sun settled on the horizon. The Louisville players purposely missed ground balls and refused to tag Spiders out between the bases, all the while issuing threats to the frightened umpire. Clarke's men wanted Weidman to stop the game, in which case the score would revert to the 4–4 tie at the end of the ninth, the last completed inning.

Somehow, the Spiders made three outs and brought Louisville to bat. The Colonels, down by an 8–4 count, loaded the bases with one out, after which Weidman suddenly declared the game over. With the tenth inning uncompleted, the game ended in a tie, and Louisville escaped defeat. "Pat, he has called the game!" bellowed Jack O'Connor.

The Spiders went ballistic. Tebeau and several others charged Weidman, and Jimmy McAleer ran in from center field to punch him in the face while the others "jerked him around like a rag baby." This assault enraged the Louisville fans, who needed little provocation to explode in anger after two days of watching the Spiders. The fans poured onto the field, and a full-scale riot ensued. One policeman pursued McAleer around the infield, while other cops and the Louisville players tried to force Tebeau and his charges to the dressing room and keep the fans from harming them. McAleer, meanwhile, picked up a bat and used it to fight his way to the bench area. One of the Louisville team directors caught a punch to the jaw while Jesse Burkett took a blow to the mouth which left him with two swollen, bruised lips. Somehow, the Cleveland players made it to their omnibus outside the ballpark, and hunkered down in their vehicle. Their driver whipped his horses and escaped down the street while some 200 enraged Kentuckians pelted the Spiders with bricks, rocks, and garbage. All the while, Patsy Tebeau cursed McAleer for belting Weidman.

The Spiders arrived at the park on Saturday, but Weidman did not; he wired league president Nick Young that he was ill and unable to perform. The players changed into their uniforms, only to learn that the game was washed out by rain. Their day was not over. Before they could leave, a squadron of local police officers arrested all the Cleveland players and loaded them, still in uniform, into their paddy wagons for a trip to the police station. The Louisville team president, Dr. Thomas Stuckey, had sworn out a complaint against the Spiders for their role in Friday's riot. Tebeau and his men grumbled as they waited in the courtroom, which filled up quickly with Louisville fans eager to see justice done. In a corner, Fred Clarke grinned at the scene.

President Stuckey accused Tebeau and his charges of not only provoking the fracas, but with turning the air blue with foul language in so doing. The stands in the Louisville ballpark were close to the action, as they were in Cleveland, and Stuckey could easily hear the obscenities which spouted forth during the three-hour contest. The fans could hear them as well, and one report claimed that the ladies in the seats "with their faces white with mortification, got up and left."[6] Judge Thompson patiently heard the testimony of both teams and dismissed several Spiders, including Cuppy, O'Connor, and Blake. Tebeau, however, drew a $100 fine for assault and disorderly conduct, while Burkett was dinged for $50, McKean for $75, and McAleer for $75. The Spiders vowed to appeal the ruling, and another hearing was set for September.

The umpire, whom *Sporting Life* condemned as "utterly incompetent," was not blameless in the matter. Weidman, who should have ejected the troublemakers before the riot broke out, had proven his lack of aptitude for the job, and the league dropped him from its roster of umpires at season's end. Still, players and managers made the life of the umpire a living hell during the 1890s, and only the bravest and strongest of them could withstand the pressure and abuse. Weidman was a bad umpire, but the conditions that existed at the time kept potentially good candidates (the growing legion of retired players, for example) from the profession.

The Spiders, no doubt happy to escape Louisville, then traveled to Chicago, where team president Jim Hart brought out a large police presence, both to keep order and to intimidate the Spiders. With cops ringing the field in full uniform, Tebeau's crew won three of four against the Colts. The first two games of the series, wins for Young and Cuppy, passed uneventfully, but in the third contest Chicago manager Cap Anson spiked Tebeau in a play at first base. Patsy's pants and socks were torn from knee to ankle. Fortunately, no rioting ensued, but the tension at the ballpark was undeniable.

Frank Robison recognized that he had a public relations nightmare on his hands, so he arranged for a boisterous welcome for his Spiders upon their return from Chicago. When Tebeau and his men arrived at Union Station in Cleveland on the morning of July 3, a brass band and about 2,000 supportive fans were ready to meet them. The players rode to the Public Square in horse-drawn carriages, then to a breakfast banquet at the Forest City House. Robison made a speech, as did Tebeau, Mayor Robert McKisson, and other local dignitaries. All in all, it was an impressive display of public support, and the Spiders, buoyed by the fan fervor, beat the St. Louis Browns 14–5 that afternoon. On the next day, the Spiders swept the Browns in their Fourth of July doubleheader.

If Robison believed that such an outpouring of local enthusiasm would discourage the National League from taking action against his misbehaving ballclub, he was sorely mistaken. The league had had its fill of Tebeau and his antics. At a special meeting in Pittsburgh on June 29, the league board of directors reviewed the Louisville fracas and the Chicago confrontation, both of which had drawn sharp criticism in the national press. The board roundly condemned Tebeau's actions and fined him $200, one of the largest in-season fines up to that time in league history. The league also gave Patsy ten days after his official notification (which was issued on July 3, the day of the parade in Cleveland) to pay it or face indefinite suspension.

Patsy refused to pay. To further complicate matters, he and Robison filed suit against the National League. On July 9, Robison and his attorneys appeared in the Common Pleas Court in downtown Cleveland and asked for an injunction to prevent the National League from collecting the fine leveled against Tebeau and to enjoin the league from suspending him. The judge granted a temporary restraining order, and Robison told the press that copies of the order would be distributed to the managers and captains of all the other 11 teams in the National League. During the next several weeks, Tebeau carried copies of the order onto the field and handed them to each umpire and opposing captain at the beginning of each series.

Tebeau, by refusing to accept responsibility for a season-long string of embarrassing incidents, now challenged the right of the National League to discipline him at all. Frank Robison, loyal to a fault, backed him, complaining that the league had targeted Cleveland while ignoring other teams, such as Baltimore, which had misbehaved in similar fashion. Robison was livid with Stuckey, the Louisville owner, for hauling his employees into court, and he was furious with Chicago president Jim Hart, who complained loudly about the Lynch incident but took no action against Anson for spiking Tebeau. Robison waxed defiant in an interview with *Sporting Life*:

> This fine of $200 is imposed upon Captain Tebeau, and if he does not pay it within 10 days (and I will not pay it), then Captain Tebeau is debarred from playing base ball, as each of the other clubs is a member of the secret and private agreement, the worst boycott that exists in this country. Captain Tebeau will not be able to earn a living at his own profession, as he will not be able to play on the Cleveland team, neither will any other club take him. Is not this a nice state of affairs?
>
> I want to say to Dr. Stuckey and President Hart and the balance of the directors

of the National League and American Association, as these people so far as I know
are the only ones that have taken part in this gigantic farce, that you can no longer
make a target of the Cleveland Base Ball Company or of the players connected with
the same. I will defend both with the last dollar I have on earth, and I give you due
notice now that I will put up with no more of it.[7]

There matters stood for more than a month before Patsy, assisted by
a squad of lawyers paid for by Robison, went to the courthouse in Cleveland on August 11 to plead his case. A handful of fans came to court to
see the proceedings; as one wit put it, "The court case draws about as well
as a Spider game." Dressed in a suit and tie, Tebeau asked for a permanent
injunction to prevent the National League from fining or suspending him.
He argued that there was no rule nor law in the league constitution that
allowed a committee of owners to unilaterally punish him for his on-field
actions. Players were covered by a schedule of escalating fines for misbehavior, beginning at $25 for a first offense and increasing by $25 incre-
ments. Tebeau was still a player, and the league, claimed the Cleveland
manager, simply ignored the fining scale entirely. Their action was, in
Tebeau's view, illegal and not supported in the league constitution.

While waiting for the court case to be decided, the Spiders played
on. Patsy and the Spiders tried to ignore the controversies swirling around
them; at Cleveland in mid–July, a fan shouted at the manager that he was
"first in war, first in peace, and first in the hands of the Louisville police."[8]
The crowd roared, and Patsy doffed his cap and smiled. Still, the Spiders
worried about the pending case. If Tebeau lost, the Spiders might be forced
to forfeit all the games they won after July 13, the deadline set by the league
for Tebeau to pay his fine.

Robison was concerned as well, but he was also at the end of his rope
about the Sunday ball question. He had banned the club from playing on
Sundays, expecting increased support at home on the other six days of
the week in return. That support never materialized, and Cleveland attendance lagged as badly as ever. In July, Robison dropped his pledge to stay
idle on Sundays. He allowed the schedule makers to put the Spiders in
action on upcoming Sundays in Louisville, Chicago, and Cincinnati. He
also threatened to hold a Sunday game in Cleveland; that threat never
came to fruition, but the Spiders played four Sunday games on the road
in July alone.

Despite the swirling controversies, the Spiders remained in the thick
of the pennant chase, buoyed by outstanding individual performances.
Jesse Burkett slumped a bit in mid-season, but the defending National
League batting champion went on a tear and shot to the top of the listings.

His average broke the .400 barrier and stayed near there for the rest of the season. Cy Young, after a slow start, righted himself and pitched like the Cy of old. On July 23 in Philadelphia, he nearly pitched the first no-hitter of his career, holding the powerful Phillies without a hit until Ed Delahanty singled with two out in the ninth. Third starter Zeke Wilson won 17 games, and Ed McKean was his usual reliable self on his way to another season of 100 runs scored, 100 runs batted in, and an average well over .300. On June 8, McKean's homer in Philadelphia helped Young to an 8–7 win, and the Cleveland shortstop belted five hits the next day as Wilson defeated the Phillies. On September 9, McKean cleared the right field wall at League Park with a homer that landed on Lexington Avenue. He was the first Spider to perform the feat that year.

Another major incident happened in Cincinnati on July 26. That day was a Sunday, and 22,000 people came to see the Reds play the battling Spiders. Cy Young, a practicing Methodist, usually refused to pitch on Sundays but made an exception on this day. Perhaps he should have stayed on the bench, as the Reds scored eight runs in the first seven innings, while Cincinnati's Frank Foreman kept the Spiders off the board. It was a frustrating day for the Clevelanders, and in the Cincinnati half of the eighth inning the tensions finally boiled over. The Reds had Eddie Burke on first and Charlie Irwin on third when Burke set out to steal second. Chief Zimmer's throw was on target, but Cupid Childs dropped the ball and Burke was safe. Perhaps Burke ran into the Cleveland second baseman too hard, or maybe Childs was simply angry at Burke for stealing a base with the Reds ahead by eight runs. In any case, Childs grabbed Burke, lifted him in the air, and body-slammed him.

Burke regained his feet and charged at Childs, landing several hard punches before his teammates jumped in to separate the combatants. This brought the crowd surging onto the field. Fortunately, the Reds had provided 50 uniformed officers to keep order, and they pushed the angry crowd off the diamond to prevent another fan riot, which the National League did not need at that point. At game's end, the fans invaded the field again, but the Spiders made a dash for their carriages, and the Cincinnati cops protected then from the wrath of the mob.

At times during the summer of 1896, Patsy Tebeau appeared to be dangerously out of control of himself. On June 13, after a third loss in a row at Brooklyn, the Cleveland manager used a bat to destroy the door to the visitors' clubhouse. The Spiders then left town and left Brooklyn management to repair the damage. On July 28 in Cincinnati, Tebeau blew up in the ninth inning of a tie game when he dropped a pop-up on the infield.

With two Reds on base, Tebeau ordered pitcher Cy Young to trade places with him. Cy went to first base while Tebeau took the mound for the only pitching appearance of his career. He faced one batter, Elmer Smith, who delivered the game-winning hit that sealed Cleveland's fifth loss in a row.

Was Patsy losing it? Ed McKean's biographer, Rich Blevins, believed so. "It's easy today," wrote Blevins in 2014, "to see the tell tale signs that Tebeau's histrionics on the field had morphed into serious manic episodes in the 1896 season." Later, though the controversy over the $200 fine was resolved in Tebeau's favor, the bad feeling left by his behavioral excesses remained. "From this day on," said Blevins, "Patsy Tebeau was more of a distraction than an inspiration, and the [Spiders] were a sports anachronism. "[9]

The 1896 pennant race was another close one, with Cleveland and Baltimore in a virtual tie for the lead after the July 4 doubleheaders, with Cincinnati one game out and Boston three and a half back. The battling Spiders kept it close for a while, but when John McGraw returned to Baltimore in mid–August the Orioles roared away from the pack. A 16–2 Baltimore run in late July put some space between the Orioles and Spiders, and a 14–2 streak in August and September left Cleveland 11 games out of first. Baltimore coasted to the pennant, leaving the Spiders to fight for second place (and a berth in the Temple Cup series) with Buck Ewing and the Cincinnati Reds.

The Brooklyn Bridegrooms had waited for months to get revenge on the Spiders for the damage they caused in June, and on September 2, when the Cleveland club arrived at Washington Park in Brooklyn to begin a three-game series, they found the visitors' clubhouse locked. Club official (and future team owner) Charles Ebbets appeared and informed Tebeau that the door he destroyed on June 13 cost four dollars to replace, and a ball that Jesse Burkett hurled out of the ballpark that same day cost $1.25. Team management, said Ebbets, would be happy to unlock the dressing room door upon receipt of five dollars and 25 cents in cash.

"Ha ha," said Patsy. He thought Ebbets was kidding.

He wasn't. After a bit of arguing, Tebeau knew he was licked. The Cleveland manager handed Ebbets a $20 bill and demanded change and a receipt.

Patsy then decided to have a little fun with the Brooklyn club. He approached Dave Foutz, the Brooklyn manager, on the field and stated in a serious tone of voice,

Now, you mind, and God help you. If you so much as injure one blade of grass on the Cleveland grounds next season you will pay for it. If you spoil the surface of the lawn by dropping a bat too hard you will pay for it. If you scratch one particle of rubber off the home plate, cut one thread in the canvas of the bases you will pay for it. Every bit of dirt that you carry off the field on your spikes you will be charged for at the current price of real estate in Cleveland. We play on grounds worth $10,000 a square foot. We will make you a present of the air and the water you drink, but don't mar the bucket by dropping the cup in too hastily or we will make you pay for that.[10]

The Reds made a fight of it, but faded late in the month. On September 19, the Reds came to Cleveland for a three-game set. Cincinnati needed to win all three games to have any chance to overtake the Spiders, but Cleveland quickly brushed off their challenge. The Spiders walloped the Reds 21–2 in the opener, then split the next two to leave the Reds in the dust. The Spiders clinched second place on September 23, as Bobby Wallace defeated Louisville with a three-hit shutout. At season's end, Cleveland's 80–48 record left them solidly in second place, nine and a half games behind Baltimore.

Cleveland's finish qualified them to face the pennant-winning Orioles for the Temple Cup for the second year in a row. This matchup, however, would be different. This time, the Orioles decided to take the post-season "championship" seriously. Baltimore had lost the Cup challenge in both 1894 and 1895, and now John McGraw and his mates were determined to win it for once. Besides, the Orioles and Spiders thoroughly detested each other, and Baltimore fans would not put up with another listless loss to the hated Clevelanders.

The Spiders entered the series at a disadvantage. They played hard all through September to clinch second place, and Tebeau's men were exhausted. Cy Young was worn out after winning 28 games and pitching 414 innings, as was Nig Cuppy, who threw 358 innings while winning 25. Baltimore, with a safe lead, was able to relax and rest its starters late in September. Tebeau scheduled several practices in Cleveland before the start of the Temple Cup series, but rain and wet grounds kept the Spiders indoors for nearly a week. Baltimore, on the other hand, played a series of tune-up games to prepare for the matchup.

With the first three games to be played in Baltimore, the Spiders boarded a train for the Maryland city on the afternoon of October 1. What followed was a 27-hour nightmare of a trip that delayed the first game by a day. Heavy rains had washed out bridges and overpasses in Pennsylvania, and at three in the morning the conductor stopped the train due to a freight derailment on the track ahead. The players, reporters, and team officials in the Cleveland party had to step off their train and walk in ankle-deep mud around the wreck, in which several tramps on board had been killed. The team did not reach Cumberland, Maryland, until noon the next day, after which several nerve-racking passages over dangerous-looking bridges followed. When the bedraggled Spiders finally arrived in Baltimore on the evening of October 2, Tebeau asked Ned Hanlon, the Oriole manager, for permission to hold a morning practice at Union Park the next day. Hanlon, predictably, turned Patsy down.

Tebeau, as usual, waxed optimistic, though his club had not played in five days. "Of course it's a rest," he told the *Cleveland Leader*, "but their eye is apt to get just a little rusty. Young is all right, though. The longer the rest, the better he is, and, rusty or not, the Baltimores will do well to get one game from us." However, the paper reported, "the Orioles are chock full of confidence and Hanlon is wearing a broad smile which he says means something."[11]

The Spiders' lack of preparation showed. The first game, held on October 3, saw Baltimore's Bill Hoffer pitch a 7–1 victory over a tired Cy Young before nearly 4,000 fans. The series may have been decided in the second inning, when Patsy Tebeau wrenched his back while swinging at a pitch and gave way to Jack O'Connor. The Cleveland manager had suffered a severely pulled back muscle and could barely walk off the field, and he saw no more action in the series. Young, too, was injured when a liner from the bat of John McGraw hit his pitching hand. Young's hand was red and swollen after the game. The second game was another runaway for Baltimore, as the Orioles pounded Bobby Wallace for four runs in the first on their way to a 7–2 win. Joe Corbett, the Baltimore pitcher and younger brother of heavyweight boxing champion James J. Corbett, struck out four and cruised to the victory.

Patsy, thoroughly discouraged, sat shivering on the bench during the second game, wrapped in a large blanket and wincing at the pain in his back. He was in no condition to manage, much less play, and Jack O'Connor took over the field leadership for the Spiders. In Game 3, Tebeau did not even join his team on the bench. He sat in the stands with DeWolf Hopper, a famous actor and rabid baseball fan (and the man who introduced the poem "Casey at the Bat" to the American public). Without Patsy on the field directing the action, cheering his own men, and abusing the opponents and the umpires, the Spiders looked lost. The Clevelanders played without their usual enthusiasm against the suddenly determined Orioles.

At least there was no rioting in this series, but there weren't many fans either. Only about 3,100 showed up to see the second contest, so Baltimore management slashed the ticket prices in half for the third game.

On a beautiful, sunny fall day, 4,250 people came to Union Park to see Nig Cuppy face off with Bill Hoffer, the winner of the first contest. The Spiders kept it close for a while, but John McGraw's three stolen bases and Joe Kelley's two outstanding catches in the outfield helped make the difference for the Orioles. Baltimore scored three times in the eighth to walk off with a 6–2 win. The two teams then returned to Cleveland with the demoralized Spiders down three games to none.

With Young battling fatigue and still hurting from his hand injury in the first game, Tebeau sent Cuppy to the mound again in a bid to prevent a Baltimore sweep. The Cleveland fans, so enthusiastic in 1895, had lost interest, as rain, wet grounds, and fan apathy kept the crowd down to 2,000 at League Park. They saw a pitching duel between Cuppy and Corbett that kept the game scoreless through the first six innings. In the seventh, the Orioles broke through with two runs, and three more Baltimore tallies in the eighth spelled the end of the scoring. The Orioles won the final game in a 5–0 shutout and swept the Temple Cup series four games to none.

Financially and artistically, the 1896 Temple Cup series was a failure. Game receipts proved disappointing, as the Orioles took home about $200 per man and the Spiders a mere $117. Cold, wet weather in Cleveland depressed the turnout at League Park, but already there were signs that the public had long since lost interest in the annual Temple Cup matchup. It was not only anticlimactic after a hard-fought pennant race, but wholly unnecessary, and only the fans in the winning city cared much about it. That November, at the annual National League meeting, several owners introduced a resolution to discontinue the Temple Cup series and return the trophy to its donor. The proposal failed, but only by two votes.

Perhaps it would have been too much to ask the Spiders to hand over the Temple Cup gracefully. On the evening of October 12, the Spiders and Orioles, along with Cleveland owner Frank Robison and Baltimore president Harry von der Horst, met in the bar of the Hollenden House in downtown Cleveland. The Spiders filled the Cup with champagne (reports stated that the silver trophy held 15 quarts of liquid), and both teams drank from it ravenously. As the players became progressively more intoxicated, the defenseless Temple Cup took a beating. The Spiders and Orioles played keep-away with the Cup, rolled it along the floor among them, and ended the evening by kicking it around the bar like a football. Finally, both sides settled down, the teams toasted each other, and the Spiders relinquished the battered Cup to the Orioles.[12]

In addition, the season could not have ended without a blast from

Frank Robison, who had all but declared open warfare against his fellow club owners. The matter of Patsy Tebeau's $200 fine still awaited a resolution, and Boston's Arthur Soden remarked to a Boston newspaper that if Tebeau and Robison remained defiant, the league would be well within its rights to revoke Cleveland's franchise. Robison was having none of it. "Well, sir," said the Cleveland magnate with a vigorous thump on his desk with his fist, "I pity the man who tries to take it up. The Ohio courts have passed on that case, and have granted a permanent injunction restraining the league from collecting the fine. They have said to the League magnates, 'hands off,' and it behooves them to keep their hands off. The man who doesn't heed that admonition will get a taste of Ohio law he'll not relish." Besides, claimed the Cleveland magnate, "Soden has presided at every League meeting since I've been a member of the League, and I have yet to hear a motion or suggestion by him that was for the good of base ball."[13]

In the end, Patsy won his case against the league when the court found a convenient loophole to rescue everyone from what had become an intolerable situation. Nick Young was both the president of the National League and its secretary, so when the board of directors ordered Young to notify Tebeau of its decision to fine him, Young apparently did so in his capacity as league secretary, not as its president. In effect, President Young had never actually issued a fine against the Cleveland manager, though Secretary Young had notified him of it. This resolution, if it could be called that, was a load of hooey, and brought no honor to anyone involved. Nonetheless, the league declared the matter closed, and Patsy was off the hook.

No one believed that Tebeau and his men had learned anything from the affair, and two incidents that occurred in late 1896 further blackened the reputation of the Cleveland club. In September, the team played an exhibition in Youngstown, Ohio, Jimmy McAleer's hometown, when an argument between McAleer and Harry Blake, who had cut in front of McAleer to catch a fly ball, erupted on the field. The Spider outfielders continued their dispute in the dressing room, and when the two men came to blows, Tebeau stepped in to break it up. He explained to McAleer that he had called for Blake to make the catch, as the right fielder was in better position to make a throw home. This explanation did not satisfy McAleer, and a few minutes later, as Tebeau washed his face at a clubhouse sink, the veteran center fielder stepped behind him and belted him in the side of the head. The manager and the outfielder soon patched up their quarrel, but news of the battle could not be covered up, as Tebeau's shiner was obvious to all on the field the next day. Once again, unflattering stories of the rowdy, undisciplined Cleveland Spiders filled the nation's newspapers.

A much more serious incident took place a month later, after the Spiders lost the Temple Cup in embarrassing fashion to the hated Orioles. Elmer Pasco of the *Cleveland Press* had the temerity to write about the McAleer-Tebeau incident, and when Tebeau spotted the reporter in the bar room of the Kennard House downtown, an argument broke out. Pasco and Tebeau (both of whom may well have been intoxicated) traded insults, then punches before other bar patrons broke it up, with Pasco getting the worst of it. Jack O'Connor, Tebeau's drinking partner that night, then took it upon himself to give the already dazed Pasco a thorough thrashing, knocking him to the floor, kicking him and stomping on him.

Pasco declined to press charges against either man, but the local papers rallied to his defense. Said the *Cleveland World*:

> [The incident] was nothing short of an outrage. On the other hand, however, it shows Tebeau up in a true light. In almost every other city in the country he has been denounced as a ruffian. Here at home we have fought his battles, claiming that he is merely aggressive, because of his great desire to win, but 'off the field was always a gentleman.' That statement can never again be shoved down the throat of the public. Hence it is just as well to retract it now as any time....
>
> The affair is bound to hurt base ball in Cleveland. The owners of the club should now insist on less aggressiveness both on and off the ball field. Or if it has come to such a pass that only ruffians can make successful ball players then will it also be a fact that only ruffians will interest themselves in ball games.[14]

The *Plain Dealer* chimed in as well:

> It is said that O'Connor acted as if he was trying to kill the man, and was only dragged away with the greatest difficulty. O'Connor is one of the best catchers in the business, but this one action makes him an unfit man for the Cleveland Club. Local patrons would far rather see the team weakened than see it disgraced in such a manner. During the base ball season O'Connor does not drink, and usually behaves himself; he has therefore made a good many friends in Cleveland, but this one example of fiendish brutality will offset all the good work he has done here. O'Connor has made all preparations to leave for his home in St. Louis to-day; it is to be hoped that he will not change his plans.[15]

Tebeau received some good news from Louisville on the day after the Pasco fight. A judge accepted a deal in which Tebeau and his three co-defendants in their August trial pled guilty to causing a "breach of the peace." The four Spiders paid fines of ten dollars each, and the matter was closed. Still, the Louisville riot was one more black mark against Tebeau and his men, one that would be remembered for years thereafter.

Perhaps neither Patsy Tebeau nor Frank Robison realized it yet, but the Pasco incident cost them the support of the local media. The main Cleveland papers were bitter rivals, but one of their own had sustained a vicious assault for doing his job. The Cleveland press corps was tired of chalking up these accumulating episodes to the team's single-minded pursuit of victory. Tebeau's take-no-prisoners attitude came with collateral damage, on and off the field, and the manager's relationships with the men who reported on his team would never recover.

ᐧᒧᐧ **11** ᐧᒧᐧ

The Cleveland Indians

"Eight or ten years ago Cleveland was one of the best paying base ball cities in the country. But the fans In the Forest City became utterly disgusted with the language of Tebeau, Burkett and O'Connor, who carried their blackguardism so far that the patrons of the grand-stand refused to attend the game. The patrons dropped off year by year, until to-day Cleveland, despite the fact that she has a strong club, is one of the poorest paying base ball cities in the League. Is it any wonder, then, that Mr. Robison wants coaching stopped?"
     —J. Earl Wagner, Washington, team president, August 1896[1]

By early 1897, Frank Robison had set himself apart from his fellow owners. Gone was the young streetcar magnate who was so excited to gain a National League franchise in 1889, and gone was the man who virtually gave his best young player, George Davis, to the New York Giants in 1893 to strengthen the circuit in the nation's largest city. Now Robison saw the trials and troubles of 1896 not as an indictment of his team's behavior, but as a dastardly plot against him personally.

> I said early in the season, and am still convinced, that there was a conspiracy among the Eastern clubs to cheat Cleveland out of the pennant. We should certainly have won the pennant had we not been harassed the way we were.... Cleveland is a comparatively small city, and patrons of the sport in the East say to the management that if a little town like Cleveland can get a winning team together why can't the big fellows of the East do the same? The managements are criticized by press and public for their failure to get as good players as Cleveland, and for that reason they are compelled to enter a conspiracy to keep the pennant in the East.

He also insisted that individual Cleveland stars were not for sale, though many other clubs expressed interest in McKean, Cuppy, Childs, and other reliable veteran performers. "My players will stick to me as long as I will keep them," declared the owner. "Other clubs will not buy them because I will not sell."[2] Apparently he meant it, as Elmer Bates of

Sporting Life reported in March that the Brooklyn club's board of directors had offered to buy the entire Cleveland team for $100,000 in cash, but Robison turned them down. Other rumors had Jesse Burkett and Cupid Childs headed to New York, Cy Young and Ed McKean to the Phillies, and the entire club shifting to Indianapolis, Buffalo, and a host of other cities.[3]

In late 1896, the National League passed a slate of rule changes to curb rowdiness and umpire abuse. Beginning in 1897, only one coach was allowed to be on the field at a time, unless the bases were full. "This change is recommended," said the *Washington Post*, "because it has been proven in the past that the presence of two coachers allow a 'cross fire' of talk between them foreign to the game and frequently of a character objectionable to spectators."[4] The league also now allowed only a team's captain to argue with an umpire, with other players required to stand at least ten feet away, and proscribed a $5 fine for defacing a ball in play.

Perhaps surprisingly, the new coaching rule was Frank Robison's idea. His Spiders had drawn withering criticism for their behavior over the years, and the rule appeared to be a direct response to Cleveland's many misadventures during the 1896 season. Fans and sportswriters speculated on Robison's motives for promoting the decree; perhaps Robison believed that a severe curb on verbal abuse would harm the equally hated Baltimore Orioles more than the Spiders. Or, maybe it was part of a plan to make the on-field product more respectable as a sop to the anti–Sunday ball forces. Players and managers grumbled that the coaching rule would, as one put it, "take all the life out of the game," but at least the league was finally making an attempt to clean up the sport.

The Spiders did not travel south for spring training in 1897. Instead, the ballclub remained in Cleveland and practiced at the former home of the Cleveland Athletic Club downtown. The manager waxed enthusiastic about how well the players would round into shape in a gymnasium instead of a baseball field. "Our training," said Tebeau, "will consist of each man taking 20 minutes' work in the handball court, 15 minutes of leg work on the running track, 10 minutes of dumb bell exercise, 15 minutes of calisthenics, and the balance of the training time will be devoted to throwing the ball and catching."[5] It was a money-saving decision by the cost-conscious Frank Robison, as attendance was poor in 1896 despite the team's second-place finish. Nonetheless, the Spiders streamed into town during the third week of March to prepare for the upcoming season.

On March 19, the first full day of workouts, the Spiders received their first look at a rookie who would dominate the headlines and draw national attention that season. Louis Sockalexis, a powerfully built 25-year-old outfielder, was a full-blooded Native American, the first recognized minority of any kind in National League history. Sockalexis (who told the team he was only 23) was a Penobscot Indian who was born and reared on the tribe's reservation in Old Town, Maine. His new Cleveland teammates had never seen anything like him.

Sockalexis, born in 1871, was a great athlete from a tribe that placed a high value on athletic prowess. After playing some semipro ball in Maine during the early 1890s, he enrolled at the College of the Holy Cross in Worcester, Massachusetts, and became the athletic star of the school. He batted .444 and .436 during two seasons of varsity baseball play and reportedly threw a ball 413 feet from deepest center field to throw out a runner at the plate. Sockalexis also made headlines as a running back and defensive end on the first Holy Cross football squad in 1896. He was a monster in track as well, but baseball was his favorite sport.

In late 1896, while National League teams focused their attention on the college sensation, Sockalexis and teammate Mike Powers, a future major league catcher, left Holy Cross and enrolled at Notre Dame University in Indiana. Sockalexis never played for Notre Dame, however, for in mid–March he abruptly called an end to his college career. Having signed a contract with the Spiders a week or so before, he boarded an eastbound train and traveled to Cleveland for spring training.

Cleveland had the inside track for the Penobscot's services, as Jesse Burkett and Chippy McGarr, Worcester residents both, coached the Holy Cross baseball team during the spring months. Burkett gave him hitting tips that Sockalexis used to great advantage. Still, it is possible that the Cleveland ballclub did not know the true reason for Sockalexis' quick departure from Notre Dame. He had intended to finish the spring semester and report to the Spiders in mid–May, but the newest Spider was free to join the club much earlier, because he was expelled from school after a drunken row at a local tavern. A Notre Dame teammate recalled the incident many years later:

> It was during the college baseball season of 1897 that Sockalexis and another Notre Dame student, whose name I don't recall, decided to paint the town of South Bend. They loaded up on Old Oscar McGroggins and wandered about in search of entertainment. They visited an establishment conducted by "Popcorn Jennie" and wrecked the place. While they were demolishing furniture, and hurling the broken parts out of windows, the local gendarmes arrived on the scene. They tried to quiet Sockalexis but only annoyed him. He became so provoked that he flattened two of the coppers with perfectly delivered rights to their jaws, but he was finally overpowered and dragged to the bastille.

Sockalexis and his fun-loving pal might have gotten out of this mess if the South Bend Tribune had not gotten hold of the story and plastered it over its front page. This greatly displeased the Reverend Father Andrew Morrissey, then President of Notre Dame, and he expelled both Sockalexis and his companion.[6]

The fracas, and the ballplayer's arrest, made headlines in the *South Bend Tribune* on March 19, 1897. "On hearing of the conduct of the two young men," the paper stated, "the university authorities ordered their effects packed and sent to them with the information that their presence at Notre Dame was no longer desired. Both were released last night.... The prompt action of the university authorities in expelling these young men should be a warning to others inclined to overstep the bounds of propriety."[7]

Though a brief item in the *Plain Dealer* mentioned the episode, no one around the team raised the issue, and the incident faded into the background as the Spiders trained. A drunken spree or two would not have been a topic of concern to most baseball people at the time; indeed, some of the Spiders had a few embarrassing incidents in their pasts as well. We now know, however, that Sockalexis had arrived in the major leagues with a serious drinking problem. For the moment, however, the Penobscot drew attention, not for his nightlife escapades, but for his prodigious talents. Tebeau hoped the rookie would solve the perennial right field problem and provide some power to the lineup too.

"Sock" arrived at practice on March 20 in top condition. Despite his muscular build, he easily defeated all his new teammates in footraces and won nearly all his handball matches. He also displayed his talent at gymnastics. "Sockalexis, who is quite a gymnast, occasionally breaks out with some caper that would tear the ordinary man in two," reported the *Plain Dealer* on March 26. "Those things are all right in a circus, Louie," said Tebeau, "but you don't need 'em to win ball games." In the March 27 issue of *Sporting Life*, former New York Giants manager John Ward, who saw the Penobscot star perform at Holy Cross, declared, "I have seen [Sockalexis] play perhaps a dozen games, and I unhesitatingly pronounce him a wonder. Why he has not been snapped up before by some League club looking for a sensational player is beyond my comprehension."

The newest Spider even inspired a new name for the team. No one much liked the name "Spiders," a relic of the early part of the decade, so when the *Plain Dealer*, in a headline on March 20, referred to the club as "Tebeau's Indians," a new identity was born. Sockalexis became the "Cleveland Indian," and the local sportswriters latched on to the new moniker with enthusiasm. For once, there was a sense of excitement around the club, and in no time the "Spiders" nickname was virtually forgotten. On

March 27, the *Plain Dealer* stated, "The Indians have a spring schedule which is bound to give them good, hard work."

The hubbub around Sockalexis drew attention from Tebeau's plans for the upcoming season. With Chippy McGarr slowing down, the manager moved the sure-handed Bobby Wallace from the mound to third base. Bobby, who had played some in the outfield the year before, heartily endorsed the move. "I'm glad that Tebeau will keep me on third," said Wallace to the papers, "as I hated to pitch. When I was an amateur, I played in the infield and pitched. Though I was

Louis Sockalexis, the "Cleveland Indian," was a sensation for three months (author's collection).

signed by Tebeau to help out with the pitching, every pitcher who can practice fielding ought to try it."[8] Tebeau, who recognized that shortstop Ed McKean, now in his thirties, had gained weight and covered less ground with each passing year, gave Wallace a simple command: "Get everything you can!"

To take Wallace's place as the fourth starter, Tebeau tried out two right-handers, John Pappalau and Jack Powell. Pappalau was a teammate of Sockalexis at Holy Cross, where Jesse Burkett had coached him, while Powell was a Chicagoan who pitched well for George Tebeau at Fort Wayne in 1896. As a fourth pitcher would not be needed right away, both men were slated to start the season either in the bullpen or in the minors, depending on their spring showing.

Tebeau was always a spring optimist, but his public pronouncements in early 1897 were extraordinary even for him. His team was set to open the season with nine games on the road against second-division clubs Louisville, Washington, and St. Louis, followed by a three-game set against the Cincinnati Reds at home. "Ten of these twelve games are already ours," said Patsy, "and I rather expect to win all 12 of them. Young and Cuppy will be in shape to go in the box right at the start, and you know how helpless these teams are against such pitchers. I want to get a lead by May 15 that no other team can possibly overtake."⁹

Despite the manager's brash prediction, the newly-named Indians lost their first five games on the road before playing the Browns to a 6–6 tie in St. Louis. They then came alive and swept the remaining three games against the Browns, then opened the home schedule in Cleveland on May 2 with another win over the Browns. Louis Sockalexis, though erratic at times in the field, hit well and made several spectacular catches in the early weeks of the campaign. He also drew fans to the parks both at home and on the road. The fans thrilled to the novelty of a real Native American ballplayer in the National League, and greeted the Penobscot with noisy war whoops and chanting. As Charles W. Mears explained in *The Sporting News* on April 24:

Pitcher-turned-infielder Bobby Wallace (National Baseball Library, Cooperstown, New York).

Everybody in Cleveland as well as in other league cities, for that matter, are talking Sockalexis, and if the young Indian isn't the best advertised new man that ever entered the big organization then it will not be the fault of the baseball paragraphers of the press. They have discovered a novelty in it. The newspaper talk concerning the youngster has stirred up great local interest in the Red Man, and of all the young players on the Cleveland Club's list he is the most talked of, and it will be his appearance that will draw the greatest number of curious people at the opening of the season.

The Indians recovered from their slow start and reached the .500 mark on May 7 with a win at home over the Chicago Colts. Cy

Young won his second game of the season, but the story was Sockalexis, who belted three singles and a triple, and contributed a running catch in the outfield with the bases loaded. The next day, more than 5,000 people, a big crowd for Cleveland in May, saw the Indians pass the .500 mark behind Zeke Wilson. The team was on an upswing, mainly because both of the club's perennial problem areas at third base (Wallace) and right field (Sockalexis) appeared to be solved. With Sockalexis providing a jolt of excitement to the Cleveland baseball scene, perhaps National League baseball could thrive in Cleveland after all.

Frank Robison apparently thought so. Now it became clear why he would turn down $100,000 for his team, though he had put it up for sale three years before for less than half that amount. Robison figured that a well-supported franchise in Cleveland would be worth much more than $100,000. To achieve that end, the attendance at League Park, already on the rise, would have to improve further. So, Robison decided to revisit the Sunday ball issue and resolve it once and for all.

That's where Jack Powell came in.

Jack Powell was a stocky 23-year-old right-handed pitcher from Chicago who, at just under six feet in height and weighing nearly 200 pounds, bore a physical resemblance to Cy Young, though Powell's best fastball was much slower than Young's. In fact, Powell's easy motion and less than impressive speed made him appear utterly hittable. Fans said that they would like to grab a bat and take their chances against the "nothing pitcher." Still, Powell threw strikes, hit his spots and worked quickly. He threw without a windup, a rarity at the time, and his deceptive quick-pitch delivery caused many arguments. His pitching style put little strain on his arm, and his build made him durable.

He was a semipro star in his hometown and occasionally threw batting practice for Cap Anson's Chicago Colts. Powell wanted to sign with the Colts, but Anson waved him off. "He hasn't anything," remarked the veteran manager. But George Tebeau, Patsy's brother and manager of the Fort Wayne Farmers in the Inter-State League, took a more positive view and signed Powell in 1896. Powell and another future major leaguer, catcher Lou Criger, boosted the Farmers to second place finish, and in 1897 Patsy Tebeau brought Powell to Cleveland. With Bobby Wallace moving from the mound to third base, he counted on Powell to fill the number four slot in the rotation behind Cy Young, Nig Cuppy, and Zeke Wilson.

Powell made his first official appearance for the Spiders on June 23, but his unofficial debut, on May 16, was one of the most memorable in Cleveland baseball history. May 16 was a Sunday, and it was the day that

Frank Robison chose to launch a frontal assault against the forces that kept League Park deserted on the Christian Sabbath. On that date, the Cleveland club scheduled a game against the Washington Senators in direct defiance of state law.

Robison's frustration with the ban on Sunday ball had reached a boiling point. His Spiders, one of the most talented teams in the National League, had finished a strong second in the twelve-team circuit in both 1895 and 1896, winning the Temple Cup in the first of those seasons. The Cleveland lineup boasted the presence of batting champion Jesse Burkett, 30-game winner Cy Young, the outfield sensation Sockalexis, and other stars. Still, the Spiders drew fewer fans to their home games than every other team in the league save Louisville. Cleveland was one of the league's top road attractions, but even the helpless Browns and Senators enjoyed a higher turnstile count at home. The Sunday ban was to blame, and rumors that the team might abandon Cleveland and move to a more accommodating city gained currency. In February of 1897, *Sporting Life* mentioned, almost in passing, that "the Cleveland team in St. Louis would be a gold mine to its owners."[10]

An unlikely coalition of interests fought hard to keep the "blue laws" in place. The politically powerful Cleveland Ministers Association opposed Sunday ball, railing from their pulpits every Sunday about the evils of breaking the Sabbath. The ministers found an unlikely ally in the league of downtown saloon owners. The Cleveland blue laws, for some reason, did not cover bars and saloons, which did their best business on Sundays in the era of six-day, 50-hour work weeks. If Sunday ball became legal, the bar owners reasoned, thousands of young working men—their core customers—would spend the afternoon cheering at the ballpark and not drinking in their establishments. "Men and boys will ... go to the games and spend the 75 cents they would otherwise leave with us," complained one tavern proprietor to a local sportswriter.[11] These two groups were strongly supported by Cleveland's mayor, Robert McKisson, and the *Cleveland Leader*.

The National League had sanctioned Sunday games in 1892, but in 1897 only five teams—Chicago, St. Louis, Baltimore, Cincinnati, and Louisville—allowed Sunday ball. The other seven did not, but the teams in Boston, New York, and Philadelphia prospered anyway due to a diverse fan base, one that was made up of both white- and blue-collar workers. The fans in Cleveland and Pittsburgh, in contrast, were mostly factory laborers who were only free on Sundays.

Robison plastered the downtown area with placards advertising the upcoming Sunday game, with a notice that if the contest was interrupted, the fans could either hold onto their tickets (for use at a later date) or demand a refund. The Cleveland owner prepared for that latter eventuality by amassing hundreds of quarters and half dollars to streamline the refunding process.

Cleveland police warned Robison on the day before the game that the players would be arrested if the game took place, and Mayor McKisson convened a Saturday meeting with the city prosecutor and several ministers at police headquarters. Still, Robison forged ahead, and on Sunday morning, waves of fans surged down Lexington Avenue and made their way to League Park. The Cleveland owner ordered the gates closed early, after some 9,500 fans had jammed into the ballpark; at least 5,000 more people, and perhaps as many as 15,000 more, were left outside. The ministers had predicted that the fans would become rowdy, and the police feared a riot if the game was interrupted; nonetheless, the crowds both inside and outside the park were noticeably well-behaved.

With every seat in League Park filled, and the overflow standing behind ropes in the outfield, the first inning proceeded uneventfully, though the fans noticed that, for some reason, first base was manned by rookie pitcher Jack Powell. Cleveland elected to bat first and went out easily. Zeke Wilson, the Cleveland starter, then retired the Senators without a run despite a single by Kip Selbach. The first inning was over, and a police captain strode to home plate, accompanied by Frank Robison.

The captain informed umpire Tim Hurst that he and the 18 players who participated in the game were to be arrested and transported downtown to the police station. The fans booed heartily, but Robison raised his arms and asked for their attention. He had a smile on his face, and his genial nature did much to quiet the fans and defuse a potentially dangerous situation.

"Ladies and gentlemen," the owner bellowed, "we are ordered by the police to refrain from fracturing a state law. The law must be respected. I will take this case into the state courts and I believe we will be victorious."[12] The fans cheered, and hundreds of them invaded the field to shake the magnate's hand. Meanwhile, the nine Spiders—McKean, Tebeau (filling in at second base for Childs), Blake, Wilson, Powell, Sockalexis, Burkett, Zimmer, and Wallace—were allowed to change clothes before boarding a police bus for transport. The Senators appeared at the station in their uniforms. All, including umpire Hurst, were released on $100 bond, which Robison posted. About half of the fans received their refunds, while the rest held onto their tickets.

This skirmish in the war on Sunday ball was won decisively by Robison, though the owner fumed at what he saw as a betrayal by the mayor. On Saturday, McKisson had reportedly agreed to allow the teams to complete five innings before being arrested; instead, the ministers and the saloon owners got wind of the agreement and bullied the mayor into reneging on it. Robison dismissed the ministers as "a lot of unheard-of divines anxious to secure free advertising in the newspapers" and promised to keep the battle going. Said the Cleveland owner:

> Sunday baseball is endorsed by the masses of this city, as was shown by the enormous crowd that wanted to see today's game. The inconsistency of the whole business is proven by the scores of Sunday amateur games that are being played in Cleveland and throughout Ohio today, to say nothing of professional ball at Cincinnati, Toledo, Columbus, and Dayton. I will admit that there is a state law, now practically obsolete, that prohibits Sunday ball, but the prohibition is under a vague statute that forbids amusements in general on Sunday. It is an unpopular law, and antagonistic to the desires of the public. I will fight this case to its finish in the courts.[13]

On Monday morning, the players returned to the central police station as the authorities prepared a two-count indictment against each of the 19 defendants. Cannily, Robison and his attorneys demanded 19 separate jury trials, after which the two sides met and hammered out a compromise. The authorities decided to try only one player for violating the prohibition on Sunday ball, and Jack Powell, the rookie pitcher, would be the legal guinea pig. Powell, who had not yet appeared in an official game, could be left behind in Cleveland without harming the team on the road. The team lawyers also filed a motion to dismiss the case outright. It was a long shot, but the New York Giants were coming to town for a weekend series, and Robison hoped to draw another huge Sunday crowd.

The Sunday ball showdown seemed to enliven the Spiders-turned-Indians, and the Cleveland club swept the next three against the Senators. Idled by rain the next two days, they split a Saturday twin-bill against the Giants, Cuppy winning the first and Young losing the second before 8,000 fans. With the court case still unsettled, Robison did not try to schedule a game for Sunday, May 23, though a driving rain would have kept the teams from playing anyway. The Phillies then came to Cleveland, only to be swept in all three games of a weekday series before the Indians split two against the visiting Orioles on Thursday and Saturday. When Tebeau's men left on Sunday for an eastern road trip, they stood in fifth place, five games above the break-even point at 17–12.

Still, the team had problems. Nig Cuppy's arm was sore, and the pitcher asked Tebeau for two weeks off to rest it. Cy Young was not himself; he had only four wins as a starter (and one more in relief) and both the Phillies and the Orioles had pounded his deliveries all over League Park. Perhaps Robison had been correct in worrying about Young's workload, as the Cleveland ace had thrown over 800 innings during the previous two seasons. The coming road trip would give the big pitcher a chance to regroup. Sockalexis was walloping the ball, with six hits in three games against the Senators, but Jesse Burkett, the two-time batting champion, wallowed in one of the worst slumps of his career. While Sock's average topped the .350 mark, Burkett's had fallen below .250.

Another major issue was a personal one. Rumors of Jesse Burkett's jealousy of the team's new outfield star became louder; as Washington's Charlie Reilly observed, Sock and the Crab "were about as popular with each other as rival tenors in an operatic company." Although Burkett had coached Sockalexis at Holy Cross and recommended him to the Cleveland team, Burkett now appeared to feel threatened by the Penobscot's popularity. Reilly reported that he teased Burkett about Sock, and Burkett exploded, "Don't ask me about that bead peddler. He's a Jonah [a jinx]. I haven't hit over .100 since he joined the team!" Burkett, according to Reilly, concluded his rant by saying, "Wait till I strike my gait and I will make him go back to the woods and look for a few scalps."[14]

The eastern trip started poorly and soon grew worse. Two losses at Brooklyn, one by the slumping Cy Young, dropped Cleveland's record to 17–14, and another loss at Boston was a total embarrassment. The Indians scored twice in the first but lost the services of Burkett, who was knocked unconscious by a fastball from Beaneaters lefty Fred Klobedanz. Boston then scored 8 runs in the first and 6 more in the second off Zeke Wilson, putting the game away almost before it began. Eight walks by Wilson and three errors by shortstop Ed McKean helped Boston to a 21–3 victory. The Beaneaters followed it up the next day with a 6–1 victory over Young.

On June 10, while the Indians battled the Orioles in Baltimore, news reached the team that Jack Powell was convicted of violating the ban on Sunday ball. The court fined the rookie pitcher only five dollars, but tacked on $153 for court costs, which Frank Robison presumably paid. At least now Powell was free to join the team, and on June 23 he pitched the Indians to a win over the Colonels by an 18–1 score. The stocky rookie won his first four contests and added much-needed support to a shaky pitching staff. Chippy McGarr, who lost the third base job to Bobby Wallace, drew his release in June, but a newcomer, catcher Lou Criger, performed well and looked like another solid addition to the club. Criger settled in as Chief Zimmer's backup.

Tebeau's men won two blowouts in Washington from the Senators, but then lost three in a row in Baltimore. The Indians had set a familiar pattern, winning against the weaker teams and losing badly to the better ones, especially on the road. By July 1, when the Indians used a five-hit performance by Sockalexis to defeat the Browns at home, the club had settled itself firmly into fifth place, 13 games out of the lead. Off the field, Louis Sockalexis and Jack O'Connor had become fast friends, hanging out with each other both in Cleveland and on the road. Because O'Connor was a heavy drinker, their new friendship spelled trouble from the outset.

The Sockalexis legend, and Cleveland's fading pennant hopes, unraveled in early July. On Sunday evening, July 3, Sock boarded a train and accompanied the team to Pittsburgh for their Independence Day doubleheader against the Pirates. Tebeau, however, did not see him until the next morning at the ballpark. Only then did Tebeau learn that Sockalexis had somehow injured his right foot and ankle over the weekend. Recalled Tebeau many years later, "His right foot was badly broken ... but he bandaged it up and went with the other players to Pittsburgh that night. I went over the next day and hurried out to Exposition Park, and there in the bus was Sox, his broken foot swollen four or five times its natural size."[15] The foot was not broken, but it was badly injured, so Tebeau sent the right fielder back to Cleveland to be examined by a physician.

The writers had no idea why Sockalexis was not in the lineup, but they remarked on the Cleveland team's ugly mood that afternoon. The Indians won the first game, but in the second contest, the Pirates loaded the bases in the sixth inning. Jesse Burkett then misplayed a line drive that got between his legs and rolled all the way to the wall. The thoroughly disgusted Burkett refused to chase the ball, forcing Ed McKean to run all the way to deepest left field to retrieve it. Four runs scored, and Pittsburgh salvaged a split of the doubleheader.

Before long, the real story of Sock's injury came out. He had gone out on the town to celebrate Saturday's win against the Browns. He was now a local celebrity, and ran with what was called, then and now, a "fast crowd" of people, many of whom wanted to buy him drinks. Sockalexis drank a large quantity of alcohol that night, and somehow the inebriated ballplayer fell or jumped from a second-story window. This fall severely injured his right foot and ankle, but Sock said nothing the next day as he and his teammates boarded the train to Pittsburgh. His injury, and the fact that he kept it a secret until the last possible moment, explains the sullen behavior of his teammates that afternoon.

The Penobscot's behavior had worried club management for several weeks. *The Sporting News* reported in late July that Sockalexis got into a serious altercation in a Chicago bar about ten days or so before his injury on the July 4 weekend. "[Sockalexis] tried to clean up a saloon," reported the magazine. "A hanger-on at the place had Socks by the neck with one hand and a big cheese knife in the other when the police interfered."[16]

The *Plain Dealer* printed the following summary of the problem on July 22, after the third game of the Cleveland-Baltimore series was canceled by rain:

> It is no longer a secret that the local management can no longer control Sockalexis, and when that management once loses control of a player it is likely to be "all off" between said management and said player. This is an unfortunate fact for the team and also for Sockalexis. When the Indian came here he was ambitious and his head was level. He was courted by a pretty lively crowd and then the troubles began. Discipline had no effect. When a player begins to realize that he is the whole thing nothing can stop him.
>
> Manager Tebeau still has hopes that the great Indian will come to his senses, and it is to be hoped that he will. He is likely to see that his popularity depends upon his ability as a player, and will not last after that ability is gone. If Sockalexis takes proper care of himself, his baseball career is bound to be a most brilliant one. If not, he will soon find that he was a nine-days wonder and that the nine days have passed. It will not take many days to decide the fate of Cleveland's great find.[17]

The team received some good news on July 9, when Judge Walter C. Ong of the Common Pleas Court handed Robison and his Spiders a major victory. The judge reversed Powell's conviction and declared the state Sunday law unconstitutional, clearing the way for the Spiders to play on Sundays pending an appeal to a higher court. Robison immediately announced that the Spiders would play Washington at League Park the next Sunday, three days hence. "It means," wrote Elmer Bates, "that 20,000 workingmen, heretofore deprived of an opportunity of seeing a National League game, can with perfect assurance of two hours of rare enjoyment go out to League Park on Sunday afternoon without fear of police interfering in their effort to enjoy personal liberty."[18]

The *Plain Dealer* said the same thing in fewer words. As a headline in the next day's edition of the paper stated, "Base Ball Playing Not a Crime."

The ruling by Judge Ong was quickly appealed by the anti–Sunday ball forces, but Robison was now free to place several Sunday games on the schedule. On July 11, rain threatened to wash out the next Sunday game and kept the crowd to only 1,500, but Jack Powell beat the Senators 15–4 for his fourth win of the season. Seven days later, 8,000 people crammed into League Park to see Powell win again, this time against

Brooklyn, and on July 25 15,000 people, the largest crowd in League Park history up to that time, saw the Indians lose to the Orioles in extra innings, with Cy Young taking the loss in relief.

More Sunday games might have lifted the Indians out of the attendance doldrums, but on August 6 Judge Thomas K. Dissette reversed the Common Pleas Court decision, reaffirming the constitutionality of the state ban on Sunday ball. Robison reserved the right to appeal and scheduled several more Sunday games at home, but the fans had lost their enthusiasm with the team stuck in fifth position and the Sockalexis-inspired excitement long dissipated. On Sunday, August 15 only 2,500 turned out to see the Indians defeat the hapless Browns in a sloppily-played game. By contrast, more than 4,000 people saw an exhibition game in Toronto the following week, in which Tebeau's men lost to the local Eastern League team.

By early August the Indians had fallen more than 15 games behind league-leading Boston, mostly due to a disastrous 2–9 mark on a road trip to Louisville and Chicago. Tebeau's men were out of the race, a fact that had to discourage even the most hopeful Clevelander. Jesse Burkett, crabby as ever, showed his disgust with the whole situation by playing the outfield with less than his usual enthusiasm. "I know that Jesse Burkett loafed on a hit to left field the other day," lamented Tebeau, "but what are you going to do? It's almost a clock that we can finish no higher than fifth notch, and we are certain to remain in that position."[19]

Burkett was even more irascible than usual during the last half of the season. On August 4 in Louisville, he started arguing with umpire Wolf during the first game of a doubleheader. The umpire tossed Burkett out of the game, and when Tebeau refused to send up a pinch-hitter for the Crab, Wolf threatened to forfeit the game to the Colonels. "Go ahead," replied Patsy. "We don't need it." The Indians were out of the race anyway. Wolf called a forfeit, much to the disgust of the Louisville fans, and when Burkett argued with the umpire again in the ninth inning of the second game, Wolf enlisted two policemen to remove the defending batting champion from the field of play. It hardly mattered, for as one paper reported, "the Indians played as if they did not care whether school kept or not in the second game,"[20] and the Colonels won that game as well.

This incident pointed to a much larger problem with the national game during the 1890s. Tebeau and the Indians accepted no responsibility for completing a game on the road; since they considered it a lost cause anyway, they had no problem with forfeiting the game and depriving the Louisville fans of a complete 9-inning contest. The National League saw eight forfeited games in 1897, three of which involved Cleveland, and 43 during the decade; by contrast, there has been only one forfeited game in either major league since 1979 (as of the end of the 2015 season).

The Indians forfeited another game in Washington on September 8. During the second game of a doubleheader, Tebeau ordered the slumping Ed McKean to get hit by a pitch. McKean duly leaned into a slow curveball from rookie right-hander Roger Bresnahan and took a blow to the shoulder. The big shortstop trotted down to first, but umpire William Carpenter ordered him back to bat. The arbiter had overheard Tebeau's instructions to McKean. Tebeau argued for a while, then pulled his team off the field. With Childs, O'Connor, McAleer, and others sidelined by injury, the Cleveland manager not only assigned star pitcher Cy Young to play first base, but batted him in the cleanup spot too. It looked as if the Indians had given up on the season.

Amazingly, the club then mounted a 12-game winning streak, though the sudden turnaround came too late to save the season. One highlight of the season's final weeks was Cy Young's no-hitter, the first of his career, against the Reds in Cincinnati on September 18. Young breezed through the Cincinnati lineup, with the only hard-hit ball a shot to third in the sixth inning by Bug Holliday. It went past Bobby Wallace, and though the official scorer originally called the play a hit, Wallace convinced the official that he should have had it. The ruling was changed to an error, keeping Young's gem intact. "It was my error, and it was an inexcusable one," said Wallace after the game. "I was playing in the right spot for Bug, and the ball came straight at me, but in some way got through me. I should feel guilty if that was charged up against 'Cy' as a hit after his wonderful work."

"It looked like a hit off me more than it did an error for Bobby," remarked Young later, "but [Wallace] sent a note to the scorer's box begging to be given an error in order to allow me a no-hit game.... I've never forgiven him for that, but it was only one instance of the good fellowship prevailing in the old Cleveland club."[21] The no-hitter was the first in the National League in more than four years.

However, the "good fellowship" that Young remembered was mostly absent at the close of the 1897 campaign. It had started with so much promise with the arrival of Sockalexis, the ascent to stardom of Bobby Wallace, and the possible resolution of the Sunday ball controversy, but ended in gloom and despair. At season's end, Ed McKean and Jesse Burkett demanded to be traded, the oft-injured Jimmy McAleer was mulling retirement, Sockalexis was lost to drink, and Patsy Tebeau's usual fire and energy were noticeably absent. Cleveland's home attendance of 153,000 was last in the league, and National League baseball's survival in the city had never looked more doubtful.

Second baseman Cupid Childs, who was not on speaking terms with his keystone partner Ed McKean, summed up the feelings of many of the Cleveland players. "We are no longer the Spiders, nor are we the Indians," grumbled the second baseman. "We are the Quitters, and we've got it up to here."[22]

⫸ 12 ⫷

The End of an Era

It is published in Boston that when the Cleveland club appears there women will not attend. They have learned by experience that if they go to see Tebeau and his followers their ears will be outraged with the grossest indecencies and their eyes afflicted with scenes of low barroom ruffianism.

—*Chicago Tribune*, 1896[1]

Perhaps Patsy Tebeau did not realize that baseball was changing. As a new century approached, there were many indications that the violent, undisciplined, and frankly dangerous game of the 1880s and the 1890s would soon become a thing of the past.

One harbinger of change took place in the waning days of the 1897 pennant race. The Boston Beaneaters and Baltimore Orioles had battled all season and met in Baltimore for a three-game weekend series in late September with the Bostons half a game in the lead. They split the first two games in front of large, enthusiastic, but well-behaved crowds, and on Monday, September 27 more than 25,000 people, the largest crowd in Baltimore history to that time, jammed into Union Park. They saw a 19–10 Boston victory in a game played cleanly on both sides. After the contest, the disappointed Oriole fans showed their sportsmanship, as "ten thousand people congratulated the visitors with handshakes and cheers and told them what good fellows and fine players they were," according to one report.[2] The Baltimore correspondent to *The Sporting News* agreed. "The conduct of the players was admirable and the cordial reception of the Boston rooters and the popular ovation tendered to the victors were in keeping with true Maryland hospitality," he wrote. "They defeated us and we feted them. The strain on the players throughout the series was something fearful and their splendid conduct under such exciting surroundings was all the more commendable."[3]

Historian Bill James called the scene "a pleasant picture, very different from the one we usually see of the period," but also opines that "the size of the crowd suggests that these were not the regular fans of the era, so much as some people who got caught up in passing excitement."[4] Or, perhaps the prospect of a well-played, riot-free game brought those fans to the ballpark. Boston, often described as a "gentlemanly" team, went on to win the pennant and end Baltimore's reign at the top of the league. The Beaneaters won the 1898 flag as well, and the rowdy Orioles of McGraw, Hanlon, and the rest were finished.

Another casualty of the 1897 season was the "King of Kickers" himself, Cap Anson. The Chicago manager, after 19 years at the helm, had not changed a bit, still berating umpires in his foghorn voice and expecting the arbiters to bend to his will. Problem was, the Chicago club (called the Colts in the 1890s) had not seriously challenged for the pennant in years, falling farther down the standings as the decade wore on. Anson's strategies and tactics were outdated, and in early 1898 the Colts declined to renew his contract. Without Anson, the papers christened the team the Orphans, but in 1898 the club jumped to fourth place and set a new attendance record without him.

The Spiders, however, planned no major changes for the 1898 season. With a roster full of veterans and one of the highest payrolls in the league ($38,000, according to one report), perhaps Tebeau and Robison believed that this aging collection of stars might have one more shot at the long-desired pennant. Or, maybe Patsy Tebeau was too set in his ways to see that his brand of take-no-prisoners baseball was becoming not only outmoded, but unpopular as well. Though the Spiders-turned-Indians were still one of the circuit's leading gate attractions on the road, their home attendance was the worst in the National League in 1897, even behind such sad-sack clubs as Louisville and Washington.

Possibly at Tebeau's urging, the team held its 1898 spring training at Hot Springs, Arkansas. The previous year's spring practice at a Cleveland gymnasium may have saved Frank Robison a boatload of money, but the team was not ready to play when the season began. The 1897 club opened its campaign with five consecutive losses and never recovered, and the 1898 training trip down South was a belated admission that the previous spring training on the cheap was a mistake.

The National League club owners, in their never-ending search for profit, made three major decisions during the winter of 1897–98. First, they extended the season dramatically, from 132 games to 154. Of course, they needed no permission from the players to make such a move, even though player salaries—and the $2,400 salary cap per man—remained the same. They also dropped the Temple Cup after the 1897 post-season match between Baltimore and Boston was poorly attended, loosely played, and totally anticlimactic after the furious pennant race. The magnates returned the Cup to its donor, William Clay Temple, with their thanks. The other new feature of 1898 was a radical attempt to control poor behavior and verbal abuse on the field.

Despite the National League's coaching restrictions of 1897, conflicts between players and umpires were as rancorous as ever that season. One argument between Baltimore's "Dirty Jack" Doyle and umpire Tom Lynch resulted in an on-field fistfight between the two men, while Cleveland's Jesse Burkett caused several incidents with his audible explosions of foul language, which could be heard clearly by the fans. Obscene language, of which the Cleveland club was still one of the National League's most egregious offenders, drew increasing criticism from fans and sportswriters, so the league adopted a set of guidelines largely created by the powerful Cincinnati Reds owner, John T. Brush. Popularly called the "Brush Rules," this 21-point standard of conduct detailed a series of fines and other punishments for players who, for example, addressed an umpire in a "villainously filthy" manner. A three-man disciplinary panel would then hear an accused player's case and could, if it so chose, expel the offender from the National League with no right of appeal.[5]

The players grumbled, but Louis Sockalexis, of all people, had an answer for the Brush Rules. "I'll cuss the umpire in Penobscot," Sock told his teammates, as related in *The Sporting News.* "And if they call me I'll say that I was telling them they are right and that you fellows are dead wrong in kicking." Sockalexis also offered to teach his teammates Indian words like "hickehowgo" (robber) and "kanylanyee" (green lobster) to use on the umpires. Jesse Burkett, according to the papers, listened enthusiastically to the Indian's impromptu language lessons.[6] Nonetheless, Tebeau was concerned enough about the new behavioral rules to order his men to work on curbing their tongues on the field during spring practice.

The league also finally recognized that a single umpire was not enough to officiate a game, so the two-umpire system came into being. The Players League of 1890 has used two umpires per game, but the National League had done so only every now and then; in 1897, about 11 percent of contests featured two umpires. In 1898, though the magnates were always loathe to spend one nickel more than necessary on much of anything, the league expanded its umpiring staff and put two at a time on the field, one to call balls and strikes and one to rule on the bases.

The 1898 campaign faced one potentially damaging crisis that had nothing to do with player behavior. War fever gripped the nation, as sensational reports of atrocities committed by Spanish colonial rulers in Cuba, 90 miles from American shores, raised a public clamor for war with Spain. On April 6, Congress declared war against Spain, and war news pushed the start of the baseball season off the front pages and out of the minds of the American public. As the American war effort swung into gear, tens of thousands of young men, baseball's core audience, rushed to enlist.

Tebeau's men assembled in Cleveland in early March for the trip down south. Sockalexis claimed to have kept away from alcohol during the winter months, but he disappointed the team once again. He reported to Cleveland on time but missed the train to Hot Springs. On his first day in Cleveland, he fell off the wagon. "I did it again, Cap," said Louis to his manager when he finally arrived in Arkansas. "A crowd got hold of me and before I knew it they had loaded me. I had not taken a drop in so long that I did not know my capacity, and before I knew it they had me. I am through for good now. My friends in Cleveland are my worst enemies, I fear, even though they don't mean to be. After this I will defy anybody to get me started."[7]

Tebeau elected to believe him, at least for the moment, because the right field situation was still unsettled. "It's a pity [Sockalexis] doesn't keep straight," sighed Tebeau to the writers. "If I can keep him in line this year he will strengthen us to a great degree. However, it looks as though Blake would start the season covering right field."[8] However, as the *Plain Dealer* commented, "it is a known fact that the club will stand no more foolishness from Sockalexis. One more slip and he will be suspended, just as sure as there is a rule to provide for such suspension ... there are too many good outfielders to put the club in any seriously embarrassing position by the suspension of one, and the rest are all conscientious workers."[9] The writers were getting tired of his escapades too. "All this talk by Sockalexis would have more weight," suggested the *Plain Dealer*, "had not the Indian told about the same story before on several occasions."[10]

While the Cleveland ballclub (which many reporters now called the Spiders again with the downfall of Sockalexis) trained in Arkansas, Frank Robison battled on the home front. The Cleveland magnate had sold most of his streetcar interests several years before, but in early 1898 he angered the local labor unions when he added more seats to League Park. The contractor completed the job with non-union labor, and though Robison claimed that he had no say in the matter, the Cleveland union bosses thought otherwise. On April 21, the local Building Trades Council and the Knights of Labor declared a boycott of the team, a sanction that kept thousands of union men away from the ballpark in 1898. This was exactly the sort of development that the attendance-challenged club did not need at this time, and further imperiled the survival of National League baseball in Cleveland. At least the Spiders got off to a good start in 1898, opening the season with a 10-game road trip to the western cities and returning with a 6–4 record.

The home opener on April 29 was cold and chilly, and took place on the same day that Cleveland's Fifth Regiment shipped off to Cuba. The newly-enlisted soldiers paraded down Superior Street to Public Square that morning, with thousands of people cheering and waving goodbye to their husbands, sons, and sweethearts. After the speeches and official farewell, the soldiers marched to the Erie railway yards, where they boarded the trains that carried them off to war. Somehow a baseball game did not seem very important that day, because only about 2,000 filed into League Park to see Cy Young defeat the Browns with a three-hitter. The next afternoon, only 100 fans braved the cold to see the Spiders sweep the Browns in a doubleheader.

Jack O'Connor and Patsy Tebeau (author's collection).

The crowds were small, but Cleveland jumped into the pennant chase. The win in the home opener started a 10–2 run that boosted the Spiders into second place, and a seven-game winning streak at home in late May left Cleveland with a 23–9 record, only one game out of the lead. Nig Cuppy's arm was still sore, but Cy Young, Jack Powell, and Zeke Wilson made a formidable starting rotation. Bobby Wallace solidified the left side of the infield (and covered for Ed McKean's diminished range), while Lou Criger and Jack O'Connor teamed with Chief Zimmer for the strongest catching unit in the league. Perhaps the Spiders could indeed squeeze one more fine season out of their collection of aging stars.

Cleveland kept winning despite a rash of injuries and tragedies. Jesse Burkett's young daughter died suddenly in mid–April, so Sockalexis played left field during Burkett's absence. Louisville pitcher Chick Fraser beaned Bobby Wallace on May 7 and knocked him cold. Fortunately, Wallace's skull was not fractured, as had been feared, and he rejoined the lineup only four days later. Jack Powell was bedridden for two weeks with pneumonia, while Tebeau left the team for a few days when his wife Kate took ill. Somehow, the Spiders stayed near the top and promised to make a race of it.

Despite the two-umpire system and the Brush Rules, one incident in a game between Cleveland and Louisville on April 24 illustrated the rowdiness and lack of discipline still present in the National League at the time. In the third inning, Louisville's Honus Wagner slid hard into Bobby Wallace in a play at third base. Wagner snatched the ball from Wallace, heaved it into left field, and scored as the Spiders erupted in protest. The good news is that the two umpires on duty declared Wagner out for interference and took his run off the board. The bad news is that it took fifteen minutes of arguing to arrive at that decision, during which umpires Cy Swartwood and George Wood reversed themselves three times. In some ways, two umpires gave the players twice as many opportunities for mischief. The new rules also did not stop two Giants players, Bill "Scrappy" Joyce and Ed Doheny, from beating up umpire Pop Snyder after a game in New York.

While the Spiders performed on the field, Frank Robison suffered a defeat on April 19 when the Ohio Supreme Court upheld the state law banning Sunday baseball. Robison, noting that the Cincinnati Reds played ball on Sundays and drew huge crowds with no interference from the local authorities, threatened to force the issue again. He defiantly scheduled Sunday games for May 1 against the Browns and May 8 against the Pirates, daring the city officials to take action. The authorities promised to stop the contests, but another skirmish in the Sunday ball war was averted when both games were washed out by rain.

Jack Powell returned in late May from his illness, while Nig Cuppy pitched his first game of the season on May 23, beating the woeful Senators by a 4–3 score. When Ed McKean missed a few games, Tebeau took his place at shortstop and performed well, and when Cupid Childs took ill in June, Patsy filled in at second base. It seemed as if the Spiders used a different lineup every day, but the team held together in the early going.

Still, the Cleveland club was once again running last in the league in attendance, and the survival of National League baseball in the city was never
more in doubt. If attendance did not pick up soon, warned the Cleveland
owner, the Spiders would have no choice but to shift their home games
to other, better-attended cities. Or, since St. Louis was a great baseball
city with a bad team, perhaps Robison could simply buy the troubled
Browns and move the Spiders westward as a unit. During the summer of
1897 Robison had sounded out Browns owner Chris von der Ahe about
that very topic.

Robison's message was clear—the fans of Cleveland would lose the
Spiders if local support did not markedly improve. "I am not in the baseball
business for fun, nor for patriotism for my own city," said the owner in
the previous spring, "and I do not propose to have a few people in Cleveland run my team to my disadvantage when I can see good money in it
elsewhere."[11] Moving games to other cities was the first step. The magnate
figured that, since the Cleveland team was one of the league's best draws
on the road, he could make more money from the visitors' percentage of
the gate in other cities than from tiny hometown crowds. The extra income
would more than offset the added travel costs for his team.

Cleveland was not the only National League team in trouble. The
Orioles saw their fan support drop sharply after their three-year run at
the top of the league ended with a loss to Boston in 1897. Perhaps the Baltimore fans were bored with winning, or maybe the war drew attention
away from baseball. The Orioles drew 6,000 fans to their home opener in
April, and that was the biggest home crowd in Baltimore all year. The
perennial sad-sack teams in Louisville and Washington, too, teetered on
the edge of viability, and talk of contracting the National League from 12
teams to ten, or even eight, grew louder.

The Spiders, perhaps distracted by attendance woes and off-field controversies, went 12–12 in June and fell back to fourth place. Many
observers believed that the club could contend for the pennant with even
fair home support, but the tiny crowds and the ban on Sunday ball hin-
dered the team. Reds manager Buck Ewing, the former Spider, faulted the
Cleveland and Baltimore players for their low fan support. "I'm afraid,"
said Ewing, "[that] the foul tactics of the Orioles in the past have served
to kill Baltimore, just as Cleveland was killed by the kicking of the Indians."[12] Arthur Irwin, the Washington manager, blamed Tebeau himself.
"The grandstand on the Cleveland grounds is so near the diamond," said
Irwin, "that the acoustic properties are as perfect as the sound effects in
the Mormon Tabernacle.... When a string of blue chatter was ejected from

Tebeau's face, the spectators in the remotest corner of the stand could hear every syllable."[13]

Tebeau, among others, blamed the war. "During a close-score game," said Tebeau in July, "[the fans] sit in the bleachers reading war extras. Why, in one of our recent games on the home grounds, Burkett pushed three runs over the plate at once. The program boys and candy butchers gave him a genial hand, but every other pair of palms in the stand were engaged in holding war extras. The war certainly has contributed a dab of rust to the turnstile in Cleveland."[14] He could have added that Robison's union troubles in a heavily unionized town and his constant threats to move the team elsewhere played a large role in keeping the fans away from League Park.

The Spiders desperately needed Sunday ball to remain viable in Cleveland, so in June Robison considered his options. Cedar Point, a resort on Lake Erie near Sandusky, Ohio, was tempting but more than 50 miles west of Cleveland. A much closer alternative was another Lake Erie resort, Euclid Beach, an amusement park that had opened three years earlier in Collinwood, only nine miles from League Park. Collinwood is now a part of Cleveland, but in 1898 it was an independent, self-governing village. Cleveland's ministers and bar owners could complain all they wanted, reasoned Robison. They had little or no power in the suburbs. Robison built a temporary wooden ballpark with 8,000 seats in only two weeks, then announced plans to play the Pittsburgh Pirates there on Sunday, June 12.

Collinwood also had an active group of ministers and church officials who opposed Sunday ball. A Congregational pastor, the Reverend George R. Berry, and a Mr. Clarke of the YMCA proved themselves every bit as vehement as their Cleveland counterparts. The Reverend Berry thundered against Sunday baseball from his pulpit, while Clarke was quoted as saying that he didn't want "the discarded filth of Cleveland dumped upon the village."[15] Despite their furious opposition, more than 6,000 fans arrived at Euclid Beach by streetcar, by train, and even by steamboat, as the ferry line that serviced the park added a boat for the occasion.

Cleveland's Jack Powell and Pittsburgh's Jim Gardner warmed up under threatening skies. Neither side scored in the first, and in the second inning the rains came. The driving rain grew in intensity, but Robison was determined to complete five innings no matter how badly the field deteriorated. There was still no score in the fourth when a torrential downpour drove most of the fans to seek cover, as the temporary ballpark had none. Still, the teams played on despite the wet ball and muddy field. After Pittsburgh scored three times in the bottom of the fifth, umpire Pop Snyder (the long-ago Cleveland catcher) pronounced the game complete. Few fans remained, as nearly all of them had used their tickets—which also gave them admission to Euclid Beach—to find alternate entertainment.

Despite the downpour, the completed game represented a victory for the Sunday ball supporters, and Robison scheduled a game against the Pirates for Collinwood the following Sunday, June 19. He was also defiant enough to plaster Collinwood with posters announcing the upcoming contest. This act made the local ministers more determined than ever to stop the game.

Though the weather was better, only 3,000 fans showed up for the second Sunday game to see Zeke Wilson square off against Jim Gardner, the winner of the previous contest in Collinwood. Garner gave up only three hits, but walked nine batters, allowing the Spiders to keep the game close. The teams battled through seven innings tied at 3, but in the eighth Cleveland loaded the bases, and Gardner hit a batter to force in a run. After eight innings, the Spiders led by a score of 4 to 3.

There would not be a ninth. At the end of the eighth inning the Collinwood marshal stepped onto the field and placed the nine active Cleveland players under arrest. He carried warrants sworn out by the Reverend Berry, a determined soul who refused to accept defeat. The fight was not yet over, and though a complete game was played, nine Spiders headed to the local magistrate's office for arraignment. They were all released on $50 bond with a hearing set for the following Saturday.

The Sunday ball controversy, and the constant threat of arrest, took a toll on the Spiders. They lost three times to the Pirates before the victory on Sunday, then lost twice to visiting Brooklyn on Monday and Tuesday with only a few hundred fans in the stands. Two wins against the Dodgers followed, but the Giants came to League Park on Friday, June 24 and pummeled the Spiders 11 to 4. Friday's game marked the debut of Bert "Cowboy" Jones, a left-handed pitcher whom Frank Robison had purchased from Connie Mack's Milwaukee club of the Western League. Jones struggled, allowing six runs in the fourth and three more in the fifth before yielding the mound to George "Pugger" Kelb, another left-handed prospect from Fort Wayne of the Interstate League. Kelb drew his release the next day, but Jones remained. With Cuppy's arm still ailing, Jones would be given at least a few more chances.

The Cleveland owner scheduled a third Sunday game in Collinwood on June 26, this time against the Giants, and on Saturday the team received some encouraging news. A local justice of the peace, ruling in a special session for the nine players arrested the previous Sunday, imposed a fine of one dollar per man and let them go. Robison took this action to mean that the authorities in Collinwood saw little or no harm in staging games at Euclid Beach on Sundays; perhaps this end run around the Cleveland ministers had proved a success. Buoyed by the seeming victory, Tebeau's men defeated the Giants that afternoon, then looked forward to another large crowd in Collinwood the next day.

However, the Cleveland ministers were not merely satisfied to bar Sunday games in Cleveland. They offered their support to the anti–Sunday ball forces in Collinwood. Thus emboldened, the Reverend Berry threatened the Collinwood mayor, gleefully boasting to the local papers that had the mayor not stopped the spread of Sunday ball in Collinwood, "he would probably have been tarred and feathered." *Sporting Life*'s Elmer Bates, thoroughly disgusted by the ministers and their scorched-earth campaign, wrote that Berry "saw in the playing of a League game in Collinwood the whole kingdom of Heaven, tottering, although the amateur games, played on that day with barrels of beer as prizes, did not ruffle his feelings."[16]

More than 7,500 fans arrived in Collinwood on Sunday, but the mayor, hounded all Saturday night and Sunday morning by the Reverend Berry and his followers, caved in. When the Spiders arrived at the temporary ballpark, they saw 25 Collinwood police officers, all in uniform and ready to enforce the state ban on Sunday baseball. The mayor informed the Robisons that the players would all be arrested if even a single pitch was thrown, so the Spiders, Giants, and thousands of disappointed fans left the park. The Sunday ball fight was over, and the future of baseball in Cleveland was doubtful as a result. "It was a bitter disappointment to a big crowd," wrote Elmer Bates. "There were 17 car loads of enthusiasts here from towns in Indiana, and plans had been made to care for 10,000 people. What will be done next is an open question. It is safe to say, however, that Sunday games between League clubs cannot be played in or near Cleveland."[17]

This debacle was the last straw for Frank Robison. He began contacting other National League teams for permission to switch Cleveland's remaining home games to other cities. At first he announced that games against the Phillies, Giants, and Beaneaters would be moved; later, the Cleveland owner decided to move as many games as possible. In the end, the Spiders played only four games at League Park after July 9, and played 83 of their final 87 games on the road. The Cleveland Spiders were now, for all practical purposes, a traveling road team, and League Park stood idle while the Spiders roamed the country on an endless, exhausting road trip.

All the while, Louis Sockalexis remained the forgotten man on the Cleveland roster. He appeared to be abstaining from alcohol, but because Tebeau preferred to fill his center and right field slots with old standbys Jimmy McAleer and Harry Blake, Sock remained pinned to the bench except for the occasional pinch-hitting assignment. He performed poorly when he appeared in the lineup, most likely due to the lack of regular work. His loss of status was reflected in the Cleveland papers, which dropped the name "Indians" and started calling the team the Spiders again.

Sock got a chance to play in a July 4 doubleheader in Chicago when Harry Blake was called home by an illness in his family. The opportunity went poorly, as Sockalexis stroked only two hits, both singles, in nine trips to the plate. Even worse, the large holiday crowd singled out the Indian for abuse. They threw so many firecrackers at the Cleveland right fielder that Sock stood in a fog of blue smoke all afternoon. The Spiders lost three of four games in Chicago as Sockalexis produced only two hits in 17 times at bat. Later that week, Blake, despite his .245 batting average, reclaimed the right field job.

By mid–July the Robisons had completed arrangements to transfer almost all of the remaining games from Cleveland to other cities. The Spiders-turned-Indians were now called the Wanderers, the Exiles, and, because of the large number of Irish players on the Cleveland club, the Wandering Micks. In late July and early August the Cleveland club played 13 games in a row in Philadelphia—five against the Orioles, four against the Phillies, and four with the Senators. Though Philadelphia, by special agreement with the rest of the National League, charged only 25 cents per ticket instead of the 50-cent rate required in other cities, Cleveland's slice of the road receipts in Philly was still bigger than the home share at League Park, even with the mounting travel costs factored in. For a few weeks, the Spiders were Philadelphia's second home team.

Jimmy McAleer, the sure-handed center fielder, retired after the 1898 campaign (author's collection).

Patsy Tebeau tried his best to keep his charges happy and motivated, but the endless road trip took its toll on the Spiders. Living out of suitcases and seeing the same faces for weeks on end proved exhausting. "We haven't gotten a close call [from the umpires] in months," complained Jesse Burkett. "I never was as tired of a baseball season as I am of this one. Most of the time we have been without a home. Without morning practice, and with the umpires against you, what chance have you? I hope I'll never have to go through another season like this one."[18]

Perhaps the pressure was getting to the Cleveland manager. On July 21, the Spiders swept a doubleheader from the Orioles in Baltimore, but Patsy became so unnerved by a heckler in the grandstand that he fired his bat into the offender's general direction. No one was hurt, fortunately, but the Cleveland manager was arrested after the game and carted off to the nearest police station. Tebeau posted bond of $2.45 and left town with the team. The league took no action against him; apparently the Brush Rules carried sanctions against "villainously filthy language," but not against heaving a dangerous projectile into the stands.

When the Spiders slipped back into Cleveland on August 24 for a three-game set against the Giants, many Spider fans were not even aware that they were home until they saw the "Direct to Ball Park" signs on the street cars. The team had been gone for more than a month, going 12–12 on its extended road trip, After that, it was off to Rochester, New York, for three games against the Brooklyn Dodgers. A Sunday game in Wee-hawken, New Jersey, against the Giants drew 11,000 people, but the small crowds in Rochester did nothing for Frank Robison's bottom line.

The Spiders held fourth place, only five games out of the lead, at the end of August, but played .500 ball as Boston pulled away from the pack. By September 16 they were nine and a half games behind, and a subsequent seven-game skid knocked the Spiders out of the race for good. When the 1898 campaign reached its conclusion, the Spiders, exhausted from their never-ending road trip, stood in fifth position, 21 and a half games behind the pennant-winning Beaneaters. Late that season, a Louisville reporter came upon a gaggle of Spiders in an all-night poker game. When queried about it, one unidentified player grumbled, "If the man who owns us doesn't give a damn whether we win or lose, why should we?"[19]

The Cleveland players were well aware that the off-field turmoil had destroyed their chances for the pennant, though Tebeau refused to cast blame on ownership. "I prefer to say nothing about it," said Tebeau to Elmer Bates, Cleveland correspondent for *Sporting Life*, in November. "The transfers of games this year was made necessary in order to pay salaries. We have a $38,000 team, and it takes a bundle of greenbacks to pay us off every two weeks. The small crowds we were drawing in June would not furnish enough money to meet the pay-rolls, and Mr. Robison was simply compelled to resort to the transfer expedient."[20]

Other players were not so reticent. Said Jack O'Connor, "I am confident we would have been as good as one-two had we stayed at home. We were right along-side Boston when the transfer of games began, and stood a good chance of beating them out." He was seconded by Ed McKean.

> I am sorry it was found necessary to transfer games. Our chances for the pennant were fair when we left Cleveland and were improved by Cuppy's return to the box in almost as good form as of old. I don't say we would have won the flag, but I am confident we would have finished in second place, and if we had been up there we would have drawn at least 2500 people per game. That would have meant a good deal more money than was taken in out on the road.[21]

Cy Young agreed. "Late in June," said the pitcher, "when we were alongside Boston, I had great hopes that the long-coveted pennant would be ours this year. I still think we could have won it by playing all our home games at home, and I regret exceedingly that a situation should have arisen making it necessary to transfer our games."[22]

Bates concluded his article with a list of what the Robisons needed to do to put the fiasco of 1898 behind them and save baseball in Cleveland. Club ownership, wrote Bates, should:

1. Drop the divisive, damaging fight over Sunday ball.
2. Make peace with the powerful labor unions.
3. Assure the public that the club will stay in Cleveland permanently.

All these things were easier said than done, though in October the local unions proclaimed themselves satisfied with Robison's apologies and called off their boycott of the team. This news came too late to save the 1898 season, and off-the-field developments were already moving quickly. Rumors of an impending transfer of Cleveland's stars to St. Louis were in the air and becoming louder by the week. Editors and columnists floated the possibility of reducing the number of league teams from twelve to ten or even eight for the 1899 season; the candidates for contraction included Louisville, Washington, and Baltimore—all holdovers from the old American Association—and Cleveland.

◦ 13 ◦

The Disaster of 1899

"I know it to be a fact that there is no intention of dropping Cleveland from membership in the National League. My information is that the 12-club League will suffer no disruptions this year whatever may happen next. Cities of 375,000 population are not lying around loose. Base ball has been profitable in Cleveland in the past and will be profitable for years to come."

—Patsy Tebeau, March 1899[1]

As the 1899 baseball season approached, the National League faced serious problems with half of its 12 franchises.

Baltimore was highly successful on the field, winning three pennants in a row from 1894 to 1896 and finishing second the next two years, but their style of play had largely turned off their own fans. Perhaps, too, the people of Baltimore had become jaded by success; their 1898 opening-day attendance of a mere 6,000 was the highest of the season. Only 123,000 people paid their way into the Baltimore ballpark in 1898, less than half the number of the year before, and the Orioles, with a veteran, star-laden roster, had trouble meeting its high payroll.

Louisville boasted one of the two best young stars in baseball in Honus Wagner (Philadelphia's Napoleon Lajoie was the other), but the Colonels owned an unbroken record of failure since joining the National League. They had finished in last place three times, had never finished higher than ninth, and had never ended a season fewer than 33 games out of first place. Their attendance had dropped to a mere 109,000 in 1898; by comparison, the Chicago club had drawn a crowd of nearly 25,000 in a single afternoon that summer. It was becoming apparent that the Kentucky city could not adequately support a major league team.

New York, the nation's largest and most vibrant city, should have been the most prosperous franchise in the National League, but in 1894 a wealthy, well-connected politico named Andrew Freedman bought the club and made it his personal plaything. Freedman, a powerful figure in the national Democratic Party, was a vain and arrogant individual who fined his players for little or no reason, left his box to argue with umpires on the field, and once fired his manager and hired a friend of his, a Broadway actor, to direct the club. He had so mistreated his star pitcher and gate attraction, Amos Rusie, that Rusie sat out the entire 1896 season. The other owners knew that Rusie could have challenged the league's reserve clause, but Freedman refused to compromise. Eventually, at Frank Robison's suggestion, the other owners reached a settlement with the pitcher. The league paid Rusie his entire 1896 salary to keep the issue out of court.

In June of 1898 Freedman made headlines when he engaged Cap Anson, recently set free by the Chicago club, as his manager. Giants fans hoped that their team had finally made a change for the better, but Freedman grew impatient after a 9–13 start and fired Anson a few weeks later. Freedman, often called the worst owner in baseball history, kept his team in chaos as the Giants slid into irrelevance.

Washington was in even worse shape. The perennially talent-starved Senators had rallied to sixth place in 1897, only to see their turnstile count drop by more than 40 percent from the year before. They reverted to form in 1898, finishing in 11th place and barely topping the 100,000 mark in attendance. Their on-field product was hopeless, and team ownership made the problem worse by employing four different managers in 1898 alone. Washington, the nation's capital, had become a millstone on the league.

If Washington was a baseball disaster area, then St. Louis was a Superfund site. Owner and "Boss President" Chris van der Ahe had turned the Missouri city, with the fourth-largest population in the country and an unrivaled passion for baseball, into a national joke. Like Louisville, the Browns had never finished higher them ninth in the National League. They had claimed 11th or 12th place in each of the preceding four years, ending the 1898 season 63 and a half games behind the leaders. A disastrous stadium fire in early 1898 (the owner had neglected to buy sufficient fire insurance) and a costly divorce put von der Ahe on the edge of bankruptcy. He tried to sell the team, but his many outstanding debts made a sale impossible. The survival of the St. Louis franchise, which should have been one of the strongest in the league, remained a question mark as the new season approached.

Von der Ahe caused most of his own problems. He had once been a sharp, clever businessman, but success and fame had changed him for the worse. As his baseball team sank in the standings, the beer baron indulged in extramarital affairs, endured an embarrassingly public divorce (one wit said that von der Ahe had been released—by his wife), and "handled $1000 bills as if they were peanuts to feed to monkeys," according to one report. Surrounded by a "numerous army of flatters and hangers-on,"[2] von der Ahe kept firing managers and hiring new ones, and on two occasions took the reins himself despite his nearly total lack of baseball knowledge. He even erected a statue of himself outside his ballpark. With each passing year, von der Ahe acted less like a baseball magnate and more like the dictator of a crumbling Third World country.

Then, there was Cleveland. The ban on Sunday ball hurt the franchise, but the Boston, New York, and Philadelphia clubs labored under the same handicap. The Spiders suffered from many self-inflicted wounds. Tebeau's rowdy style of play proved increasingly unpopular, while Robison's constant battles with the Cleveland ministers and the local labor unions had drained the team of support. The Spiders could not even finish their home schedule in 1898. Though the Spiders represented the sixth-most populous city in the United States, the team ranked dead last in league attendance in both 1897 and 1898.

In October of 1898, Robison and the unions forged a truce in which the Cleveland magnate promised to use only approved union labor on future building projects. However, it was too little and too late to save National League baseball in Cleveland. Robison angered the fans when he moved most of the team's games out of town during the last half of 1898, and the relationship between team and city was damaged beyond repair. Besides, Frank Robison's gaze had turned westward, where Chris von der Ahe was about to lose control of the St. Louis Browns. It should have been no surprise that Robison, in February of 1899, ventured to the Mound City to make a deal to bring his Spiders, as a unit, to Missouri and abandon Cleveland.

While Robison dickered with St. Louis interests, Patsy Tebeau stoutly denied that the Spiders would move. Either he was sincere in his belief that he and his men would represent Cleveland in 1899, or he had been counseled by Robison to feign ignorance about the impending deal. In any case, Patsy assured his charges that they would play the upcoming season in League Park as usual. As late as March 14 Tebeau told a reporter, "The people can rest assured the Cleveland team will not only play in Cleveland, but it will be among the most formidable bidders for championship honors. I never had any doubt that the team would remain in Cleveland, notwithstanding all the reports that have been circulated concerning the removal of the club to St. Louis."[3]

"To prove to you that I am sincere," said Patsy to the correspondent from *Sporting Life*, "I have only to say that I have just ordered 20 new uniforms, and the word Cleveland will be printed across the breast of every one of the shirts. If we are switched to St. Louis all this work will have been wasted, I am going right ahead making plans to play right here, and I honestly believe that we wll."[4] Still, the idea of managing a strong, well-supported club in his home town must have been tempting for the veteran manager. He led his men to Hot Springs, Arkansas, for spring training in early March, conducting workouts and awaiting further developments.

Von der Ahe tried his best to fight off his many creditors, but his ruin was by now so complete that a court-appointed receiver took control of the Browns. In March, the court approved the sale of the club at a sheriff's auction, less than a month before the start of the 1899 season. A local merchant named Edward Becker, one of von der Ahe's main creditors, won the bidding, purchasing the franchise for $33,000. Several days later, Becker reached an agreement with Frank Robison, handing the Cleveland

The Spiders and the Browns together at spring training in Hot Springs, Arkansas, 1899. Top: McAllister, Heidrick, Young, Bristow, Burkett, Zimmer. Middle: Stenzel, McKean, Schreckengost, O'Connor, Tebeau, Childs, Wilson, Blake, Wallace. Bottom: Powell, Criger, Paschal, Long, Bates (author's collection).

owner 51 percent of the stock in the St. Louis club. Robison put up no money of his own; instead, he paid for his half-ownership of the Browns by moving the entire Cleveland team to St. Louis. By March 20 the news was out; Cy Young, Jesse Burkett, Ed McKean, Patsy Tebeau, and all the other Cleveland stars would wear St. Louis uniforms in 1899.

Frank Robison now owned two National League franchises, and the *Plain Dealer* wondered aloud what would happen when Cleveland and St. Louis played each other. "Of course there is bound to be a whole lot of suspicion," said the paper, "as long as two clubs are controlled by the same management, with one at the top and the other at the bottom."[5] But what would Robison do with Cleveland? Possible sales to Detroit, Buffalo, or Indianapolis interests never proceeded past the talking stage; neither did a proposal from Tom Loftus, the baseball entrepreneur who had managed the Spiders in 1889, their first season in the National League. Loftus was now in charge of the Western League team in Columbus, and designed new uniforms for his men with a large letter C on the shirt. C could stand for Cleveland as well as Columbus, and if given a chance, Loftus was ready to move his team into Cleveland if the Robisons abandoned it. That idea never went anywhere either.

Robison would have preferred to simply fold the Cleveland franchise, but the new season was ready to begin, and it was too late to contract any teams. Besides, an 11-team league would be difficult to schedule, especially at this late date, and no other club was willing to close up shop. So, Robison prepared to operate both the Browns and the Spiders in 1899. He put his brother Stanley, the mild-mannered bachelor, in charge of the Cleveland branch of the baseball operation. Stanley Robison's immediate task was to assemble a new team of Spiders from the leftovers of the Browns-Spiders merger. Most of those new Spiders were men who played for the

Stanley Robison, Frank's younger brother, took charge of the Cleveland Spiders in 1899 (Library of Congress).

1898 Browns, a team so wretched that it lost 111 of the 150 games it played. The rest of the roster would be filled with rookies, prospects, and aging former stars that no other team wanted.

Tommy Tucker was one of those former stars. He made a strong start in baseball, winning the Association batting title in 1889 for Baltimore with a .372 mark (still the single-season record for a switch-hitter). He was a solid first baseman for Boston's pennant winners of the early 1890s, but his attitude made him unpopular with his teammates and manager Frank Selee. Called "Foghorn," or "Tommy Talker," Tucker did not know when to shut up. His profane tirades at umpires and opponents were excused as "enthusiastic coaching" by some of the local writers but irritated Selee, who valued a professional demeanor on the field. One day Tucker arrived at the park drunk and berated Selee so vehemently that the manager had him removed from the clubhouse by the police. Opponents hated him for his fielding style, which included a pickoff play in which he would fall on top of the runner and keep him from the bag. Not surprisingly, he led the league five times in being hit by pitches.

Tucker hated the Orioles in general and John McGraw in particular, and in 1894 Tucker set off perhaps the most memorable on-field brawl in baseball history. He and McGraw fought, both teams joined in, the Boston fans rioted, and somehow the ballpark caught fire and burned to the ground, taking much of Boston's South End with it. They don't make bench-clearing brawls like that anymore.

Worst of all, Tucker stopped hitting. In 1893, when the pitching distance changed, he and Jake Virtue were two of the very few batters whose production dropped. Selee tried hard to trade Tucker, hoping for a decent player in return, but not until 1897 would the Senators take him off Boston's hands for a mere $800. The onetime star first baseman fell down the baseball ladder to the awful Brooklyn team, then to the even worse Browns in 1898. St. Louis had no use for him in 1899, so they sent him to the Spiders, the only team that would have him.

In center field was another veteran near the end of the line, but one with a better reputation than Tommy Tucker. This was Tommy Dowd, a 30-year-old former college star at Brown University who debuted with Boston's pennant-winning Association team in 1891. That club was the only good one that Tommy Dowd would ever play for. He spent most of the 1890s with the worst teams in the National League, bouncing from Washington to St. Louis, then to a short stint with a decent Philadelphia club before landing again with the woeful 1898 Browns. Dowd hoped to remain in St. Louis, but Patsy Tebeau preferred to keep Harry Blake instead, and Tommy was exiled to Cleveland. He was a solid but unspectacular player, a somewhat below-average hitter (though not as bad as Blake) and decent fielder. These attributes, mediocre as they were, made him one of the best players on the new Spider team.

The new Cleveland pitching staff, however, would have to improve substantially to reach mediocrity. "Wee Willie" Sudhoff, a righty who stood only five feet and seven inches tall, posted an 11–27 record and walked more men than he struck out for St. Louis in 1898. Incredibly, he was the best of the rejects from St. Louis, along with "Coldwater Jim" Hughey and Wilfred "Kid" Carsey. Hughey, who came from Coldwater, Michigan, was a right-hander who went 7–24 for the Browns, while Carsey, a onetime 20-game winner on his way down, compiled a 2–12 log. These three less-than-stellar performers were expected to carry the pitching load for Stanley Robison's team.

Sudhoff was a native of St. Louis, but wrote his own ticket out of town. The Robisons offered him $2,100 to pitch in the Mound City, but Sudhoff demanded $300 more, a sum that would put his salary at the National League maximum. Instead, Frank Robison banished him to Cleveland. This move not only saved the owner some money, but demonstrated to the rest of the players what could happen to them if they complained about the size of their paychecks.

To fill out the pitching staff, the Spiders signed Bill Hill, Jack Stivetts, and, in early May, Charlie Knepper. "Still Bill" Hill, a Tennessean from moonshining country, had pitched fairly well for Cincinnati in 1898, but the Reds could not abide his off-field behavior, which featured a string of drunken antics and bar fights. Hill, a left-hander, wired the Robisons that he was in no shape to attend spring training, but traveled to camp anyway. He showed up about 20 pounds overweight. Knepper, a right-handed curveball specialist, was 28 and had yet to reach the major league, but a 20-win season at Youngstown in 1898 won him a spot on the Spiders. Stivetts, another righty, had been a star, winning 35 games for Boston in 1892. He also was a fine hitter, the best-hitting pitcher of his era, and played the outfield for the Beaneaters as his arm lost its magic. The Spiders hoped Stivetts could regain his pitching form; if not, perhaps he could give the Cleveland outfield a much-needed boost.

At least the new Cleveland ballclub would have one familiar face. Chief Zimmer, the 39-year-old catcher, had business interests in Ohio and was not interested in moving to St. Louis. With Jack O'Connor and the promising youngster Lou Criger handling the catching duties for Tebeau, the Robisons granted Zimmer's wish to stay in Cleveland. It remained to be seen how Zimmer would get along with his new teammate Tommy Tucker, the man who broke the Chief's collarbone six years earlier. Ed McKean was similarly reluctant to travel westward, as he and a partner had recently opened a tavern, called the Short Stop Inn, at Seneca and St. Clair streets in downtown Cleveland. McKean did not want to leave Ohio, and only signed his contract for 1899 in early March after he was assured by Tebeau that the Spiders would stay put. One wonders why the Robisons did not hire the fading, but still popular, shortstop as the Spiders' playing manager. However, Patsy Tebeau, loyal as ever to his veterans, wanted McKean at short in St. Louis, so McKean joined the rest of his longtime teammates in the Mound City.

To manage what amounted to an expansion team, the Robisons looked at several candidates. Tim Hurst, the volcanic umpire, had directed the Browns in 1898, but his one-year foray into the dugout was a disaster for all concerned. The Browns finished last, and the players hated Hurst so much that they even talked among themselves about putting poison in his coffee, if newspaper reports can be believed. Hurst was not a candidate for the Cleveland job, but Bill "Scrappy" Joyce, former skipper of the Senators and Giants and a childhood friend of Tebeau's, was. Joyce, however, wanted too much money, and Mike Griffin, the former Brooklyn field captain whom Frank Robison had recently signed, wanted nothing to do with the Cleveland situation. Besides, with Jimmy McAleer officially retired from active play, Griffin was needed in the St. Louis outfield. McAleer would have been a good choice, but the Robisons no doubt wanted a playing manager to save money on salaries. In the end, the Robisons selected a 33-year-old infielder named Lafayette Napoleon Cross, known as Lave, to the post.

Lave Cross, whose real name was Vratislav Kriz, was one of the first major league players of Eastern European descent. He had begun his career in Louisville as a catcher in 1887, and spent seven years at third base for the Phillies before his trade to St. Louis in 1898. Cross was a dependable, well-respected, but unspectacular performer (writer Ernest Lanigan once called him "the hard-working, but utterly useless Lave Cross") who had been displaced from his third base position by Bobby Wallace. Accompanying Cross to Cleveland was second baseman Joe Quinn, a 34-year-old veteran who lost his job to Cupid Childs. The presence of Cross and Quinn would, at least, offer the new Spiders a small touch of respectability.

While other National League teams made spring training trips to Hot Springs, New Orleans, or other warm places, the Robisons rented a high school gymnasium in Terre Haute, Indiana, for the Cleveland players.

Terre Haute was cold and overcast, leading the *Cleveland Press* to label the eight players who showed up on the first day of training as "a handful of half-frozen has-beens from an alleged training camp at Terre Haute."[6] The office staffs of other teams busied themselves with publicity, but the Robisons did not even bother to take a team picture or print schedules. With Stanley Robison in charge, austerity was the rule of the day, and the local papers started calling the team the Forsakens and the Misfits. The Robisons did not even bother to buy new uniforms for the 1899 Spiders. Their flannels were the same uniforms worn by the 1898 Browns, and the players could clearly see the outline of "ST. LOUIS" in stitching marks under the "CLEVELAND" letters on their uniform shirts.

While the Spiders shivered in Terre Haute, Tebeau and the St. Louis squad practiced in Hot Springs. Expectations were high for the coming season, and because all involved wished to put as much distance as possible between the horrid Browns and the current club, the papers cast about for a new team nickname. Before long the papers were calling the new St. Louis nine the "Perfectos," borrowed from a popular and expensive cigar. Many newspapers picked the Perfectos to bring the Mound City its first National League pennant.

However, their main competition for the flag would come not only from Boston's defending champions, but from a team that had finished in 10th place in 1898. Brooklyn, like St. Louis, was a great baseball town with a bad team, and owners Charles Ebbets and Frederick Abell decided to follow Frank Robison's script. Abell and Ebbets strengthened their club by purchasing the Baltimore Orioles and shifting most of that team's stars to Brooklyn. Oriole manager Ned Hanlon and many of his key players, including Willie Keeler, Joe Kelley, and Hugh Jennings, moved to Brooklyn and created an instant contender. The papers began calling the newly star-laden club the "Superbas," after a popular vaudeville act. The only key Orioles who refused to go to Brooklyn were John McGraw and Wilbert Robinson, who owned business interests in Baltimore. Those two players were left to anchor the decimated Orioles, with the 26-year-old McGraw as manager and Robinson as his chief assistant.

These machinations, which the papers called "syndicate baseball," left a bad taste in everyone's mouths. Hanlon now owned pieces of Brooklyn and Baltimore and served as president of the Orioles and manager of the Superbas simultaneously. The Robisons also owned and operated two teams and had no qualms about moving players from one city to another as needed. The weakened teams in Cleveland and Baltimore were expected to serve as farm clubs for their more powerful partners.

Fittingly, the 1899 Cleveland Spiders opened the season in St. Louis against Patsy Tebeau's newly-named Perfectos. Every member of the St. Louis starting lineup was a Cleveland transplant, while all but one of the Cleveland nine played for the unlamented Browns the year before; indeed, the contest was a virtual matchup between the 1898 Browns (representing Cleveland) and the 1898 Spiders (representing St. Louis). Cy Young, in his first start for St. Louis, breezed through the Cleveland lineup, allowing only six hits in a 10–1 romp before 16,000 fans on a Saturday afternoon.

The outmanned Cleveland club made a game of it on Sunday, with 18,000 in the seats, but the Perfectos won again by a 6–5 count behind Jack Powell. The Spiders made the Perfectos look like world beaters, and with 34,000 people paying their way into the St. Louis ballpark (renamed Robison Field) in only two days, Frank and Stanley Robison no doubt congratulated themselves on their business acumen. The Spiders then traveled to Louisville, where they lost two games before gaining their first win of the season on April 22 in the first game of a Saturday doubleheader. The Colonels put the Spiders in their place in the second game, belting the Clevelanders by a 15–2 score. Lave Cross and his talent-poor team then lost two blowouts in Cincinnati. After eight games, the Spiders had already fallen six and a half games out of the league lead, and had given up ten or more runs in a game five times.

Cross, despite all evidence to the contrary, waxed optimistic to the press. The new Cleveland manager allowed that his team might not win many games in April, but "they are playing willing ball, and are bound to finish well up in the second division."[7] Almost everybody expected that the Robisons would wind up transferring games as they did in 1898, but George W. Muir, the Cleveland team's secretary, did

Lave Cross managed the 1899 Spiders for 38 games, winning only eight (author's collection).

his best to reassure the fans. "Say to the readers of *Sporting Life*," said Muir to Elmer Bates, "that every one of the 77 games scheduled for Cleveland this year will be played here regardless of the attendance. You may say to them, too, that it is our purpose to strengthen the new team from week to week in an effort to make it a first division possibility if not a probability."[8]

Jimmy McAleer wasn't fooled. "I left the diamond last fall for good, and nothing would induce me to return," he said. "I am sorry for the boys playing under the name of Cleveland. They had no practice, and cannot be expected to play winning ball. As I feel now I wouldn't play on that team for a million dollars a minute." The Cleveland players also knew the score. They indulged in some gallows humor when the 1–7 Spiders arrived at League Park on May 1 for their home opener. Cleveland pitcher "Still Bill" Hill remarked, "I am glad that I am not a catcher. I would have the satisfaction of not being shot in the back when I play the first game." Pitcher Willie Sudhoff was happy the streets around League Park were recently paved, wondering aloud "what we might have got if the streets were full of paving stones."[9]

Cleveland, with its ragtag roster and shoestring operation, was now the league's Siberia, but one man knew that the 1899 Spiders represented his last chance in baseball.

His name was Louis Sockalexis.

Sockalexis, who worked out on his own in Cleveland while the rest of the 1899 Spiders attended spring training in Terre Haute, Indiana, ran into local writer Elmer Bates one day in late April and waxed optimistic. "I expect to be back in the game for good within a week," said Sockalexis to Bates. "I have cut out the red stuff for good, and am feeling fine. With Zimmer and I back on the team, it will help out the boys who have been playing out of form." Sock also boasted to the *Plain Dealer*, "I will be in right field when the bell tinkles Friday, and if I feel as I do today, I'll knock the ball over to Lexington Avenue."[10]

Problem was, the Penobscot was not the Sockalexis of old. He weighed more than 200 pounds–"big as an alderman," said teammate Dick Harley—and his speed was a memory. As Chief Zimmer, the aged catcher, commented, "I can give him twenty yards and beat him in a hundred.... You would not know the big Indian if you saw him now."[11] He took a public pledge of abstinence once again, but the fans, reporters, and teammates had heard it all before. He officially joined the club on May 1, the date of Cleveland's home opener, a twin bill against the Louisville Colonels. Sock watched from the bench as the Spiders lost both games in front of only

500 fans. Cleveland split another doubleheader the next afternoon, as Louis struck out in a pinch-hitting assignment.

Lave Cross hoped that the big Indian would come to his senses and regain at least some of his stardom. Patsy Tebeau had given up on him, but Sockalexis had no negative history with Cross and could start with a clean slate. However, just to be safe, the manager left Sockalexis in Cleveland while the rest of the team traveled to Chicago for a weekend series. Cross did not want the 28-year-old outfielder to fall prey to the temptations of the big city.

Still, the signing of Sockalexis appeared to be a desperation move on Cross' part, as was a tryout he offered to the 40-year-old pitcher Tony Mullane. Mullane had not played in the National League since he walked off the 1894 edition of the Spiders in mid-season. Mullane failed the tryout, though it is hard to imagine how he could have done worse than the younger pitchers on the Cleveland roster.

The Chicago Colts, called the Orphans ever since their long-time manager, Cap Anson, left the team the year before, arrived in Cleveland on May 3 and beat the Spiders three times in a row by lopsided scores. Cleveland's decimated roster simply could not compete with the better National League teams, and even middle-of-the-pack clubs like the Orphans found no difficulty in walloping the Spiders. Rumor had it that, despite the string of blowout losses and the promise of many more to come, Stanley Robison's extreme cost-cutting operation allowed the team to turn a small profit. It must have been a very small profit, as only 125 Cleveland fans bothered to attend the third game of the series against Chicago, an 11–2 defeat that left the Spiders at 3–12 for the season.

Sockalexis stayed in Cleveland while the Spiders ventured to Chicago for two games, the second of which ended in perhaps the most heartbreaking loss of the season. Pitcher Willie Sudhoff, who owned two of Cleveland's three wins, held the Orphans at bay for most of the game, and the Spiders entered the bottom of the ninth with a 7–5 lead, The Orphans put two men on base with one out, and then Chicago's Harry Wolverton blasted a home run over the scoreboard to win the game, 8 to 7. After this defeat, the Spiders returned to Cleveland to face the Perfectos in a four-game series beginning on Tuesday, May 9. For the first time, Patsy Tebeau, Cy Young, Ed McKean, and all the other ex-Spiders would return to League Park as the visiting team.

More than 1,500 curious fans turned out to see their longtime favorites. It was a rematch between Cy Young of St. Louis and Cleveland's Jack Stivetts, who had opposed each other in that memorable 11-inning post-season contest in October of 1892. The game was also notable as the first start of the season for Louis Sockalexis, who manned right field for the Spiders. The Clevelanders kept it close for a while, but Stivetts ran out of gas in the late innings as Young breezed to an 8–1 win. Apparently the fans saw all they wanted to see, as only 300 people attended the next game on Wednesday, a 12–2 Spider loss, and 150 turned out to see another defeat on Thursday by an 8–6 score. On Friday, the Spiders and Perfectos put on perhaps the best game of the year, with both teams playing errorless ball and making fine fielding plays. The game ended in the tenth inning when Ed McKean, the longtime local fan favorite, pounded a walk-off homer off Kid Carsey to win the game for St. Louis.

The Thursday game was the last hurrah for Sockalexis. He belted four singles and a double, showing a glimpse of the immense talent that had captivated the city two short years before. However, Sock's bad fielding and poor baserunning largely negated his work with the bat. He dropped two easy fly balls in the outfield and got himself thrown out at the plate on a double steal. Sock appeared to be daydreaming most of the time in the field, letting several fly balls drop for hits because he did not notice them coming his way. As the *Plain Dealer* acidly commented, "A wooden Indian might get through the season without an error, and so might some of the Cleveland players if they continue to keep away from the ball."[12]

A two-game series in Pittsburgh not only brought the woeful Spiders two more losses, but also spelled the end for Louis Sockalexis. Sock, the starting right fielder in the first game against the Pirates, went hitless and humiliated himself in the field. Twice he fielded bouncing balls cleanly, but fell over with a thud as he straightened up to throw. He was drunk on the field again. Cross, like Tebeau before him, had seen enough of the Penobscot. Two days later, after the Cleveland police arrested Sock in a disturbance at a downtown theater, the Spiders released him. The team had lost all seven games it played with the former star in the lineup.

Incredibly, the Spiders won four of their next six games, one each against the Phillies, Colonels, Senators, and Orioles, but the team soon reverted to its losing ways. Another skein of losses demonstrated to all that the Cleveland situation was utterly hopeless, so Stanley Robison, in a cost-cutting move, released the popular catcher Chief Zimmer, who was leading the team in batting at the time. With Zimmer's departure, the Spiders boasted exactly two solid National League players in Lave Cross and Joe Quinn. Pitcher "Coldwater Jim" Hughey, the apparent ace of the staff, was well on his way to a 30-loss season, while he and the other starters gave up run totals in the double digits almost daily.

It appeared that the opposing National League teams tried extra hard against the Spiders lest they be embarrassed by losing to this collection of nobodies and has-beens. On July 17 the Orioles, managed by John McGraw, lost to the Spiders in the first game of a doubleheader. The enraged McGraw fined and suspended his starting pitcher, Jerry Nops, whom he suspected of being hung over on the mound. McGraw and the Orioles took out their frustrations in the second game, walloping the Spiders by a score of 21 to 6. The Spiders were a national joke, and Elmer Bates sarcastically offered a list of reasons why one would follow such a terrible team:

- There is everything to hope for and nothing to fear.
- Defeats do not disturb one's sleep.
- An occasional victory is a surprise and a delight.
- There is no danger of any club passing you.
- You are not asked 50 times a day, "What was the score?" People take it for granted that you lost.[13]

In the meantime, Patsy Tebeau and his Perfectos struggled mightily in St. Louis. Ed McKean, a 13-year veteran, could no longer cover much ground on the infield, and his bat now only occasionally produced anything but a single. McKean had hit the end of the line, but Tebeau, ever loyal to his veterans, kept the fading shortstop in the lineup. Bobby Wallace sparkled at third, but the other two infielders—Childs and Tebeau—were on the downside of their careers. Still, Tebeau soldiered on with his aged infield intact as the Perfectos, after leading the league briefly in April, fell to sixth place by late July.

The Cleveland club, with all hopes for the season long dashed, did some more salary cutting in June. Out went Jack Stivetts, the onetime good-hitting pitching star who by this time could no longer pitch (0–4 for the Spiders) or hit (a .205 batting average). Stivetts was only 31 years old, but his major league career was over. Still Bill Hill followed Stivetts out the door, only to be snapped up by the Orioles, who decided that the 24-year-old lefty might still have a future. He pitched no better for Baltimore, and his 1899 season was, as for so many Spiders, his last in the majors.

The Spiders suffered two losses on June 5 in Brooklyn. First, they dropped their fifth straight game, losing to the Superbas by a 14–2 score. Jim Hughey gave up 19 hits while the Spiders stroked only four of their own, all singles. It was their fifth blowout loss in a row, and the fifth straight game in which the Spiders gave up 11 or more runs. After the game, the team absorbed an even more devastating blow when Patsy Tebeau, or perhaps Frank Robison, make the obvious move. The Perfectos recalled Lave Cross from his purgatory at Cleveland, installing him as the new St. Louis third baseman and shifting the rising star Bobby Wallace to shortstop. Ed McKean took a seat on the bench and made a few pinch-hitting appearances during June and July, but on July 27 he turned down a transfer to the Spiders and announced his retirement instead.

Willie Sudhoff, who led the Cleveland pitching staff with three wins (against eight losses) accompanied Cross to St. Louis. Apparently Frank Robison was satisfied that Sudhoff had been punished enough for his salary dispute in the spring. The Spiders received a young catcher named Ossee Schreckengost and a 23-year-old pitcher named Creed Napoleon Bates, but the players were not terribly important. Cross, who led the Spiders to only eight wins in 38 games at the helm, and Sudhoff drew larger salaries than two rookies, so the shift further drove down the Cleveland payroll.

The Robisons appointed Joe Quinn, the Cleveland second baseman, as the new manager of the Spiders. Quinn, a respected 16-year veteran, was the first major leaguer born in Australia. His parents emigrated from Ireland but bypassed North America, settling Down Under where Joe was born in 1864. Eventually, the Quinns tired of Australia and relocated to Dubuque, Iowa, a baseball-mad town that had hosted Charlie Comiskey and other future stars. Quinn, like Comiskey, wound up in St. Louis and started a career that took him to Boston, where he played for two championship teams, then back to the Mound City, where he managed the woeful Browns for part of one season. All the while, Quinn built a reputation for honesty and fair play, and in 1893 *The Sporting News* named him the most popular ballplayer in America.

Quinn would have preferred to stay in his adopted hometown of St. Louis in 1899, but Patsy Tebeau gave preference to his Cleveland mates. Besides, Quinn, a non-drinking, soft-spoken gentleman, was not Patsy's type of player, and having a former manager on the roster might prove awkward. With Ed McKean at short and Cupid Childs at second, there was no place in St. Louis for either Quinn or Lave Cross, both of whom were shuttled off to Cleveland to give the ragtag Spiders some thin veneer of respectability. When the aging McKean ran out of gas in June, Cross was summoned to St. Louis, leaving Quinn to manage the Cleveland mess as best he could.

Incredibly, Quinn worked in St. Louis as an undertaker during the winter months in a funeral home founded by his father-in-law. This led to any number of jests at the Spiders' expense, as an undertaker would be a fitting field boss for a team as lifeless as Cleveland.

Creed Bates, who sometimes shows up in reference books as "Frank," was a right-hander from Tennessee who had shown some promise in a trial with Cleveland the year before. He won two of his four late-season starts for the 1898, and pitched well enough for the Robisons to keep him in St. Louis at the start of the 1899 season. But after two appearances for the Perfectos, Bates was sent back to Cleveland with the rest of the rejects. Whatever potential he may have possessed soon evaporated; as the *Cleveland Press* complained, Bates was "turning almost every game in which he participates into a howling farce."[14] In other words, he fit right in with the Spiders.

By late June, the Spiders were so desperate for pitching that they signed a crazy man.

Frederick (Crazy) Schmit was one of baseball's nuttiest people, variously described as a "colorful character" and a "vile drunk." Both assessments are probably true. Schmit was a 33-year-old left-hander who had pitched, with a notable lack of success, for several National League teams between 1890 and 1893. He had bounced around the minors and the semi-pro ranks since then, but because the Spiders needed a lefty starter, they signed him to see what he could do. They knew of his eccentricities, but the Cleveland club had nothing to lose by giving him a chance.

Schmit was Crazy, all right. He had angered one manager after another by treating curfew rules as optional, not mandatory. He spoke in a German accent, but only sometimes, and it was hard to tell which of the several voices he used was his real one. John McGraw, his manager in Baltimore, once saw Schmit standing on a soapbox outside the park after a game, hawking baseballs that he had stolen from the team for five dollars each. Despite his 5–17 career won-lost record, Schmit nonetheless considered himself a star and demanded to be treated as one. As he told one reporter,

> I am the most popular player on the circuit and the only man who knows how to coach as a science. If some of these managers knew something of the theatrical business they would wire on and advertise I am to pitch a certain game. When it is known I am to pitch I have often brought enough into the box office in a single game to pay my whole salary for the season several times over. We played before 14,000 people in Chicago and of that number fully 5,000 came to see me.[15]

All in all, Crazy Schmit did not pitch badly in his debut, though he lost the game to the Giants by a 6–1 score. He allowed only five hits and lined out two singles of his own. Poor fielding did him in, and only one of the six runs he allowed was earned. His next start was more Schmit-like, a 14–0 drubbing at the hands of the Beaneaters in a game that lasted only six innings.

With the season lost and the home fans totally indifferent, the Robisons prepared the public for the move that virtually everyone had been expecting. They wanted to move the rest of Cleveland's games to other cities. Said Stanley Robison to the *Plain Dealer*, "I cannot keep running a club with a salary list of $30,000 for an attendance of 100 per day. And if I could, the other clubs would not stand it. I have been notified by several clubs that they will not return here, but I do not know what to do with the scheduled games."[16]

This time, the other National League teams played a major role in the decision. Many clubs now refused to play in Cleveland, where they could not meet their travel expenses from their share of the gate receipts. The Eastern clubs lost money whenever they traveled to Cleveland, and they were tired of it. Some of the clubs would simply have expelled the Spiders from the league and been done with them, though that proposal never got off the ground. In theory, the Spiders could have won games by forfeit if their opponents refused to show up. The situation could have become an even uglier mess than it already was, and transferring games out of Cleveland appeared to be the only practical solution.

There was another important factor at play. On June 10, 850 employees of the biggest local streetcar firm, the Cleveland Electric Railway Company, voted to strike in a dispute over wages and working conditions. Management responded by hiring strikebreakers, and within days the city was convulsed by rioting. A wild scene erupted on June 20, when 8,000 union supporters laid siege to the company's storage barns, threatening the lives of strikebreakers and destroying streetcars. In July, the Cleveland mayor brought in a local military unit, called Troop A, to control the violence, which flared intermittently throughout the summer. Downtown Cleveland was a dangerous place during the summer of 1899, and the violence made the Spiders even more eager to move their games to other cities.

In late June, the Robisons applied for permission to play the rest of the 1899 campaign on the road. League president Nick Young left the decision up to each opposing club, and all but two agreed. Boston and New York, however, did not. Boston had a four-game set against the Spiders in August as part of a Louisville to Cleveland to Chicago swing, and manager Frank Selee did not want to dash back to Boston in the middle of it. Likewise, the Giants did not want to reschedule an August trip from Pittsburgh to Cleveland to Louisville. Besides, the Beaneaters and Giants believed (wrongly, as it turned out) that their clubs would draw fans anywhere, even in Cleveland. When all was said and done, the Spiders were set to return to Cleveland for a seven-game homestand in late August. All the rest of their games would be played on the road.

With that, the once-proud Cleveland Spiders finally hit bottom, and the disaster of 1899 was complete.

⚙ **14** ⚙

The Bitter End

"Cleveland [was] the sorriest shell of a team ever seen in the major leagues. This was the team that won 20 and lost 134 games, the worst record ever made in the majors, good for a ghastly percentage of .130."
—Lee Allen, Hall of Fame historian, 1961[1]

While the miserable, dejected Spiders traveled the country, losing games in bunches, Patsy Tebeau had his own problems in St. Louis. Attendance in the Mound City was much greater than it had ever been in Cleveland, and the popularity of Sunday ball assured Frank Robison of a healthy profit. However, the Perfectos underperformed on the field, and a team that was expected to bring St. Louis its first National League pennant struggled to stay in the first division. By June 5, when Bobby Wallace took over at shortstop and pushed Ed McKean to the bench, the Perfectos had fallen to fourth place, and a 12–13 record in June dropped them to sixth by the July 4 holiday.

Many of Tebeau's old standbys were rapidly aging. Harry Blake's hitting fell off, Cupid Childs was fading at second base, and Tebeau himself batted only .246 in 1899. Still, Patsy cast the blame for his team's poor performance elsewhere. Though his own ancestry was partly German, Tebeau was given to complain publicly about "dumb Dutchmen" who were not as mentally quick as Irishmen. His attitude caused friction in the clubhouse and angered the many German-American fans who had supported baseball in St. Louis since the American Association pennant-winning days of the 1880s. In early July, Tebeau discharged the veteran outfielder Jake Stenzel, a holdover from the 1898 Browns who was popular with the German fans. "Why did you release Stenzel?" shouted a fan from the bleachers.

"I released him," replied Tebeau angrily, "because he couldn't think fast enough and was Dutch." The fans exploded in anger, and only a quick intercession by the park police kept the manager from being assaulted by a mob of irate German-Americans. "Tebeau is a great baseball general," said Baltimore's John McGraw to a reporter, "but his temper will get him in a peck of trouble if he doesn't apply a bridle to his untamed wrath."[2]

At least Patsy found a new way to get his old enemy McGraw booted from a game. In late June, when the Orioles played a four-game set in St. Louis, Tebeau sidled up to rookie umpire Al Mannassau before the first contest. "See here, old sport," said Tebeau, "that little chap at the bat is Muggsy McGraw. Perhaps you've heard of him. Now, if he makes any breaks at you, don't stand for it. Chuck him out of the game and your reputation as a game fellow will be made." Moments later, Mannassau ejected McGraw.[3]

Patsy remained as feisty as ever. In one game, a shoving match with McGraw grew out of control and incited the St. Louis fans to throw eggs and garbage at the Oriole players. One afternoon in Baltimore, Patsy cursed a heckler so viciously that the fan had the St. Louis manager arrested. Patsy posted bail, but the fan eventually dropped his complaint. In September, Tebeau assaulted umpire Arlie Latham, a former star player for the Browns, though he somehow avoided punishment for manhandling the arbiter. By this time, he had benched the fading Childs and Blake, and recalled Ossee Schreckengost from Cleveland to play first base. "I will probably never play again," he told a reporter. "Schreckengost will make a star first baseman and I will manage from the bench hereafter."[4] Patsy, at age 35, recognized that his playing days were over.

Schreckengost, a promising young catcher called Schreck in the box scores, had been sent to Cleveland when Lave Cross went to St. Louis, but performed so well for the Spiders that Tebeau brought him back. His departure, and Chief Zimmer's release, left Cleveland with only one catcher, Joe Sugden. To help Sugden, Lew McAllister took a few turns behind the plate. McAllister was normally an outfielder, but could also play the infield if needed, and he had pitched a few times for Cleveland in 1897 and 1898. He was a versatile player, if not a particularly talented one.

Creed Bates, the pitcher who came to Cleveland with Schreckengost in June, was a Spider to the core. He lost his first four games, won one (a stunning come-from-behind win against the defending champion Beaneaters at League Park), and lost his next 14 in a row. He was also a stubborn individual, resisting advice and trusting his mediocre curveball despite all evidence to the contrary. By August 12, when Bates lost an embarrassing 13–2 decision to the Giants in New York, the Cleveland papers were fed up with him. "Bates doesn't even seem to be a second-rater," complained the *Plain Dealer*. The *Press* was even more brutal: "The games which Bates pitches should be thrown out of the count. It can be conclusively shown that he is ineligible—from lack of ability and refusal to accept advice—to pitch in the same league with Young, Nichols, Griffith, et al."[5] This loss at the Polo Grounds was Cleveland's 83rd in 100 games, and wrote another chapter in what the *Plain Dealer* called "the daily downfall."

Harry Colliflower was a 30-year-old left-handed pitcher who was well known in the amateur and semipro ranks in and around Washington. His recent fine pitching for the Eastern Athletic Club came to the attention of the Spiders, so in a classic oh-what-the-hell move, the Cleveland club signed him to a one-game contract, issued him a uniform, and sent him out to face the Senators in the first game of a doubleheader in Washington on July 21. Some 2,500 fans—a large crowd for the hapless Senators—turned out to watch the local boy in his major league debut, and the papers reported that many in the stands were rooting for Colliflower and the Spiders.

Incredibly, Colliflower must have joined his new teammates on a particularly good day, or caught the Senators on a bad one, for he pitched the Spiders to a 5–3 victory. Colliflower allowed only six hits and belted two of his own, and for a moment it looked as if the Spiders had made a lucky find. The Cleveland management signed him for the rest of the season.

Colliflower's magic did not last. He made 11 more starts for Cleveland in 1899 and lost them all, leaving him with a 1–11 record and an earned run average of 8.10 at season's end. He could hit a little, batting .305 for the season (though with little power), so Joe Quinn played him at first base or the outfield when he wasn't being hammered on the mound. Colliflower—they called him the "Pitching Vegetable"—returned to the amateur ranks after his Spiders adventure and never played major league ball again.

At least the woeful Spiders managed to pull off a feat that Tebeau's club could never accomplish. On August 18, in a game at Brooklyn, the Spiders turned a triple play. The score was tied at 1 in the second inning with Bill Dahlen on first and Tom Daly on second for Brooklyn. The runners were moving when Doc Casey smashed a hot liner directly into Joe Quinn's glove at second; Quinn tossed the ball to Tommy Tucker at first to catch Dahlen before he could get back to the bag. Daly was nearly around third by this time, so Tucker returned the ball to shortstop Harry Lochhead, who stepped on the bag for the third out. Though Cleveland eventually lost the game by a 4–2 score, their tenth defeat in a row, this play stands as the only triple play executed by the Spiders in the National League.[6]

The high points, such as they were, were rare. The discouraged Spiders—dismissed as the Misfits, Exiles, and Wanderers in the press, both local and national—trudged from one city to another, losing game after game. The players insisted that they were trying to win; indeed, many of the Spiders did their best to cover their despair with a veneer of optimism, at least in public. As Tommy Dowd recalled afterward, "At least fifty times the past season we have gotten together at the hotel before going to the grounds and said, 'We'll win that game today or break our necks.' We would mean it too, but all the other teams would jump up at the start and skin us so bad that we'd come off the field with our heads hanging down and our good intentions shattered."[7] In late August, Stanley Robison cut expenses even further by handing two players their 10-day notices of release. The two were pitcher Creed Bates, whose 1–18 record stood out for its awfulness even among the Spiders, and first baseman Tommy Tucker, whose "enthusiastic coaching" was wasted with so many empty seats in the stands.

The Spiders returned to League Park in August for three games against the Giants and four against the Beaneaters, but many Clevelanders did not even know their team was home. There was little publicity, and though the local union violence had largely abated, not many people were willing to pay their way into League Park to see a team that was already 56 games out of first place. With Frank and Stanley Robison in attendance, the Spiders won a 4–2 decision against the Giants on August 25 when Charlie Knepper pitched his best game of the season, a three-hitter with six walks, before about 100 people. The rare win failed to energize the fans, as only 200 turned out the next day, a Saturday, to see the Giants beat Crazy Schmit in a rain-shortened 5-inning affair.

The Saturday loss set the Spiders on the path to another unwanted distinction. It was the first defeat of a 24-game losing streak, the longest in National League history.[8] They actually lost 25 consecutive games, as the Spiders played a Sunday exhibition contest in Johnstown, Pennsylvania, on September 2. They were opposed by a team of local amateurs who figured to provide little resistance to a major league club, even one as talent-poor as the Spiders. Instead, the Johnstown amateurs defeated Creed Bates and the Cleveland misfits by a 7–5 score.

Only one game in the streak was close. On September 7 in Chicago, the Spiders erupted for eight runs in the eighth inning as Charlie Knepper entered the ninth with a two-run lead. He hit opposing hurler Jack Taylor with a pitch, but two quick outs put Cleveland on the brink of a rare win. Two Chicago singles followed to load the bases, and Chicago's Bill Bradley grounded to Harry Lochhead at short. First baseman Tommy Tucker missed Lochhead's throw but stood motionless as the ball skittered away into foul territory. Perhaps he was seething about his impending release, or maybe he finally had his fill of playing and coaching for the worst team in the history of baseball. Tucker refused to chase the ball, and all three runners scored, giving Chicago a 7–6 win. Tucker left the team a few days later, and the career of "Foghorn Tommy" was over.

The record-setting 24th loss in a row was a typically frustrating day at the ballpark. On Saturday, September 16, in front of 400 fans in Washington, the Senators scored one in the first off Knepper, but the Spiders racked up eight runs in the second inning on six hits and three Washington errors. However, the Senators chipped away, bunting three times in a row against the overmatched Cleveland infielders on their way to four runs in the fourth. Knepper held on until he tired in the seventh, but pitchers— especially Cleveland pitchers—were expected to finish their games then. With no reliever riding to the rescue, Washington belted Knepper around for five runs and took an 11–8 lead. The final score, after four more Senator runs in the ninth, was 15–10. For Washington pitcher Jack Fifield, it was his 21st, and final, major league win.

There was no game on Sunday, but the Misfits, as the papers called them, finally broke the streak on Monday, September 19. The St. Louis club had signed a 21-year-old right-hander named Jack Harper from a minor league team in Springfield, Ohio. Frank Robison sent Harper to Cleveland to gain some experience, and Joe Quinn put him on the mound. In his major league debut, Harper kept the Spiders close enough to send the game in extra innings tied at 4. Harper retired the Senators in the top of the 10th (Washington batted first that day), and in the bottom of the inning Tommy Dowd doubled off Washington's Bill Magee. A single by Dick Harley moved the winning run to third. Washington drew their infield in and got Otto Krueger on a popup, but Magee was too careless in giving Charlie Hemphill an intentional walk. Hemphill reached over the plate and slapped the ball to right, scoring Dowd and ending the game.

Magee was no doubt doubly, or triply, embarrassed by the loss. Washington was the third team he had pitched for in 1899, following short, unsuccessful stints with Louisville and Philadelphia. He lost to the Spiders three times that season, once for each team.

The Spiders had no time to celebrate, as the game was the first of a doubleheader, but the victory was their 20th of the season. It was also their last. They dropped the nightcap 8–5 to start a new 16-game losing streak that lasted until the end of the campaign. Harper's win over the Senators was the last in Cleveland Spiders history.

Eddie Kolb was a 19-year-old Cincinnati boy who pitched amateur ball in and around his hometown with some success. A right-hander, Kolb dreamed of a career in professional ball while serving as pitcher and captain for a team in the Cincinnati suburb of Norwood. By day, the teenager worked as a cigar boy at the Gibson Hotel downtown. There he became acquainted with Cleveland manager Joe Quinn and the rest of the ragtag Spiders, who stayed there while in town to play the Reds.

The Spiders made their final road trip of 1899 to Cincinnati, where the Spiders and Reds closed their schedules with a four game weekend series. The teams played single games on Thursday and Saturday, with the season slated to end in a Sunday doubleheader on October 15. While chatting at the Gibson Hotel sometime that weekend, Eddie Kolb pleaded with Joe Quinn for what he believed would be the opportunity of a lifetime—to start the last game of the season for Cleveland against his hometown Reds.

Kolb possessed exactly two qualifications for the task. He was (1) a good local amateur pitcher, and (2) breathing.

Still, Quinn had long since passed the what-the-hell stage of the season. With the Spiders a record 112 games under the .500 mark and more than 80 games out of first place, it wasn't as if Kolb could possibly embarrass the Cleveland ballclub. Besides, Quinn had signed Harry Colliflower in a similar situation in Washington in August, and Colliflower had posted a win against the Senators. It was Colliflower's only win of the season in 12 starts, but maybe lightning would strike again. Also, the local boy might help the Reds by drawing a few extra people to the ballpark. Quinn gave Kolb the go-ahead, found him a uniform, and penciled him in to start the second game of the Sunday twin bill.

Though the Reds were headed for a respectable fifth-place finish, their fans had stopped paying attention to the club weeks before, after their pennant hopes had evaporated. Only 100 people showed up on Thursday to see Harry Colliflower, still winless after his debut, give up four runs in the first inning. He pitched well the rest of the way, but the Reds marched to an easy 6–2 win that was notable for the lack of enthusiasm on both sides. On Saturday, in what the local paper called "another disgusting exhibition" with 400 fans in the seats, the Reds walloped Jim

Hughey for 17 hits in a 12–4 rout, Cleveland's 132nd loss of the campaign. Six errors, three by shortstop Harry Lochhead, doomed Coldwater Jim to his 30th loss against only four wins. He was the last major league pitcher to lose 30 games in one season, giving the Spiders another unwanted distinction in a campaign full of them.

On Sunday, Quinn tapped utility man Lew McAllister to pitch the opener of the doubleheader. McAllister had pitched only twice previously that year; perhaps he, too, had begged Quinn for the assignment. Lacking any better options, Quinn sent McAllister to the mound with predictable results. The Reds lit him up for 17 hits while the Clevelanders made only six of their own. Before about 1,500 bored fans, Cincinnati belted its way to a 16–1 win. Now it was Eddie Kolb's turn.

The teenaged pitcher quickly discovered that major leaguers play on a much higher level than Cincinnati amateurs. The Reds pushed across four runs in the first and three more in the second to start another rout. Kolb walked five, hit a batter, and struck only one Red, who no doubt heard about it from his teammates for years thereafter. Kolb stayed upright long enough to complete the game (and belt a single too), but the Reds walked off with a 19–3 win. Finally, the long, disappointing 1899 season was over.

Legend has it that the Spiders repaired to the Gibson Hotel after the final game, where the players awarded a shiny new watch to their traveling secretary, George W. Muir. "We are doing this for you," the players said, "only because you deserve it. You are the only person in the world who had the misfortune to watch us in all our games."[9] If the story is true, it would have been a fitting remembrance of a disastrous campaign. The Spiders packed their bags and boarded a train to Cleveland, where they received their final paychecks and collected their belongings and equipment from the League Park clubhouse. Then they scattered to their hometowns to reunite with their families and line up jobs for the winter months. With that, the 1899 Cleveland Spiders passed into history.

The Brooklyn Superbas, which featured most of the stars of the mid– 1890s Baltimore champions, pulled away from the Beaneaters and Phillies in the season's final month and won the 1899 pennant by an eight-game margin. Boston claimed second place with Philadelphia in third. Fourth place was occupied by the surprising Baltimore Orioles. Though Brooklyn had stripped the Orioles of most of their stars, John McGraw, in his first season as a manager, drove his team of leftovers into the first division. If a Manager of the Year award had existed in 1899, McGraw probably would have won it. At the other end of the league, the Spiders stood alone in the cellar. The official National League statistics came out a few months later and revealed that the Spiders

- finished at 20–134 with a winning percentage of .130, the worst in major league history;
- finished 84.5 games out of first place, a major league record, and 45 games behind 11th-place Washington;
- lost 40 of their final 41 games;
- compiled a 24-game losing streak from August 26 to September 16, a National League record (the Philadelphia Phillies nearly matched it in 1961 with 23 losses in a row);
- occupied last place from May 24 to the end of the season;
- gave up 1,252 runs and scored only 534 of their own;
- went 9–32 at League Park and 11–102 on the road; and
- drew only 6,088 fans to their 41 home contests, an average of 148 per game.

The Spiders played all 154 of their scheduled contests, with 14 games against each of the 11 other National League teams. They went 0–14 against both Cincinnati and Brooklyn, and 1–13 against Chicago, New York, and St. Louis. They won no more than four games against any one team.

The Spiders used 15 different pitchers during the 1899 campaign, but no Cleveland pitcher won more than four games. Jim Hughey, the staff ace, went 4–30, with Charlie Knepper (4–22), Creed Bates (1–18), Crazy Schmit (2–17), and Harry Colliflower (1–11) close behind. Bates lost his final 14 games, while Colliflower won his debut and followed with 11 consecutive defeats. By comparison, Still Bill Hill (released with a 3–6 record) and Willie Sudhoff (3–8 before his return to St. Louis) looked like MVP candidates.

The Spiders were an embarrassment, and their spectacular failure laid bare the evil of syndicate baseball. Though Frank Robison turned a nice profit in St. Louis by stripping his Cleveland club of all its stars, and the previously lackluster Brooklyn team won the 1899 pennant by raiding the Baltimore Orioles, the National League owners finally admitted to themselves that the situation needed to change. The 12-team league was too large, and multiple team ownership cheated the fans and destroyed the integrity of the pennant races. The sporting press was disgusted with what the league had become, with an editorial in *Sporting Life* blasting the magnates for their "gross individual and collective mismanagement, their fierce factional fights, their cynical disregard of decency and honor, their open spoliation of each other, their deliberate alienation of press and public, their flagrant disloyalty to friends and supporters and their tyrannical treatment of the players."[10]

Accordingly, in March of 1900 the National League dropped four teams from its roster. Three of them were Washington, Baltimore, and Louisville, all of which had moved into the National League from the defunct American Association in 1892. The fourth was Cleveland, which had lost its best players to St. Louis, the other remnant of the 1892 merger. The league reportedly spent about $150,000 to buy out the four franchises, with Frank Robison receiving $25,000 to close up shop in Cleveland. The National League became an 8-team circuit again, and would remain so until 1962.

The league took possession of Washington's players and distributed them around the league. The Brooklyn club, which already owned the Orioles, was allowed to sell off the extra players on the Baltimore roster, while Louisville's best men, including Honus Wagner and manager Fred Clarke, wound up in Pittsburgh after a complicated series of transactions. Robison's payout for the Cleveland club included $10,000 for the franchise itself and $15,000, payable over two years, for League Park. A few of the Spiders—rookie pitcher Jack Harper and manager Joe Quinn among them—returned to St. Louis, and Robison sold a couple of others to other teams.

The St. Louis owner simply released the rest of Cleveland's players. Apparently no one wanted any of them.

Epilogue

"They're trying to tone down baseball and they are killing the interest. You don't have to poke anyone in the jaw, step on or kick a player to win, but you don't have to wear kid gloves, either. There's a difference between rowdiness and aggressiveness. The aggressive player will be on top when the parlor boy is at the bottom. Off the field, oh, well, that's different. On the field fight 'em to the last."

—Patsy Tebeau, 1913[1]

At the end of the 1899 season, **Cy Young** owned 267 major league wins.

His career was barely half over.

Cy grew increasingly discontented with his lot in St. Louis. His displeasure only intensified when Frank Robison, a usually genial man with a temper that flared every now and then, chose the wrong time to throw a tantrum. Disappointed by the outcome of the 1900 season, he sent angry letters to his players, letters that accused them of indifferent play, gambling, and drunkenness. The owner told his charges that he had decided to withhold their last paycheck of the season and was ready to cut salaries sharply in 1901. Amazingly, Robison exempted Jesse Burkett, John McGraw, and Wilbert Robinson from criticism, while venting his spleen at reliable stalwarts such as Young and Bobby Wallace. Burkett had sulked all season, largely because he detested the presence of McGraw and Robinson, while the two ex-Orioles had seemed more interested in making bets on horses than in winning baseball games. Young and Wallace, however, had performed admirably. Young was taken aback by the criticism and proclaimed that he was "surprised beyond anything I had ever imagined."

The big pitcher was also angry. Already the new American League had stepped up its efforts to lure Cy away from the established circuit, and the pitcher had often expressed his distaste for the muggy, hot

190

climate in Missouri. If Young still harbored any doubts about leaving the Cardinals, Robison's ill-advised letter removed them. "Your treatment of your players," said Young, "has been so inconsiderate that no self-respecting man would want to work for you if he could do anything else in the world."[2] When Boston offered him a significant raise, Cy couldn't beat it out of St. Louis quickly enough.

In 1901, the American League's first season as a major, Young won 31 games for Boston, and in 1903, his 14th major league campaign, he finally pitched for a pennant winner. He won three games as Boston defeated Pittsburgh in the first modern World Series that year,

Cy Young, at age 42, returned to Cleveland in 1909 and pitched for three more seasons (National Baseball Library, Cooperstown, New York).

and in 1904 he pitched a perfect game, the first of the 20th century. Cy was indestructible, too, throwing his third no-hitter in 1908 at age 41 and winning 19 games for Cleveland the following year. He wound up throwing more innings than any pitcher who ever lived, and his records of 511 wins and 315 losses will most likely last for all time.

Cy was widowed in 1933, and passed the last two decades of his life on a farm in Tuscarawas County, Ohio, not far from where he grew up. Visitors to the village of Newcomerstown might have spotted an elderly man in coveralls and a straw hat, sitting in a chair and smoking a pipe, chatting with the locals at the gas station. That man was Cy Young, the winningest pitcher in the history of baseball. After Cy died in 1955 at 88, major league baseball created a new annual award to be presented to the game's best pitcher. They called it the Cy Young Award.

Jesse Burkett also lived a long life. He played until 1905, then played for and managed minor league teams in New England for more than a decade after that. He even coached for his old enemy John McGraw on the New York Giants for a while in the early 1920s, though that job ended badly. The players hated the Crab so much that when the Giants won the World Series in 1921, they refused to vote coach Burkett a share of the winners' purse, not even a partial one.

Jesse never lost his ill temper. One day, while managing in the minors, he sent himself up to pinch-hit. When the umpire asked him who he was batting for, Jesse snarled, "None of your blankety-blank business!" The umpire then turned to the crowd and announced, "Burkett batting for exercise." The crowd roared, and roared again when Jesse struck out.[3]

Burkett lived out his years in Worcester, Massachusetts, and was rescued from total obscurity by his election to the Hall of Fame in 1946. His reaction was as Crablike as ever: "It took them a long time," remarked the bedridden 77-year-old. "I thought they weren't going to, because everybody had forgotten me."[4] Still, Jesse took great pride in the honor, though he was never able to travel to Cooperstown due to his fragile health. A few years later, the city of Worcester organized a Little League. When a newspaperman informed Jesse that the organization would be called the Jesse Burkett Little League, the feisty old ballplayer actually cried. "I am not a forgotten man after all," said Burkett, "thanks to fellows like you." Jesse Burkett was 84 years old when he died of a heart attack in 1953.

Bobby Wallace, elected to the Hall of Fame a few years after Burkett, was a baseball lifer. After an uneventful 1901 campaign with the Cardinals, Bobby and six of his teammates (including Burkett and Jack Powell) jumped to the St. Louis Browns of the American League in 1902. There, Wallace established himself as the premier shortstop in the new circuit. Though he never hit as well as he had in Cleveland, his glovework kept him in the lineup for the next decade and a half. He finally hung up his spikes in 1918, when he was nearly 45 years old, and was the last of the old Cleveland Spiders to play in the majors. Bobby managed the Cincinnati Reds for a short time in 1937, and worked as a coach and scout until the day he died in 1960.

Chief Zimmer was another long-lasting old Spider. Though he was 39 years old when the Spiders released him in June of 1899, he played for a few more seasons, spent one year as a National League umpire, and even served as president of a short-lived players' union. He retired to pursue his business interests, which included a bowling alley, a cigar factory, a billiard hall, and real estate, at which he was highly successful. In 1921 the 60-year-old Zimmer and his old battery mate, 54-year-old Cy Young, donned their old Cleveland uniforms and played two innings at League

Park in an old-timers game. As one newspaper reported, "A quarter of a century seemed to make no difference. They worked together ... as if they had been playing continuously until now."[5] In 1932, at age 71, Zimmer told a reporter from the *Plain Dealer*, "Not a thing wrong with me. I work in my garden every day, stay up as late as I like, eat what I like and run around like a youngster."[6] Zimmer and Young remained close friends until Zimmer died in 1949 at 89.

The Chief sold thousands of units of his "Zimmer's Base Ball Game" during the 1890s, but today, in the early 21st century, fewer than ten of the game boards are known to exist. One game in top condition sold at auction in 2008 for nearly $20,000.

Louis Sockalexis found only tragedy in his post–Cleveland life. He performed fairly well for Waterbury in the Connecticut State League after his flameout with the Spiders in 1899, but when the spring of 1900 rolled around he was nowhere to be found. He was so completely lost to alcohol that he spent a few years as a homeless vagrant, with the occasional arrest for drunkenness popping up in the papers. Sock sobered up enough to hit .288 for Lowell of the New England League in 1902, but at age 31 his baseball career was over. He wound up back home with the Penobscot tribe in Maine, working as a logger and piloting a ferry from the Indian Island reservation to the mainland. He was an avid reader of the newspapers that his passengers left behind, especially the Sporting News.

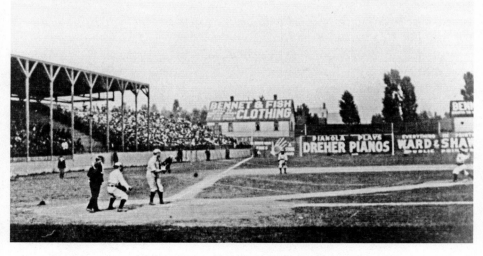

League Park, home of the Spiders, was built in 1891 and hosted major league ball until 1946 (National Baseball Library, Cooperstown, New York).

Sockalexis, while working with a logging crew deep in the Maine woods on the day before Christmas in 1913, suffered a heart attack and died at the age of 42. A few days later, the *Cleveland Leader* interviewed Ed McKean, who paid tribute to his onetime teammate. "[Sockalexis] was a wild bird," said McKean. "He couldn't lose his taste for firewater. His periodical departures became such a habit [that] he finally slipped out of the majors. He had more natural ability than any player I have ever seen, past or present."[7]

After Sock's death, Patsy Tebeau did his best to protect the Penobscot's memory. He concocted a story that Sockalexis had never tasted alcohol before he arrived in Cleveland; after delivering a game-winning hit in June of 1897, said Tebeau, his teammates introduced him to liquor in a post-game celebration. This is what started the great athlete on his slide to oblivion. The story was poppycock, of course, but the sportswriters picked up on it and reported it as the truth for decades thereafter.

Neither **Ed McKean** nor his longtime double play partner found much happiness after their baseball careers ended. McKean, whose ever-increasing weight hastened his exit from the major leagues, never played major league ball again after leaving St. Louis in July of 1899. He ran a tavern called the Short Stop Saloon in Cleveland for a while, then returned to baseball in 1902 as playing manager for Rochester of the Eastern League. He lasted only half a season there, but continued in the minors until 1908, when he was 44 years old. After that, he worked for a whiskey distributor in Cleveland and opened a tavern, often tending the bar himself. He had always been a heavy drinker, and his daily proximity to alcohol was a detriment to his health. He developed gastric ulcers, exacerbated by his drinking, and died in 1919 at age 55.

Cupid Childs, too, felt the effects of a life lived hard. He hated St. Louis, where the fans roasted the fading ballplayer mercilessly, and demanded that Tebeau send him elsewhere. Sold to Chicago in 1900, he played mediocre ball and was released in July of the following year. His oddly-shaped body aged poorly, as Cupid was out the major leagues at age 33. He did not want to give up on the sport, so he kept at it until his .245 average in the New York State League convinced him that it was time to quit. He and his family returned to his native Baltimore, where he owned a coal delivery service, but years of heavy drinking had damaged his kidneys beyond repair. Childs' health failed in his early forties, and he was bedridden during the last year of his life as his business tottered toward bankruptcy. He died of Bright's disease in 1912 at 45, and after his death many of his old Cleveland teammates contributed to a fund to pay his medical expenses.

Cy Young, Jesse Burkett, and Bobby Wallace are the three long-term Spiders of the 1890s who gained election to the Baseball Hall of Fame. Short-term Spiders Buck Ewing, George Davis, and John Clarkson are also honored there. Many baseball experts believe that Ed McKean and Cupid Childs deserve enshrinement as well. There are only three middle infielders in major league history with at least 1,600 hits and a .300 career batting average that are not in the Hall of Fame. Two of them are McKean (.302, 2,084 hits) and Childs (.306, 1,721 hits).[8]

Jimmy McAleer attained greater heights. He managed Cleveland's American League entry in 1900, and during the circuit's first decade he led the St. Louis Browns and Washington Senators, where he helped develop a right-handed rookie pitcher from Idaho named Walter Johnson. In 1912 he headed a group that bought the Boston Red Sox and became team president. He was rewarded with a pennant and a World Series victory over the New York Giants in Boston's new stadium, Fenway Park.

However, the Red Sox stumbled in 1913, torn apart by internal squabbles between Protestant and Catholic factions in the clubhouse, and McAleer fired manager Jake Stahl. This move upset H. W. Mahan, a major Red Sox investor who was also Stahl's father-in-law. It also angered league president Ban Johnson, who soured on McAleer's stewardship and maneuvered to push the old Spider out of Boston. While McAleer was out of the country with John McGraw and Charlie Comiskey on a baseball tour of the world, Johnson convinced McAleer's partners to sell out to Joseph Lannin, a Boston real estate magnate. When Jimmy returned to Boston, Johnson brusquely informed him that he was no longer the president of the Red Sox and may as well sell his shares too. Just like that, McAleer was out of baseball.

Filled with understandable bitterness at Johnson, who had a history of dismissing people when their usefulness to him had expired, the old center fielder never returned to the game and never spoke to Johnson again. Instead, he managed his real estate investments in his native Youngstown. In 1931, widowed, recently remarried, and fighting a losing battle with cancer, he shot himself in the head and died the next day. He was 66 years old.

Jack O'Connor was also driven out of baseball by Ban Johnson, in an even more spectacular way. Rowdy Jack, hired as manager of the St. Louis Browns in 1909, finished last in both of his seasons at the helm. In 1910, with Detroit's Ty Cobb and Cleveland's Napoleon Lajoie in a tight race for the batting title (and a Chalmers automobile that was offered as a prize to the winner), the Cleveland club played O'Connor's Browns in a season-ending doubleheader. Lajoie, a much more popular player than the widely disliked Cobb, went 8 for 9 in the twin bill, most of his hits coming on easy bunts down the third base line. The St. Louis third baseman played far back on O'Connor's orders, so deeply that it looked as if the Browns had two left fielders.

League president Johnson reacted to this display in two ways. He awarded the batting title to Cobb (though modern researchers have determined that Lajoie actually won it) and arranged for O'Connor's dismissal as manager. Jack, whose contract ran for one more year, sued the league and won part of his 1911 salary, but he was through with the American League. He managed in the new Federal League in 1913 but was booted out of that circuit, too, after he broke an umpire's jaw with a punch.

Rowdy Jack moved back to his hometown of St. Louis, where he promoted boxing matches and other events. Four years before he died in 1937, he gave an interview to *The Sporting News* in which he called baseball "a game for sissies."[9]

Jack Powell not only pitched big league ball until he was 38 years old, he also became O'Connor's brother-in-law when he married Rowdy Jack's sister Nora in 1902. The marriage broke up after only five years, though Powell and O'Connor apparently remained on friendly terms. Powell spent most of his long career in St. Louis with the talent-poor Browns, and his career won-lost record of 245–254 would no doubt have been much better on a good team. Powell hung up his spikes in 1912, though he attempted a comeback with the Browns in 1918 at the age of 44. He died in Chicago in 1944 at 70.

Some of the shorter-tenured Spiders died young. **John Clarkson**, who quit the team in a huff in 1894, never pitched again, though rumors of his possible comeback popped up in the papers for several years thereafter. Clarkson ran a cigar store in Bay City, Michigan, for a while, but his mental health deteriorated so sharply that in 1905 his family had him confined to an insane asylum in his native Massachusetts. Clarkson was only 47 when he died there four years later. **Buck Ewing** left Cleveland and managed his hometown team, the Cincinnati Reds, for several seasons. He left baseball a wealthy man, having invested his money wisely in real estate, but diabetes and kidney failure destroyed his health. Ewing was 45 years old when he died of Bright's disease in 1906. **Harry Blake**, who dropped out of the majors after a mediocre 1899 season with St. Louis, died in a rooming house fire in Chicago in 1919 at 45. **Jake Virtue** lived to be 77, but his baseball career ended abruptly after the Spiders released him. In early 1895, while preparing to attend spring training with the

Louisville Colonels, Virtue suffered a stroke that left his right side paralyzed for the rest of his life. When he died in 1943, *The Sporting News* reported that he was left "a helpless cripple."

Chippy McGarr did not live long either. He worked as a National League umpire in 1899 but was not rehired for the 1900 season. Despondent over losing his job, he became so depressed that he would up in the Worcester Home for the Insane in his Massachusetts hometown. There he spent his last few years as his health failed; one report claimed that he suffered from "general paralysis of the insane and exhaustion," but it may well have been a fatal case of syphilis. McGarr died in 1904 at age 41.

Nig Cuppy's arm never came around, though he kept pitching for several years after leaving Cleveland, and in 1901 he joined Boston's American League team as a teammate of Cy Young. Manager Jimmy Collins hated Cuppy's slow working pace, and the story goes that Collins tried to speed up his delivery by stationing a teammate behind him during practice. The teammate carried a hatpin, and if Cuppy did not deliver the ball by a count of eight, the player was instructed to jab Cuppy with the hatpin. Cuppy left baseball after that season and wound up in the tobacco business in his native Indiana. He was also a victim of Bright's disease, dying in 1922 at 53.

George Davis, however, disappeared. After a long, productive major league career that lasted until 1909, Davis fell off baseball's radar. No one in the baseball world heard any more about him, though Davis was a popular star who spent most of his 20-year career in the nation's two largest media markets, Chicago and New York. During the 1960s, Lee Allen, historian of the Baseball Hall of Fame in Cooperstown, New York, became obsessed with finding out what happened to George Davis. Allen ran down leads, made phone calls, and wrote letters in a quest that lasted for many years until 1968, when Allen discovered that Davis, who worked as a used car salesman in his post-baseball life, died in Philadelphia in 1940.

In early 1899, Frank Robison considered several candidates for the manager's job in Cleveland before settling on Lave Cross. **Bob Leadley**, Tebeau's predecessor as manager of the Spiders, was definitely not in the running, and Robison could not have hired Leadley if he had wanted to.

Leadley was missing, and no one could find him.

Leadley, a well-regarded figure in the baseball world, turned out to be an embezzler and a con artist. He had worked for several years as the clerk of Detroit's Police Court, and in 1897 had nearly lost his job when more than $4,000 went missing from his accounts. Leadley repaid the money and smooth-talked his bosses into keeping him, though the *Detroit*

Free Press demanded his dismissal. In early 1899 the ex-manager disappeared, and so did more than $10,000 of court funds. A warrant was issued for his arrest, but he and his wife had fled to Mexico, where he remained for more than a decade. Not until the 1920s, after the heat had died down, did the former Cleveland manager slip back into the United States, living out his years in California, where he died in 1936.

Few of the 1899 Spiders ever played major league ball again. One whose career ended with the worst team in history was **Tommy Tucker**, who had finally talked himself out of baseball after his egregious refusal to chase a loose ball turned a rare Spider win into another stunning loss. Said historian David Nemec, Tucker "grew increasingly unpopular with each passing year, so that by the time he took his last throw at [first base] in a [major league] game, no one was sorry to see him go."[10] He played a few more years in the minors, then went to work in the paper mills of Holyoke, Massachusetts, his hometown. He died in 1935 at 71.

Another of the Misfits who dropped out of the majors after 1899 was **Harry Colliflower**, who notched his only major league win in his debut, then tried for the rest of the season to recapture the magic of his one good game. Colliflower served briefly as an American League umpire in 1910, then went into business in his native Washington, D. C., where he spent the rest of his life. He was the next-to-last living ex-Spider when he died in 1961 at 92. **Charlie Knepper**, who went 4–22 for Cleveland in 1899, failed several trials in the high minors and eventually gave up the sport and returned to Indiana, where he worked as a heating technician in a gear factory. He died in 1946. **Creed Bates** simply disappeared. He worked as a laborer in his native Tennessee after he left baseball, and filled out a World War I draft card in 1918, but there is no record of him thereafter. He is one of the few major league players whose date and place of death remain a mystery.

Amazingly, **"Coldwater Jim" Hughey** was able to continue his pitching career despite his four wins and 30 losses for the Misfits. He wound up in St. Louis in 1900, playing for Patsy Tebeau on the Cardinals. After a few more years in the minors, Hughey returned to his hometown of Coldwater, Michigan, where he and his wife operated a general store for many years until his death in 1945. His career won-lost log of 29–80 gave him a winning percentage of .266, the lowest in baseball history for a pitcher with 100 or more decisions; he is also the last pitcher to lose 30 games in a season and the only man to throw 100 or more complete games without a single shutout.

For **Lave Cross**, the debacle of 1899 was a mere speed bump in a long career. After leaving Cleveland, he played third base for three pennant winners (Brooklyn in 1900 and the Philadelphia A's in 1902 and 1905). When he ended his 21-year major league career in 1907 at age 41, he stood in third place on the all-time list in games played. He played in the minors for a few more years, then worked in an auto plant in Toledo, Ohio, until his death in 1927. The other manager of the doomed 1899 Spiders, **Joe Quinn**, left the game in 1901. He had earned his certification as a funeral director, having passed his exams while still an active player, and he rejoined his father-in-law's funeral home in St. Louis, which he eventually came to own. He died in 1940 at 75.

What happened to **Eddie Kolb**, who pitched the last game in the history of the Cleveland Spiders? He played and managed with some success in the lower minor leagues, then moved to the Canadian province of Alberta and ran a prosperous restaurant for two decades. During the late 1930s, an oil boom promised to lift Alberta out of the Depression. Before long, Eddie Kolb the cigar boy had become E. W. Kolb, a wealthy oil executive who served as secretary and treasurer of the Western Canada Petroleum Association. He died in 1949, 50 years after his only major league game.[11]

Crazy Schmit remained as crazy as ever. When the National League adopted the five-sided home plate in 1900 (it was a diamond before then) Schmit wrote a letter to *The Sporting News* claiming credit for the idea. He also stated, "I pitched some 14 exceptional good games for Cleveland last summer [though he went 2–17 in 1899]. I am like a gnarled oak and am getting better every year.... I was a drawing card in Chicago, Cincinnati, Philadelphia and Baltimore and drew in my salary at the gate many times over."[12] Offered a tryout by John McGraw with the Orioles in 1901, Schmit showed up drunk, fell off the mound, and was fired. By 1908 he was pitching semipro ball in Chicago's City League. He died in 1940.

Frank Robison dreamed of bringing a pennant to St. Louis, but his wish went unfulfilled. His club, called the Cardinals beginning in 1900, was decimated by American League raids, losing Cy Young, Lou Criger and others before the start of the 1901 campaign. In early 1902, seven more of his players, including Jesse Burkett, Jack Powell, and Bobby Wallace, jumped to the new Browns of the rival circuit. Robison could only watch helplessly as his Cardinals sank in the standings, and a stadium fire in 1903, caused by lightning, added to the general despair. At least Robison, unlike his predecessor Chris von der Ahe, was smart enough to carry sufficient fire insurance on his ballpark.

In 1906 he ceded control of the seventh-place club to his brother

Stanley, who became team president, though Frank remained on the board of directors. Frank Robison retired to his lakefront manor outside Cleveland, where he died suddenly of a stroke in 1908. He was only 56 years old. **Stanley Robison**, the lifelong bachelor, ran the team until his death in 1911, after which the Cardinals passed to Frank's daughter, Mrs. Helene Robison Britton, baseball's first female owner. Of the eight teams that remained in the National League after the contraction of 1900, the Cardinals were the last to win a pennant. They gained their first league title in 1926, long after the Robison family had sold its stake in the team.

Cleveland, in fact, won a pennant before St. Louis did. Abandoned by the National League, the city hosted a franchise in the new American League in 1900. Managed by Jimmy McAleer, the team was called the Lake Shores, then the Blues, and used the name Bronchos for a while. When superstar Napoleon Lajoie signed on in 1902, the team became the Naps in his honor. Lajoie played in Cleveland for 13 seasons and managed the club for five. His Naps came within a whisker of their first league title in 1908, but lost a close race to Detroit and faded away to mediocrity thereafter.

In 1911, the team finally gained the right to play at home on Sundays, and in 1915, after Lajoie left, owner Charles Somers reached into the past for a new name. He called his team the Indians, the moniker that the city embraced during the too-brief stardom of Sockalexis. Five years later, the Cleveland Indians won the American League pennant and defeated the Brooklyn Dodgers in the World Series. Finally, after nearly half a century of professional baseball, the fans of Cleveland celebrated a real championship.

Patsy Tebeau, like several of his Spider teammates, did not live long enough to see it.

Patsy remained in St. Louis for the 1900 season, and because the team wore uniforms trimmed with cardinal red letters and piping that spring, he is known to this day as the first manager of the St. Louis Cardinals. But Patsy's heart was not in it. A decade and a half of baseball warfare had worn him out, and he managed from the bench in 1900. He took the field only once, but committed three errors and went hitless. Tebeau was finished as a player, and because he drew his managerial energy from his presence on the field, his usual feistiness and spirit were gone. He appeared listless and uninterested.

His old enemy John McGraw joined the Cardinals in 1900 and said all the right things, telling Patsy to "do what you think is best" and accepting an appointment as captain of the team. Still, conflict was inevitable.

The Orioles and Spiders had hated each other for a decade, and now McGraw and his former Baltimore teammates Wilbert Robinson, Dan McGann, and others were expected to work in harmony with Jesse Burkett, Jack O'Connor, and company. The ex-Spiders grumbled because McGraw, the new captain, believed in daily morning practice, while Tebeau had long since given up on it. "Pat seemed to think," recalled McGraw, "that his [regular] men were all right and all they needed to get out and win was to get out a short while before the game and take the customary fifteen minutes' practice."[13] McGraw's intensity meshed poorly with Tebeau's laissez-faire attitude, and the Cardinals split into squabbling factions.

McGraw hit well, but was injured much of the year and spent many of his afternoons at a harness racing track across the street from the ballpark. Also, some of the imports from Cleveland resented the fact that McGraw, not Jack O'Connor, had assumed the captain's post and the salary boost that went with it. The ex-Spiders and ex-Orioles sniped at each other all year, and as the Cardinals floundered, Patsy Tebeau decided that he had had enough. A 5–15 record in June extinguished whatever pennant hopes the team might have entertained, and July was not much better. With the talent-laden Cardinals falling into the second division, Tebeau submitted his resignation to Frank Robison before the season was half over. Robison refused to accept it, urging Patsy to stay a while longer and wait for a turnaround.

The turnaround never came, and on August 19, when a loss to the Reds left the team in seventh place, Patsy convinced Robison that he was finished. Patsy explained to the local press, "Yes, I'm out. The continued poor showing of the team was too much for me.... I did my best, and know the players did, too, but we couldn't get going, so I thought the best thing I could do was to drop out."

He had no idea what to do next. "I feel like a kid out of school," he said. "For the present, I don't know what my plans will be."[14]

Though the veteran manager was only 36 years old, he was finished with baseball and baseball was finished with him. Patsy packed up his family and returned to the Goose Hill neighborhood where he grew up. Friends offered to set him up as a club president, perhaps by buying the Cardinals, but Tebeau was not interested. "I'm not one of those fancy guys," he said. "I've been a player, that's all, and they'll never put me on one of those swinging chairs."[15] Instead, he opened a tavern in his old neighborhood with another old ballplayer, Bill "Scrappy" Joyce. There he remained, occasionally popping up in the pages of the St. Louis-based *The*

Sporting News as a critic of the modern game. Baseball had passed him by, and he appeared to be perfectly fine with that.

The partnership with Joyce, a childhood friend of Patsy's, lasted only a few years. Joyce, a ten-year major league infielder who had also managed the Senators and Giants for a while, was known for two things: he once hit four triples in a single game to set a record that still stands, and he earned his nickname in every game he played. He was a Tebeau type of player, so perhaps it was no surprise when the partners settled a business dispute in February of 1903 with a vicious fistfight. Patsy got the worst of it, and the partnership eventually dissolved, leaving Tebeau as sole owner.

In 1907, Patsy's brother George offered him the managerial post in Kansas City. "White Wings" Tebeau had become a minor league impresario, and owned Western League clubs in Louisville and Kansas City. Patsy thought about it, but decided to remain retired. "The extra $5,000 [in salary] would have come in handy," Patsy told a reporter, "but the family end of it doesn't look good to me. George and I always got along all right during the two years he played for me in Cleveland, and he told me I could be absolute boss of the Kansas City club, but still this thing of working for your relatives is apt to lead to trouble. So I turned the offer down."[16]

Like many old ballplayers, Patsy believed that the men of his era played a better, tougher, and more competitive game of baseball. Players of the younger generation were not as dedicated to winning; they treated their opponents as friends, not bitter enemies as the Spiders had. The old manager saw games at Sportsman's Park in St. Louis every now and then, but could not abide any displays of camaraderie between opponents. To Patsy Tebeau, baseball was, and should be, a blood sport. He said to a reporter in 1913,

> Show me a ball club out there fighting every inch of the way, and I'll show you a team that is after the pennant. We never thought of greeting our opponents. Our idea was to get out there and lick 'em, and lick 'em good and quick. I can see some guy sliding back to first with me playing the bag and getting his head bumped with the ball. Think I'd apologize? Not Patsy Tebeau. "Get your mutt out of the way and you won't get hurt," would be more like it.[17]

Drinking and illness turned him old and bitter before his time, and in 1918 his wife Kate filed for divorce and moved back to Cleveland with their children. This was a blow from which the old ballplayer could not recover. On May 23, 1918, Patsy Tebeau killed himself with a handgun in his tavern. He was 53 years old. Patsy was buried in Cleveland, the scene of his many triumphs and defeats.

That last man alive who played for the Cleveland Spiders was **Lew**

(Sport) McAllister, who died in 1962 at the age of 87. With his death, the Cleveland Spiders passed into history.

It was, in the main, a disappointing run. A half-pennant in 1892 (followed by a 5–0 sweep in the postseason) and a Temple Cup win in 1895 (which few outside of Cleveland cared about) were the only titles the Spiders brought to their home city. In the end, mediocre third base play for most of the decade, and poor offensive production from their center and right fielders, kept the Spiders from passing the better-rounded Baltimore and Boston champions.

More importantly, the Spiders reveled in a kind of play that was detrimental to the game itself. Though the wild and wooly Baltimore Orioles of John McGraw and Ned Hanlon are more famous for their antics today, largely because they won three pennants while the Spiders won none, Tebeau's Cleveland club outdid the Orioles in rowdiness, umpire abuse, and on-field mayhem. It was a winning formula, as the Spiders finished in the first division in each of Tebeau's seven full seasons at the helm, but not a championship one. Cleveland's take-no-prisoners approach to winning may have been exciting for the rougher fan element, but probably kept many others from the ballpark. The lack of Sunday baseball was not the only reason that Cleveland regularly suffered from poor attendance, even when the Spiders were winning.

Strangely enough, one of the Cleveland team's major weaknesses was Tebeau himself. He was a good fielder and natural leader, but his bat was mediocre at best; most teams count on superior offensive production from the first base position, but Tebeau posted a career batting average of .279 and a slugging percentage of .364 in the hottest-hitting era of baseball. The Spiders could have carried Jimmy McAleer's weak bat in center field, but the team simply could not generate enough offense to cover the lack of production from third base, right field, and Patsy himself at first. As a manager, his preference for weak-hitting glove men and his loyalty to performers (such as Chippy McGarr and, later, Ed McKean) who had passed their prime years kept his teams from the top.

In the end, the Cleveland Spiders are largely forgotten today, remembered mainly as Cy Young's first major league club, and for a disastrous final campaign in which they compiled the worst one-season record in history. The battling, brawling Spiders won no pennants, so it cannot be said that Patsy Tebeau and his men left a winning legacy, or even a highly successful one.

But it was certainly was an interesting one.

Chapter Notes

Introduction

1. Bill James, *The Bill James Historical Baseball Abstract* (New York: Villard Books, 1987), 38.
2. *The Sporting News*, February 10, 1894, 4.
3. *Sporting Life*, October 24, 1896, 7.
4. *Sporting Life*, October 14, 1899, 5.
5. Lee Allen, *The National League Story* (New York: Hill and Wang, 1961), 72.

Chapter 1

1. Alfred H. Spink, *The National Game, 2nd edition* (St. Louis, Missouri: National Game Publishing Company, 1911), 301.
2. Robison's middle name is often spelled DeHaas, but legal records, Cleveland city directories, and newspapers of the period spelled it DeHass, which is correct. "De-Hass" appears on his tombstone as well.

Chapter 2

1. McKean's biographer, Rich Blevins, believes that McKean was actually five years younger than his stated baseball age. He makes the case in his book, *Ed McKean: Slugging Shortstop of the Cleveland Spiders* (Jefferson, NC: McFarland, 2014).
2. Blevins, 11.
3. James Egan Jr., *Base Ball on the Western Reserve* (Jefferson, NC: McFarland, 2008), 145.

4. David Nemec, *Major League Baseball Profiles 1871–1900 Volumes 1 and 2* (Lincoln, Nebraska: University of Nebraska Press, 2011), 38.
5. Nemec, 183.
6. Egan, 153.
7. *Sporting Life*, July 27, 1887, 4.
8. *Sporting Life*, July 27, 1887, 2.
9. *Cleveland Plain Dealer*, August 22, 1887.
10. David Nemec, "Jay Faatz," article at SABR BioProject web site, http://sabr.org/bioproj.
11. Egan, 156.

Chapter 3

1. *The Sporting News*, June 22, 1889.
2. *Washington Evening Star*, January 21, 1905, 9.
3. Franklin Lewis, *The Cleveland Indians* (New York: G. P. Putnam's Sons, 1949), 35.
4. Hatfield's older brother John held the record for the longest baseball throw; Gil had a great arm too.
5. *Sporting Life*, May 26, 1889, 5.
6. Bill Deane, *Finding the Hidden Ball Trick: The Colorful History of Baseball's Oldest Ruse* (Lanham, Maryland: Rowman & Littlefield, 2015), 169.
7. *Sporting Life*, September 25, 1889, 2.
8. *Sporting Life*, September 25, 1889, 4.
9. John Phillips, *The Astonishing Cleveland Babes of 1889* (Cabin John, Maryland: Capital Publishing, 1994), October 2 entry.

Chapter 4

1. Ethan M. Lewis, "A Structure To Last Forever: The Players' League And The Brotherhood War of 1890," Internet article at http://www.ethanlewis.org.
2. *Sporting Life*, March 26, 1890, 1.
3. Rich Blevins, *Ed McKean: Slugging Shortstop of the Cleveland Spiders* (Jefferson, NC: McFarland, 2014), 107.
4. Scott D. Peterson, *Reporting Baseball's Sensational Season of 1890: The Brotherhood War and the Rise of Modern Sports Journalism* (Jefferson, NC: McFarland, 2015), 119.
5. Egan, 189.
6. *Cleveland Plain Dealer*, June 6, 1890.
7. Blevins, page 107.
8. *Detroit Free Press*, August 31, 1891.
9. *Detroit Free Press*, March 13, 1899. The quoted player was Count Campau.
10. David Nemec, *The Great Encyclopedia of Nineteenth Century Major League Baseball* (Tuscaloosa, Alabama: The University of Alabama Press, 2006), 573.
11. "Chief and Cy," article at Baseball History Daily website, https://baseballhistorydaily.com.
12. *Washington Herald*, July 30, 1911.
13. Albert G. Spalding, *Base Ball: America's National Game* (New York: American Sports Publishing Company, 1911), 287–288.
14. *The Sporting News*, October 25, 1890.
15. *Cleveland Plain Dealer*, October 5, 1890.

Chapter 5

1. Art Ahrens, "An Assist for Jimmy Ryan," SABR archives website.
2. Rich Blevins, *Ed McKean: Slugging Shortstop of the Cleveland Spiders* (Jefferson, NC: McFarland, 2014), 107; original source is *Sporting Life*, November 29, 1890, 9.
3. Jimmy Keenan, "Cupid Childs," article at SABR BioProject web site, http://sabr.org/bioproj.
4. John Phillips, *The 1898 Cleveland Spiders* (Cabin John, Maryland: Capital Publishing Company, 1997), 46.
5. *Sporting Life*, May 16, 1891, 7.

6. *The Sporting News*, February 10, 1894, 4.
7. G. W. Axelson, *Commy: The Life Story of Charles A. Comiskey* (Chicago: Reilly and Lee, 1919), 74.
8. Robert L. Tiemann and Mark Rucker (editors), *Nineteenth Century Stars* (Kansas City, Missouri: Society for American Baseball Research, 1989), 52.
9. Axelson, 80.
10. Axelson, 103.
11. Phillips, 17.
12. *Sporting Life*, August 1, 1891, 7.
13. *Sporting Life*, July 18, 1891, 2.
14. *Worcester Telegram*, January 11, 1953.
15. Bill James, *The New Bill James Historical Baseball Abstract* (New York: Free Press, 2001), 659.
16. *Worcester Telegram*, January 11, 1953.
17. Clipping from an unidentified newspaper, dated September 13, 1890, in the Jesse Burkett file, National Baseball Library, Cooperstown, New York.
18. John Phillips, *The Riotous 1896 Cleveland Spiders* (Cabin John, Maryland: Capital Publishing Company, 1995), 16.
19. Phillips, *The 1898 Cleveland Spiders*, 67.

Chapter 6

1. *Brooklyn Eagle*, October 8, 1892, 2.
2. *Logansport* (Indiana) *Pharos-Tribune*, August 8, 1900.
3. "The Human Rain Delay," article at the Baseball History Daily website, https://baseballhistorydaily.com.
4. Daniel E. Ginsburg, *The Fix Is In: A History of Baseball Gambling and Game Fixing Scandals* (Jefferson, NC: McFarland, 1995), 78.
5. *The Sporting News*, January 14, 1959.
6. *Sporting Life*, September 19, 1896; Michael Glazier (editor), *The Encyclopedia of the Irish in America* (South Bend, Indiana: University of Notre Dame Press, 1999), 46.
7. Stephen V. Rice, "Chief Zimmer," biography at SABR BioProject web site, http://sabr.org/bioproj.
8. *Sporting Life*, April 7, 1906.

9. *Sporting Life*, November 23, 1891, 1. Reprinted from the *Cleveland World*.
10. Peter Morris, *A Game of Inches: The Stories Behind the Innovations That Shaped Baseball* (New York: Ivan R. Dee, 2006), 229.
11. *Sporting Life*, July 16, 1892, 3.
12. *Sporting Life*, April 23, 1892, 13.
13. *The Sporting News*, April 6, 1963, 37.
14. *Sporting Life*, October 8, 1892, 3.
15. *Sporting Life*, October 15, 1892, 1.
16. *Sporting Life*, October 8, 1892, 3.
17. *Sporting Life*, October 8, 1892, 11.
18. *Sporting Life*, October 22, 1892, 2.
19. *Sporting Life*, October 22, 1892, 4.
20. *The Sporting News*, October 29, 1892, 4.
21. L. Robert Davids, *Insider's Baseball: the Finer Points of the Game, as Examined by the Society for American Baseball Research* (New York: Scribner's, 1983), 21.

Chapter 7

1. *Sporting Life*, July 15, 1893, 12.
2. *Sporting Life*, February 18, 1893, 1.
3. *Sporting Life*, March 4, 1893, 3.
4. *The Sporting News*, March 11, 1893, 3.
5. *The Sporting News*, March 11, 1893, 1.
6. *The Sporting News*, March 11, 1893, 3.
7. *Sporting Life*, September 9, 1893, 3.
8. John Phillips, *Buck Ewing and the 1893 Cleveland Spiders* (Cabin John, Maryland: Capital Publishing, 1992), July 19 entry.
9. *Brooklyn Eagle*, June 16, 1893, 2.
10. *Sporting Life*, July 29, 1893, 12.
11. *Sporting Life*, August 2, 1890, 5.
12. Frank Russo and Gene Racz, *Bury My Heart at Cooperstown: Salacious, Sad, And Surreal Deaths in the History of Baseball* (Chicago: Triumph Books, 2006), no page number.
13. David Jones, "Jesse Burkett," biography at SABR BioProject web site, http://sabr.org/bioproj.
14. *Sporting Life*, September 2, 1893, 12.
15. *Sporting Life*, August 26, 1893, 3.
16. *Brooklyn Eagle*, August 28, 1893, 2.
17. *Sporting Life*, September 30, 1893, 10.

Chapter 8

1. *The Sporting News*, January 13, 1894, 4.
2. "Panic of 1893," article at United States History web site at http://www.u-s-history.com/pages/h792.html.
3. *Sporting Life*, December 9, 1893, 4.
4. *Sporting Life*, January 27, 1894, 2.
5. *The Sporting News*, February 10, 1894, 4.
6. *Sporting Life*, January 27, 1894, 6.
7. *The Sporting News*, February 10, 1894, 4.
8. *Cincinnati Enquirer*, March 4, 1894.
9. *The Sporting News*, March 10, 1894, 1.
10. John Phillips, *The 1894 Spiders* (Cabin John, Maryland: Capital Publishing Company, 1991), June 3 entry.
11. *The Sporting News*, June 2, 1894, 1.
12. David Nemec, *Major League Baseball Profiles 1871–1900 Volume 1* (Lincoln, Nebraska: University of Nebraska Press, 2011), 616.
13. John Phillips, *Cleveland Spiders Who Was Who* (Cabin John, Maryland: Capital Publishing Company, 1993).
14. *Ibid.*
15. *The Sporting News*, August 11, 1894, 1.

Chapter 9

1. *Sporting Life*, August 22, 1893, 3.
2. *Sporting Life*, April 13, 1895, 4.
3. John Phillips, *The 1895 Cleveland Spiders, Temple Cup Champions* (Cabin John, Maryland: Capital Publishing, 1990), April 21 entry.
4. Phillips, June 4 entry.
5. *The Sporting News*, January 12, 1949.
6. *The Sporting News*, May 23, 1918, 4.
7. David Nemec, *Major League Baseball Profiles 1871–1900 Volumes 1 and 2* (Lincoln, Nebraska: University of Nebraska Press, 2011), 28.
8. *Sporting Life*, May 11, 1895, 3.
9. *Sporting Life*, July 13, 1895, 19.
10. *Boston Record*, July 29, 1897.
11. *The Sporting News*, May 23, 1918, 4.
12. David Nemec, "Eddie O'Meara," biography at SABR BioProject web site, http://sabr.org/bioproj.

13. Charles Alexander, *John McGraw* (New York: Viking Penguin, 1988), 44.
14. *Cleveland Plain Dealer*, October 4, 1895.
15. *Cleveland Plain Dealer*, October 6, 1895.
16. *Ibid.*
17. *Ibid.*
18. Frank Ceresi, "The Battle of 1895: The Temple Cup Games," on the FC Associates Internet site at http://www.fcassociates.com/nttemplecup.htm.
19. Henry Chadwick (editor), *Spalding's Base Ball Guide and Official League Book for 1896* (New York: American Sports Publishing, 1896), 58–59.
20. *Brooklyn Eagle*, October 11, 1895, 5.

Chapter 10

1. *Sporting Life*, February 15, 1896, 6.
2. *Sporting Life*, February 15, 1896, 6.
3. *Sporting Life*, January 25, 1896, 2.
4. Charlie Bevis, *Tim Keefe: A Biography of the Hall of Fame Pitcher and Player-Rights Advocate* (Jefferson, NC: McFarland, 2015), 231.
5. David Vincent, "So, You Want to Be an Umpire?" article posted on the Project Retrosheet website, http://www.retrosheet.org.
6. *Sporting Life*, July 4, 1896, 7.
7. *Sporting Life*, July 11, 1896, 9.
8. John Phillips, *The Riotous 1896 Spiders* (Cabin John, Maryland: Capital Publishing, 1997), 66.
9. Rich Blevins, *Ed McKean: Slugging Shortstop of the Cleveland Spiders* (Jefferson, NC: McFarland, 2014), 192–193.
10. *Sporting Life*, September 12, 1896, 6.
11. *Cleveland Leader*, October 2, 1896.
12. This scene was described by Nig Cuppy, as quoted in Phillips, no page number.
13. *Sporting Life*, November 7, 1896, 7.
14. *Sporting Life*, October 24, 1896, 7.
15. *Ibid.*

Chapter 11

1. *Sporting Life*, August 15, 1896, 4.
2. *Chicago Tribune*, September 28, 1896, 8.
3. *Sporting Life*, March 20, 1897, 7.

4. *Washington Post*, February 8, 1897.
5. *The Sporting News*, March 27, 1897.
6. H. G. Salsinger, "The Facts About Sockalexis," *Baseball Digest*, June 1954, 54–56.
7. *South Bend (Indiana) Tribune*, March 19, 1897.
8. John Phillips, *Chief Sockalexis and the 1897 Cleveland Indians* (Cabin John, Maryland: Capital Publishing, 1991), June 6 entry.
9. *Sporting Life*, April 10, 1897, 3.
10. *Sporting Life*, March 27, 1897.
11. *Sporting Life*, February 13, 1897.
12. Phillips, May 16 entry.
13. *Ibid.*
14. *Washington Post*, May 27, 1897.
15. Lee Allen, *The National League Story* (New York: Hill & Wang, 1961), 74.
16. *The Sporting News*, July 24, 1897.
17. *Ibid.*
18. *Sporting Life*, June 19, 1897.
19. Phillips, September 11 entry.
20. *Wheeling (West Virginia) Register*, August 5, 1897. Burkett was born in Wheeling, though he lived in Worcester most of his adult life, and the Wheeling papers closely followed his career.
21. Al Kermisch, "Cy Young Not Proud of First No-Hitter," *Baseball Research Journal #28* (1999), 142.
22. *Cleveland Plain Dealer*, August 14, 1897.

Chapter 12

1. *Chicago Tribune*, June 29, 1896, 8.
2. Bill James, *The Bill James Historical Baseball Abstract* (New York: Villard Books, 1987), 53.
3. *The Sporting News*, October 2, 1897.
4. James, 53.
5. David Quentin Voigt, *American Baseball: From Gentleman's Sport to the Commissioner System* (University Park, Pennsylvania: Pennsylvania State University Press, 1983), 230.
6. *The Sporting News*, April 2, 1898.
7. *Cleveland Plain Dealer*, March 14, 1898.
8. *The Sporting News*, March 12, 1898.
9. *Cleveland Plain Dealer*, March 11, 1898.
10. *Cleveland Plain Dealer*, April 1, 1898. The paper also stated that Sock would

receive his salary as long as he "keeps away from the firewater."

11. *Cleveland Plain Dealer*, March 23, 1897.

12. John Phillips, *The 1898 Cleveland Spiders* (Cabin John, Maryland: Capital Publishing, 1997), 43.

13. John Phillips, *The '99 Spiders* (Cabin John, Maryland: Capital Publishing, 1988), July 29 entry.

14. Phillips, *The 1898 Cleveland Spiders*, 67.

15. James Egan, Jr. *Base Ball on the Western Reserve* (Jefferson, NC: McFarland, 2008), 274.

16. *Sporting Life*, July 2, 1898, 8.

17. *Ibid.*

18. Phillips, *The 1898 Cleveland Spiders*, 119.

19. *Sporting Life*, September 17, 1898, 7.

20. *Sporting Life*, November 5, 1898, 9.

21. *Ibid.*

22. *Ibid.*

Chapter 13

1. *Sporting Life*, March 11, 1899, 9.

2. Edward Achorn, *The Summer of Beer and Whiskey* (New York: Public Affairs, 2013), 258.

3. John Phillips, *The '99 Spiders* (Cabin John, Maryland: Capital Publishing, 1988), March 14 entry.

4. *Sporting Life*, March 11, 1899, 9.

5. *Cleveland Plain Dealer*, May 18, 1899.

6. *Cleveland Press*, April 2, 1899.

7. *Sporting Life*, April 22, 1899, 3.

8. *Sporting Life*, April 15, 1899, 7.

9. J. Thomas Hetrick, *Misfits! Baseball's Worst Ever Team* (Clifton, Virginia: Pocol Press, 1999), 28.

10. *Cleveland Plain Dealer*, April 25, 1899.

11. *The Sporting News*, May 27, 1899.

12. *Cleveland Plain Dealer*, May 11, 1899.

13. Lee Allen, *The National League Story* (New York: Hill and Wang, 1961), 79–80.

14. Hetrick, page 102–103.

15. "Crazy Schmit in Cleveland," article at Baseball History Daily website, https://baseballhistorydaily.com.

16. *Cleveland Plain Dealer*, June 29, 1899.

Chapter 14

1. Lee Allen, *The National League Story* (New York: Hill and Wang, 1961), 79.

2. John Phillips, *The '99 Spiders* (Cabin John, Maryland: Capital Publishing Company, 1988), July 12 entry.

3. Phillips, August 14 entry.

4. Phillips, September 27 entry.

5. *Cleveland Press*, August 17, 1899.

6. The Blues of the American Association had recorded a triple play against Cincinnati on June 30, 1887.

7. J. Thomas Hetrick, *Misfits! Baseball's Worst Ever Team* (Clifton, Virginia: Pocol Press, 1999), 172.

8. Louisville of the American Association lost 26 in a row in 1889, while Brooklyn of the National Association, precursor to the National League, lost 31 in a row in 1875.

9. Allen, 80.

10. *Sporting Life*, October 2, 1900, 4.

Epilogue

1. *Pittsburgh Press*, July 16, 1913.

2. Robert Burk, *Never Just a Game: Players, Owners, and American Baseball to 1920* (Chapel Hill: University of North Carolina Press, 1994), 150.

3. David Jones, "Jesse Burkett," article at SABR BioProject web site, http://sabr.org/bioproj.

4. *The New York Times*, May 28, 1953.

5. Stephen V. Rice, "Chief Zimmer," article at SABR BioProject web site, http://sabr.org/bioproj.

6. *Cleveland Plain Dealer*, May 30, 1932.

7. *Cleveland Leader*, January 4, 1913.

8. The other is Buddy Myer, who played in the American League from 1925 to 1941, mostly for the Washington Senators.

9. *The Sporting News*, February 23, 1933, 3.

10. David Nemec, *Major League Baseball Profiles 1871–1900 Volume 1* (Lincoln, Nebraska: University of Nebraska Press, 2011), 333.

11. Peter Morris, "Eddie Kolb," article at SABR BioProject web site, http://sabr.org/bioproj.

12. *The Sporting News*, March 24, 1900, 2.

13. *St. Louis Globe-Democrat*, November 23, 1900.

14. *Spokane Spokesman-Review*, September 2, 1900.

15. Undated article by Sid Keener in the Patsy Tebeau file at the National Baseball Library, Cooperstown, New York.

16. *Pittsburgh Press*, July 3, 1907.

17. *Pittsburgh Press*, July 16, 1913.

Bibliography

Books

Achorn, Edward. *The Summer of Beer and Whiskey*. New York: Public Affairs, 2013.

Alexander, Charles. *John McGraw*. New York: Viking Penguin, 1988.

Allen, Lee. *The National League Story*. New York: Hill & Wang, 1961.

Axelson, G. W. *Commy: The Life Story of Charles A. Comiskey*. Chicago: Reilly and Lee, 1919.

Blevins, Rich. *Ed McKean: Slugging Shortstop of the Cleveland Spiders*. Jefferson, NC: McFarland, 2014.

Burk, Robert. *Never Just a Game: Players, Owners, and American Baseball to 1920*. Chapel Hill: University of North Carolina Press, 1994.

Burns, Ken, and Geoffrey C. Ward. *Baseball: An Illustrated History*. New York: Alfred A. Knopf, 1994.

Casway, Jerrold. *Ed Delahanty in the Emerald Age of Baseball*. Notre Dame: University of Notre Dame Press, 2004.

Deane, Bill. *Finding the Hidden Ball Trick: The Colorful History of Baseball's Oldest Ruse*. Lanham, Maryland: Rowman & Littlefield, 2015.

DeValeria, Dennis, and Jeanne Burke DeValeria. *Honus Wagner: A Biography*. New York: H. Holt, 1996.

Egan, James, Jr. *Base Ball on the Western Reserve*. Jefferson, N.C.: McFarland, 2008.

Hetrick, J. Thomas. *Misfits! Baseball's Worst Ever Team*. Clifton, Virginia: Pocol Press, 1999.

James, Bill. *The Bill James Historical Baseball Abstract*. New York: Villard Books, 1987.

Johnson, Lloyd, editor. *The Encyclopedia of Minor League Baseball: The Official Record of Minor League Baseball*. Durham: Baseball America, 1997.

Lewis, Franklin. *The Cleveland Indians*. New York: G.P. Putnam's Sons, 1949.

Light, Jonathan Fraser. *The Cultural Encyclopedia of Baseball*. Jefferson, NC: McFarland, 1995.

Morris, Peter. *A Game of Inches: The Stories Behind the Innovations That Shaped Baseball*. New York: Ivan R. Dee, 2006.

Nemec, David. *The Beer and Whisky League*. New York: Lyons and Burford, 1994.

_____. *The Great Encyclopedia of 19th-Century Major League Baseball*. New York: Donald I. Fine Books, 1997.

_____. *Major League Baseball Profiles 1871–1900 Volumes 1 and 2*. Lincoln: University of Nebraska Press, 2011.

Phillips, John. *The Astonishing Cleveland Babes of 1889* Cabin John, Maryland: Capital Publishing, 1994.

_____. *Buck Ewing and the 1893 Cleveland Spiders.* Cabin John, Maryland: Capital Publishing, 1992.

_____. *Chief Sockalexis and the 1897 Cleveland Indians.* Cabin John, Maryland: Capital Publishing, 1997.

_____. *The 1898 Cleveland Spiders.* Cabin John, Maryland: Capital Publishing, 1997.

_____. *The 1895 Cleveland Spiders, Temple Cup Champions.* Cabin John, Maryland: Capital Publishing, 1990.

_____. *The 1894 Spiders, Temple Cup Champions.* Cabin John, Maryland: Capital Publishing, 1991.

_____. *The '99 Spiders.* Cabin John, Maryland: Capital Publishing, 1988.

_____. *The Riotous 1896 Spiders.* Cabin John, Maryland: Capital Publishing, 1997.

_____. *The Spiders: Who Was Who.* Cabin John, Maryland: Capital Publishing, 1991.

Seymour, Harold, and Dorothy Seymour Mills. *Baseball: The Golden Age.* New York: Oxford University Press, 1971.

Spink, Alfred H. *The National Game, 2nd edition.* St. Louis: National Game Publishing Company, 1911.

Tiemann, Robert L., and Mark Rucker, editors. *Nineteenth Century Stars.* Kansas City: Society for American Baseball Research, 1989.

Voigt, David Quentin. *American Baseball: From Gentleman's Sport to the Commissioner System* University Park: Pennsylvania State University Press, 1983.

Newspapers

Brooklyn Eagle
Chicago Tribune
Cleveland Leader
Cleveland News
Cleveland Plain Dealer
Cleveland Press
New York Times
Pittsburgh Press
St. Louis Globe-Democrat
South Bend (IN) *Tribune*
Toledo Blade
Washington Post
Wheeling (WV) *Register*
Worcester (MA) *Telegraph*

Magazines

Baseball Digest
Baseball Magazine
Baseball Research Journal
The National Pastime
Sporting Life
The Sporting News
Sports Illustrated

Internet

Baseball History Daily https://baseballhistorydaily.com
Baseball Reference http://www.baseball-reference.com
Library of Congress http://www.loc.gov
National Baseball Hall of Fame and Museum http://www.baseballhalloffame.org
Project Retrosheet http://www.retrosheet.org
SABR Baseball Biography Project http://sabr.org/bioproject
Society for American Baseball Research SABR http://www.sabr.org

Index